Working Out Gender

Working Out Gender

Perspectives from labour history

Edited by

Margaret Walsh

Ashgate

Aldershot • Brookfield usa • Singapore • Sydney

Published by
Ashgate Publishing Limited
Gower House
Croft Road
Aldershot
Hants GU11 3HR
England

Ashgate Publishing Company
Old Post Road
Brookfield
Vermont 05036–9704
USA

Ashgate website: http://www.ashgate.com

British Library Cataloguing-in-Publication data

Working out gender. – (Studies in labour history)
    1. Women – Employment – History   2. Sexual division of labour – History
    I. Walsh, Margaret
    331.4'09

Library of Congress Cataloging-in-Publication data

Working out gender: perspectives from labour history / edited by Margaret Walsh.
    (Studies in labour history)
    Includes index.
    1. Sexual division of labor – United States – History.   2. Sexual division of labor –
    Great Britain – History.   3. Sex discrimination in employment – United States –
    History.   4. Sex discrimination in employment – Great Britain – History.
    5. Women – Employment – United States – History.   6. Women – Employment –
    Great Britain – History.
    I. Walsh, Margaret.   II. Series: Studies in labour history (Ashgate)
    HD6060.65.U5 W674 1999
    306.3'615'0941—dc21   99-33636
                                                                                                   CIP

ISBN 0 7546 0058 0

Typeset in Times by N²productions and printed on acid-free paper and bound in Great Britain by MPG Books Ltd, Bodmin, Cornwall

Contents

Tables

Contributors

Pat Ayers is Liverpool born and studied Economic History at the University of Liverpool. From 1986–90 she worked on the Leverhulme-funded Docklands History Project and is currently Senior Lecturer in History and Economic History at Manchester Metropolitan University.

Robert Bennett is currently training to be a Careers Guidance Officer at the University of Huddersfield while also completing his PhD. He has lectured in British Social History and Gender and Economic History at the University of Leeds.

Fiona Brown has a BA Hons in History from the University of Birmingham (1990), an AM in American History from Harvard University and is currently writing a PhD thesis (University of Hull) about women in the American legal profession from 1920 to 1940.

Valerie Burton began her academic career in the UK. She is now Associate Professor of Maritime History at Memorial University of Newfoundland where the vast archive of British merchant seafarers' work contracts from the nineteenth and twentieth century is housed. She has published research from these contracts on themes relating to seafaring work and maritime communities.

Krista Cowman teaches history at Leeds Metropolitan University. She has published several articles on suffrage and socialism and has a forthcoming book, *Mrs Brown is a Man and a Brother! Women in Political Organisations on Merseyside, 1890–1920.*

Janet Greenlees is a postgraduate student at the University of York. Her D. Phil. examines the impact of women on the development of patterns of work organization in the cotton industries of Lancashire and New England between 1790 and 1860.

June Hannam is a principal lecturer in history at the University of the West of England, Bristol. She has written a biography of *Isabella Ford, 1855–1924* (1989) and has published articles on women's involvement in socialist and feminist politics in the nineteenth and twentieth centuries. She is writing a book with Karen Hunt, *Women and Socialism, 1880–1930* (forthcoming).

Colin Heywood is a Senior Lecturer in Economic and Social History at Nottingham University. He is the author of *Childhood in Nineteenth-Century France* (1988), *The Development of the French Economy* (1995) and various articles concerned with modern French and European history.

Karen Hunt teaches women's history at Manchester Metropolitan University. She is the author of *Equivocal Feminists: the Social Democratic Federation and the Woman Question* (1986) and is currently writing a book with June Hannam on socialist women.

Sheila Rowbotham is the author of several books on women's history, as well as on women's contemporary movements and conditions, including *Hidden from History* (1973), *Women in Movement* (1993) and *Homeworkers Worldwide* (1993). She edited *Dignity and Daily Bread* (1994) and *Women Encounter Technology* (1995) with Swasti Mitter. Her most recent works are *A Century of Women: The History of Women in Britain and the United States* (1997) and *Threads Through Time: Writings on History and Autobiography* (1998). She was awarded an honorary doctorate from the University of North London in 1994 and is a University Research Fellow in the Sociology Department at Manchester University.

Jutta Schwarzkopf teaches British social history with a particular focus on gender at the University of Hannover. She is author of *Women in the Chartist Movement* (1991) and her current research examines the social construction of gender in the labour process in the Lancashire cotton weaving industry, 1880–1914.

Deborah Simonton lectures in History, Cultural History and Women's Studies at the University of Aberdeen where she is a Continuing Education Organizer. She is the author of *A History of European Women's Work, 1700 to the Present* (1998) and articles on gender history. She is currently working on a social and cultural history of women in Western Europe since 1700.

Margaret Walsh is Reader in American Economic and Social History at the University of Nottingham. She is author of *The Manufacturing Frontier* (1972), *The American Frontier Revisited* (1981) and *The Rise of the Midwestern Meatpacking Industry* (1982). She is currently working on a book on the long distance bus industry in the United States.

Studies in Labour History
General Editor's Preface

Labour history has often been a fertile area of history. Since the Second World War its best practitioners – such as E.P. Thompson and E.J. Hobsbawm, both Presidents of the British Society for the Study of Labour History – have written works which have provoked fruitful and wide-ranging debates and further research, and which have influenced not only social history but history generally. These historians, and many others, have helped to widen labour history beyond the study of organized labour to labour generally, sometimes to industrial relations in particular, and most frequently to society and culture in national and comparative dimensions.

The assumptions and ideologies underpinning much of the older labour history have been challenged by feminist and later by postmodernist and anti-Marxist thinking. These challenges have often led to thoughtful reappraisals, perhaps intellectual equivalents of coming to terms with a new post-Cold War political landscape.

By the end of the twentieth century, labour history had emerged reinvigorated and positive from much introspection and external criticism. Very few would wish to confine its scope to the study of organized labour. Yet, equally, few would wish now to write the existence and influence of organized labour out of nations' histories, any more than they would wish to ignore working-class lives and focus only on the upper echelons.

This series of books provides reassessments of broad themes of labour history as well as some more detailed studies arising from recent research. Most books are single-authored but there are also volumes of essays centred on important themes or periods, arising from major conferences organized by the Society for the Study of Labour History. The series also includes studies of labour organizations, including international ones, as many of these are much in need of a modern reassessment.

Chris Wrigley
British Society for the Study of Labour History
University of Nottingham

Acknowledgements

I am grateful to the contributors for their faith in both the Spring 1998 Conference of the Society for the Study of Labour History and the ensuing book. I also wish to thank Chris Wrigley for his help and support at every stage. The Departments of American and Canadian Studies and History at the University of Nottingham provided valuable support in the running of the conference.

Margaret Walsh

Introduction

Margaret Walsh

Gender has become a dynamic and contentious category of analysis since the mid 1980s when Joan Scott challenged historians to look again and rethink their perspectives. Inspired in part by the approaches of French critical theorists as well as by the resistance of traditional historians to shift the emphases of the 'master' narrative to include women and everyday experiences, her aim was to use gender as a lens through which to examine all aspects of the past.[1] In the ensuing debate about the nature and scope of gendered inquiry some historians have raised concerns that the still developing women's and feminist histories have been sidelined in favour of a gender history which incorporates women and men into a relational situation, thereby losing the sense of female centrality and female oppression.[2] Gender history could become simply another way of returning control to men. Other historians have been more worried that history has been talked out of the major principle of its established canon, namely a focus on events and actions, in favour of taking the linguistic turn and shifting the agenda towards a concern with the textual features of historical writing.[3] Certainly these anxieties are legitimate concerns of historians and they have stirred highly contentious and lengthy debates. However, gender history as a form of inquiry that challenges sex-blindness, both in lived relations and as a symbolic system, needs to move forward by producing new perspectives on and insights into the past.[4]

The basic hypothesis of *Working Out Gender* is that gender is important in historical analysis because the different circumstances of the sexes makes women and men experience and understand events and interpretations in dissimilar ways. These differences and any similarities between the sexes need to be understood if historians are to be concerned with a more informed knowledge of the past. Any such gendered approach owes much to the modern feminist movement and to the flowering of women's research, writing and teaching during the past quarter century.[5] In this way *Working Out Gender* is fully committed to advancing the position of women and making their lives central to historical learning. This collection of essays is also committed to examining men as gendered persons and to discussing the social construction of masculinity and manhood, thereby rendering an improved understanding of history. In achieving this understanding the linguistic turn is not ignored because language can construct different meanings of the past and can produce oppression and inequality. The authors, however, have each chosen their own path to gendering their essays and the volume as a whole is thus both context specific and context dependent in its approach towards seeing the formerly unseen.

Working Out Gender examines gender from the perspective of labour history in its broadest context. Traditionally, labour history has been concerned with the workplace outside the home and the ways in which workers have organized to fight for their rights. Class has been the leading category of analysis, and oppression the driving mechanism. In Europe, workers' politics and their representation in political parties have also been of major importance. The 'new' currents which spread through all branches of history in the 1960s and 1970s also brought change to labour history, mainly in the shape of moving it back into the communities and examining varieties of working classes. Indeed working class studies became a major focus for social historians as much as for labour historians.[6] This Thompsonian approach did not, however, carry all before it. In the USA, in particular, where class has struggled to become a major analytical tool, race, ethnicity and women became important categories and created their own separatist strands of history. As part of the social reform movements which pervaded society in the 1960s and early 1970s and which had direct links with academic research and writing, these fields also altered the parameters of labour history and pressed for recognition of so-called minority groups.[7]

But gender should be more than a pressure to remould the labour history canon.[8] More recently, moving in tandem with the general trend in history to bring gender into focus, labour historians have in their turn presented vibrant case studies showing the importance of gender.[9] Much of this work has been carried out in the USA, and the results have been well received both there and in Europe. The outstanding volume, *Work Engendered. Toward A New History of American Labor* edited by Ava Baron is now an essential tool to understanding gender and labour and its introduction is frequently cited on both sides of the Atlantic.[10] *Labor History* followed this publication with a special double issue on gender which aimed to air 'a collection of attitudes and subjects which are rather new to the writing of working-class history'. The essays, most of which were originally presented at the 1991 North American Labor History Conference, were written mainly 'by a younger generation of scholars, breaking free from the restraints of past schools of thought'.[11] Gender was also discussed by the British Society for the Study of Labour History in the early 1990s. Then a conference on gender and labour history was agreed. This meeting was in part delayed by the general desire to discuss first the future of labour history in terms of old and new trends.[12] As a result the gender conference was scheduled for the spring meeting of 1998 at the University of

Nottingham. By this time the Society had already signalled its interest in and commitment to gender in another way by sponsoring a special issue of *Labour History Review* on Gender and Work with guest editors Pamela Sharpe and Harriet Bradley.[13] Gender was clearly a category of labour history analysis in Britain which was dynamic and was moving from the margins of the discipline.

The Gender and Labour Conference, from which the articles in this book originate, was designed to illustrate a variety of ways of making gender more central to labour history.[14] The work site has been basic to any understanding of labour history, whether this is outside or inside the home. Work organizations have also been a major part of labour history as has the involvement of both organized labour and workers in political organizations. These strands are represented in *Working Out Gender* as is the newer strand of masculinity or, in this context, the gender identity of working men. The essays are placed in a Trans-Atlantic framework, though the balance is tilted heavily towards Europe. They also span a long period stretching from the eighteenth to the twentieth century. Collectively they illustrate the diverse ways in which primarily European historians have interpreted gender as a valuable lens for refocusing issues connected with work, workers, the working classes and their politics.

Sheila Rowbotham's thoughtful and committed journey through women's labour history in the USA surveys the terrain from which first wave feminist historians emerged and through which they and the second wave of feminist historians now tread. There is a mixture of achievement and caution. Women's historians have indeed come far since the early days of passion, discussion and action in the mid to late 1960s, and American women's labour history is now often judged to be the best exemplar of that field in the world. The diversity of approaches has offered opportunities to redefine the whole territory of labour history. We are reminded, however, that the roots of this scholarship owe much to the work of an older generation of left historians as well as to the modern feminist movement, and that British women's historians were ploughing some of the same fields and were possibly producing more subtle analyses than their American sisters. We are also reminded that the challenges faced by both femininst and labour historians remains to contest a dominant culture and to democratize knowledge so that history can explore a whole range of social relationships.

The two articles which pay closer attention to Europe other than England offer insights into the diversity of gendered work experiences. Deborah Simonton's wide-ranging examination of labour in eighteenth-century cities raises the oft-forgotten point that women often formed a majority of the urban population and that both married and unmarried women worked. Some managed to defy traditional restrictions imposed by guilds, corporations or patriarchal customs and became involved in trading networks and in workshops. But industrial and economic innovations restructured occupations

3

and influenced status, while ideological and social changes redefined gender roles in terms of public and private spheres. Many men then specified their artisan status in terms of masculinity, ensuring at least that women could not threaten their position. Women were perceived as subordinate to men and as their domestic helpmates. If they earned their living they did so as unskilled secondary workers. The need to clarify skill and redefine work in the eighteenth century contributed to the reshaping of femininity which was taking place in Europe.

Colin Heywood raises the important question of how the experience of work and the workplace may have shaped gender identification during childhood and youth. Weaving anthropological perspectives into a broad survey of gender socialization which incorporates large and small families from urban and rural locations and examples from both sides of the Atlantic, he questions the rigid sex typing of work. Certainly girls had less freedom to seek employment outside the home and were encouraged to adopt the feminine values of nurturance and obedience. Boys did not like domestic tasks and were recommended to be competitive and self-reliant. But there was no rigid biological division of labour. Poverty, labour shortages, location, family size, employers' recruitment strategies and cultural norms all contributed to an amazing diversity of work experience.

As gender is increasingly understood as a matter of human invention which can be shaped and reshaped by different generations, historians have paid more attention to analysing the cultural constructs of femininity and masculinity. Much work has already been undertaken on femininity, albeit indirectly, because of the volume of information which has been generated on women's history. Masculinity, by contrast, has been neglected and the history of working-class masculinity is still in the making. Pat Ayers and Valerie Burton demonstrate two ways in which working-class men's gender identity influenced and was influenced by employment. Both emphasize the importance of examining gender for understanding not only male workers and men's work, but for understanding men's relationships with their employers and with their next-of-kin.

Pat Ayers examines the meanings of masculinity in docklands Liverpool in the years between the two World Wars. Port employment, the persistence of casual labour and the experience of seafaring dominated men's lives and created a web of economic poverty within which men worked out their gender identities. Their formal credentials as males were defined by the labour market, but events such as getting married or becoming a father offered further evidence of manhood while religious affiliation often reinforced male dominance and fraternalism. Valerie Burton explores the masculinity of British merchant seafaring labour in the nineteenth century. She draws attention to two contrasting images: the rough work culture espousing recklessness and

4

prioritization of individual needs and the artisanal culture embracing male breadwinning. Increasingly seafarers wished to be accepted as responsible workers both by employers and by the public, and this desire was facilitated by the Board of Trade. When sail power declined and with it the conditions which helped define the 'rough' notion of living for the moment and unruly behaviour, the masculinity of sailors became more respectable.

Masculinity is very much part of the image of labour politics in Britain in the late nineteenth and early twentieth centuries. Though some historians might consider the notion of male dominance appropriate to the era before women voted, increasingly women's historians have attempted to locate women in the late nineteenth and early twentieth centuries, both as activists in parties like the Independent Labour Party (ILP) or the Social Democratic Federation (SDF) and as persons for whom politics mattered. June Hannam and Karen Hunt examine the stories of British socialism and find them wanting in terms of where they placed women and the woman question. Women are missing, marginalized and cast in inaccurate stereotypes. The authors contend that it is time to integrate the contributions of feminist historians both in assessing women's political endeavours and in deconstructing the dominant narratives so that gender becomes an important category of analysis.

Krista Cowman also examines the female role in early British socialism. Her voice gives credence to women's agency in the ILP and she thus enters the historiographical debate which Karen Hunt and June Hannam discuss. In optimistic mode she suggests that the ILP was woman-friendly; this appeal lay not perhaps so much in the radical views of the 'New Woman' which may have alienated many female contemporaries, but in tactics which have subsequently been designated anti-feminist. Discussions of improving the domestic lot were a viable means of recruiting women into the party, while appeals to feminine characteristics, such as respectability and motherhood could be used to advantage by the party. Women could affirm power within the ILP at the same time as celebrating their separate roles.

Examinations of the workplace have been a central feature of all varieties of labour history. Five case studies suggest ways in which gender can offer new meanings to workers and their work. All three sectors, primary, secondary and tertiary are represented as are nineteenth and twentieth century experiences on both sides of the Atlantic. A complex picture emerges suggesting that much research remains to be done if the variety and variability of gender is to be understood. In agriculture Margaret Walsh probes the continuing presence of the family economy and the household as the unit of production. Despite the ruling ethos of commercialization and efficiency in American farming since the Revolution, all family members needed to contribute to ensure survival, let alone success. Though standard texts have associated farming with male ownership and output, women and children participated in farm enterprises in diverse ways. Newer views need to bring the 'other' or hidden work force and the small-scale communal values into clearer focus to engender farming.

In the manufacturing sector Jutta Schwarzkopf and Janet Greenlees demonstrate how recent research can throw fresh light on a traditional section of British industrialization: the Lancashire cotton textile industry. Their painstaking and detailed investigations suggest how historians can use gender as a means of developing new conceptual frameworks for labour history. Jutta Schwarzkopf inverts established patterns when examining gender and technology in the weaving section of the industry prior to the First World War. The notion of a breadwinning wage is central to her study. She suggests that employers tried to defuse the opposition of trade unions to the introduction of new machines by offering a family wage to their male workers. This collaboration failed because conflicting ideas of masculinity and the desire to maximize profit overrode any solidarity along gender lines. Janet Greenlees examines wage relationships in cotton manufacturing in the first half of the nineteenth century. Questioning the reliability of traditional sources she draws on meticulous research in mill company records to suggest diverse gender-earnings ratios. There was no conventional pattern of employing women as a cheap source of labour. Local market conditions and individual employers' needs influenced gender task divisions and payment within the Lancashire cotton industry. Clearly in parts of Lancashire at least, there were flexible gender work patterns.

In the tertiary sector, case studies in banking and the civil service in the United Kingdom, and the legal profession in the USA throw new light on male and female careers. Having examined conventional attitudes to marriage bars and women's clerical employment, Robert Bennett considers the policy of marriage bars for workers of both sexes and within the context of a gendered language. Employers were worried about the respectability and financial stability of their workforce and were concerned about the need for a family wage at a point in men's careers when they might expect to be married. In this setting they encouraged a specifically middle-class masculine culture based on a dependent family. Fiona Brown examines the prospects for women who became lawyers in interwar America, a period when women's participation in the traditional professions was declining. Oral testimony provides insights into individual attitudes and choices and suggests that women did not see gender discrimination as an insurmountable problem. Certainly female lawyers, especially if they were married, faced many difficulties when working in a masculine ethos but most remained optimistic and confident in their own ability. They found a variety of ways of resolving the dilemmas of professionalism and femininity.

Labour historians on both sides of the Atlantic have, in recent years, been concerned about the future of their subject. Intense debates about loss of

6

direction and decline in the number of practitioners, often focusing on older categories like class and labour organizations, have created a sense of unwarranted pessimism. Certainly some historians may currently prefer to call themselves social historians, cultural historians, women's historians or historians of industrial relations. Yet such distinctions are purely academic. The articles in this volume suggest that discussions about key issues in the workplace, politics and working-class history are very much alive when viewed through a gendered lens. New stories as well as new versions of old stories emerge to create a variety of rich experiences. There is no dominant narrative, but a profusion of suggestions, both theoretical and experiential. The essays in this volume are a small contribution to reshaping labour history so that it is capable of understanding women, men and work.

Notes

I am very grateful to Malcolm Chase, Colin Heywood and Deborah Simonton for their comments on earlier versions of this introduction. I am also very grateful to Deborah Simonton for suggesting the title of this volume on gender and labour.

1. Scott, Joan W. (1986), 'Gender: A Useful Category of Historical Analysis', *American History Review*, **91** (5), 1053–75; Scott, Joan (1988), *Gender and the Politics of History*, New York: Columbia University Press.
2. Rose, Sonya O. (1993), 'Gender History/Women's History: Is Feminist Scholarship Losing Its Critical Edge?' and subsequent comments by Canning, Kathleen, Clark, Anna, Valverde, Marianne and Sawyer, Marcia R., *Journal of Women's History*, **5** (1), 89–128.
3. Hoff, Joan (1994), 'Gender as a Postmodern Category of Paralysis', *Women's History Review*, **3** (2), 149–68; Gordon, Linda (1990), 'Review' of Joan Scott, *Gender and the Politics of History*, in *Signs*, **15** (4), 853–8. For reactions to Hoff see Kent, Susan K. (1996), 'Mistrials and Diatribulations: a reply to Joan Hoff', pp. 9–18 and Ramazanoglu, Caroline (1996), 'Unravelling Postmodern Paralysis: a response to Joan Hoff', pp. 19–23, both in *Women's History Review*, **5** (1). See also, Newman, Louise M. (1991), 'Critical Theory and the History of Women: What's At Stake in Deconstructing Women's History', *Journal of Women's History*, **2** (3), 58–68.
4. One of the most illuminating justifications for gender history still remains the introduction of The Editorial Collective (1989), 'Why Gender and History', *Gender & History*, **1** (1), 1–6. See also Bock, Gisela (1989), 'Women's History and Gender History: Aspects of an International Debate', *Gender & History*, **1** (1), 7–30.
5. Women's historians attempting to place women's history in the context of both gender history and the history of masculinity have offered thoughtful views on the importance of gendering. See, for example, Cott, Nancy F. (1990), 'On Men's History and Women's History', in Carnes, Mark C. and Griffen, Clyde (eds), *Meanings for Manhood. Constructions of Masculinity in Victorian America*, Chicago: University of Chicago Press, pp. 205–11.
6. Thompson, E.P. (1963), *The Making of the English Working Class*, London:

7

Victor Gollancz. Two collections of essays which reflect the Thompsonian approach and discuss his influence are: Rule, John and Malcolmson, Robert (eds) (1993), *Protest and Survival. The Historical Experience. Essays for E.P. Thompson*, London: The Merlin Press; and Kaye, Harvey J. and McClelland, Keith (1990), *E.P. Thompson. Critical Perspectives*, Cambridge, Polity Press. For a sympathetic survey of Thompson's approach see Palmer, Bryan D. (1994), *E.P. Thompson. Objections and Oppositions*, London: Verso. The comparative approach is examined in Kirk, Neville (1994), *Labour and Society in Britain and the USA*, Vol. 1 *Capitalism, Custom and Protest, 1750–1850*, Vol. 2, *Challenge and Accommodation, 1850–1939*, Aldershot: Scolar Press.

7. Montgomery, David (1972), 'The Conventional Wisdom', *Labor History* **13**, 107–36; Montgomery, David (1980), 'To Study the People: The American Working Class', *Labor History*, **21** (4), 485–512; Brody, David (1993), 'Reconciling the Old Labour History and the New', *Pacific Historical Review*, **62** (1), 1–18.

8. In this sense gender is synonymous with women as it was often treated in the early days of women's history. See, for example, Pleck, Elizabeth H. (1983), 'Women's History: Gender as a Category of Historical Analysis' in Gardner, James B. and Adams, George R. (eds), *Ordinary People and Everyday Life Perspectives on the New Social History*, Nashville, Tenn.: American Association of State and Local History, pp. 51–65.

9. Buhle, Mari Jo (1989), 'Gender and History' in Moody, J. Carroll and Kessler-Harris, Alice (eds), *Perspectives on American Labor History. The Problems of Synthesis*, De Kalb: Northern Illinois University Press, pp. 55–79; Kessler-Harris, Alice (1989), 'A New Agenda for American Labor History. A Gendered Analysis and the Question of Class', in Moody and Kessler-Harris, *Perspectives on American Labor History*, pp. 217–34.

10. Baron, Ava (ed.) (1991), *Work Engendered. Toward A New History of American Labor*, Ithaca: Cornell University Press; Baron, Ava (1991), 'Gender and Labor History: Learning from the Past, Looking to the Future' in Baron (ed.) *Work Engendered*, pp. 1–46.

11. Leab, Daniel J. (1993), 'Foreword', *Labor History*, **34** (2–3), 167. For essays by older and well-established labour historians surveying the question of gender and labour history in this issue of *Labor History* see Kessler-Harris, Alice, 'Treating the Male as "Other": Redefining the Parameters of Labor History', pp. 190–204 and Fink, Leon, 'Culture's Last Stand? Gender and the Search for Synthesis in American Labor History', pp. 178–89.

12. Discussions of conferences, Society for the Study of Labour History, Executive Committee meetings, 1993–1997. The 1997 Spring Conference held in Manchester on 'Is there a future for labour history?' had sessions on labour as politics, labour as work, ethnicity, race and labour history, the culture of labour, class, and postmodernism and labour history.

13. *Labour History Review* (1998), **63** (1) contains essays by Michael Roberts, Jane Humphreys, Sîan Reynolds and Penny Summerfield.

14. The only article which was not originally given as a paper at this conference is Walsh, Margaret, 'From the periphery to the centre'. An early version of this piece was given at the Social History Society's conference in Glasgow in January 1996. All papers have been rewritten, revised and refereed.

CHAPTER ONE

New Entry Points from USA Women's Labour History

Sheila Rowbotham

When and Where I Enter is the title of a book by Paula Giddings about the impact of black women on race and class in America.[1] However, it also has a wider application, expressing the significance of entry points in setting the pattern of cultural assumptions. The creation of labour history itself involved such a challenge to historical perspective, bringing into view working-class experience which had been obliterated in a narrow definition of political history as the story of rulers. However, the initial focus of labour history was to be on the workplace, on unions and on the political organization of labour. Though women were sometimes included they were marginalized.

In both Britain and the USA, the period when the women's liberation movement emerged coincided with creative changes in radical history which were closely linked to the rejection of Stalinist forms of Marxism by the New Left. It is, of course, precisely what is taken for granted and thus not explicit, which often proves to be the most elusive aspect of a past consciousness. And indeed it is rarely noted that the new cultural syntheses of feminist historians in the late 1960s and early 1970s were formed out of a broader framework of scholarship and thinking. This background was to be crucial in providing the context of assumption from which women's history was to take off and is consequently vital for any understanding of the origins of recent feminist historiography.

Feminist historians in both countries were able to draw on the work of such historians as E.P. Thompson, Eric Hobsbawm, Christopher Hill, Richard Cobb, Edith Thomas, George Rudé, C.L.R. James, Herbert Gutman, Staughton Lynd and David Montgomery to name but a few. It is not what they said, or did not say, about women which is the point here – only Edith Thomas was writing on 'women'; it was to be the innovative ways in which they were looking at social existence, consciousness and action which were to be influential.

This reorientation in radical history suggested a whole series of questions and approaches to those of us inspired by the early women's liberation groups in the 1970s to look back into the past with women in mind. C.L.R James and

Edith Thomas, deserve mention as early pioneers of the 'history from below' which was being rediscovered by historians of the French Revolution such as George Rudé and Richard Cobb. Eric Hobsbawm's 'primitive rebels' and Christopher Hill's recovery of the extreme left groups and radical culture in the English Civil War pointed to lost traditions of participatory democracy, direct action and utopianism; while E.P.Thompson's dynamic approach to class and class consciousness, his rejection of teleological approaches to class and his recognition of the significance of community were to be particularly important – in the USA even more so than in Britain.

In the USA, Herbert Gutman's interest in the processes of class formation and the diverse expressions of the consciousness of subordinated groups was to be suggestive for a generation of young American historians influenced by the New Left.[2] Staughton Lynd's concern to involve working-class people in labour history and David Montgomery's use of his own experience as a manual worker,[3] were to revive the questioning of hierarchies of knowledge which had been present in the beginnings of labour history in the nineteenth and early twentieth centuries. These approaches towards historical enquiry were to be disseminated beyond the academy in the journal *Radical America*, which also published early articles and pamphlets on women's history.[4]

The North American preoccupations had their parallels in the Society for the Study of Labour History and at Raphael Samuel's yearly History Workshop Ruskin College meetings in which Ruskin trade union students participated. Their papers not only examined work and strikes but described family life, schooling and culture. This idea of drawing on personal experience, along with the resolve to write a history which could reach outside academia, were to be passed on from labour history to women's history. Another interest in common was oral history, which had originated in the left social documentary work of the 1930s, becoming an academic field of study only in the 1970s.

There were very close links indeed between the renewal occurring within labour history and the women's liberation movement. In Britain, for instance, the first women's liberation conference came out of a History Workshop Conference on working-class history organized by Raphael Samuel, which was held at Ruskin College, Oxford, in autumn 1969. Sally Alexander, Anna Davin and the American historian Barbara Winslow, along with myself, were among a small group of women who met to consider holding a women's history conference at Ruskin. We decided on a general women's liberation conference instead.[5]

The legacy was constantly being subjected to impassioned critiques, but it was nonetheless to be formative. Sally Alexander reflected in her introduction to *Becoming A Woman*, 'I had forgotten how much my habits of thought owed to the Marxist historians with whom I argued'.[6] It is of course the people with whom you find it worth arguing that set the terms of your own innovations.

And so women's history, in its origins, in both Britain and the USA, defied, and yet was significantly shaped by, the work of an older generation of left historians.

There were also greater similarities between the political and theoretical perspectives of the early movements in Britain and the USA than has been recognized. Most histories of the women's movement in the USA have downplayed the early interconnections between the New Left and feminism and have also disregarded the awareness of class, as well as race, in many of the early women's liberation groups. In an interview with Carol Lasser in 1981 in *Visions of History*, Linda Gordon, describes returning from London to Boston in September 1968:

> I became part of a group of women, most of them a bit younger than me, and most of them veterans of SDS (which I was not), who were beginning to discover sexism. We organized the women's liberation collective that later started Bread and Roses. ... By 1969 it seemed completely natural and logical that as a feminist and a historian just finishing a dissertation, I should do something about women ... I was carried away by the political necessity of the historical research. ... There was a very strong sense of collective process. For a number of years we had a kind of ever-changing, free-floating, women's history discussion group here in Boston. It included, in its first life, Mari Jo Buhle, Meredith Tax, Ellen DuBois, Maureen Greenwald, Priscilla Long, Lise Vogel and myself. From time to time there was also Kathryn Sklar, Nancy Cott, Ros Baxandall.[7]

All the women she mentions have made significant contributions to women's history, including Linda Gordon herself, who has written extensively on birth control, work and welfare.

Because looking at women meant asking new questions, the early groups of feminist historians kept finding themselves confronted by a series of sticking points embedded within the existing formulations of labour history. It was to be these aspects of experience and consciousness that did not fit within the existing paradigms which were to lead them towards other theoretical sources. The first wave of women's history was not hermetically sealed from the broader theoretical developments on the left, and the late 1960s to early 1970s was a period when the works of western Marxist theorists were appearing in translation. Such writers as J.P. Sartre, Henri Lefevbre, Antonio Gramsci or Michel Foucault could be mined for ideas on subjective identity, everyday life and cultural hegemony – the microcosms of domination. On both sides of the Atlantic, these insights were inspirational, not because of theoreticism, but because they illuminated aspects of women's oppression which were not part of conventional socialist ways of seeing. They were to be appropriated and transmogrified. Put through a gender lens, these abstract concepts began to yield completely new perceptions about women's past. They provided a

11

means of structuring dissatisfactions and pursuing hunches, enabling feminist historians to find new entry points into the past.

The background to the shift in understanding which the creation of women's history involved was not of course simply a matter of books. When they wrote the introduction to their influential documentary history *America's Working Women* (1976) Rosalyn Baxandall, Linda Gordon and Susan Reverby stated that the 'orientation' of their work came not simply from the women's liberation movement, but also from '... the civil rights and New Left movements'.[8] The civil rights movement had demonstrated the close connection between community resistance and trade unionism; it had also revealed the importance of alternative values – 'the beloved community'.[9] It presented a very different view of politics than 'the ends justifies the means' which had contributed to Stalinism. Moreover, civil rights and the subsequent Black Power movement challenged the Marxist view that class was the primary division in society by asserting the significance of race. The impact of both movements created an opening for raising the issue of 'gender'. Black power's emphasis on culture as an aspect of domination was similarly influential and gave women's liberation the term 'chauvinism'. In the same period that synchronicity of thinking which is always so difficult to unravel and explain was apparent. Attempts were being made in many countries to link the individual's perception of subordination to a social context. Subjectivity had erupted on the posters of the anarchical rebellion of 1968 in France while 'the personal is political' was originally a slogan from the American student movement and was part of its desire to prefigure the desired future society through counter-institutions.[10]

Radical theories and radical activities were thus to interact with ideas coming out of the women's liberation movement itself in the first half of the 1970s. Particularly important for women's history was the interest in the personal account as a way of finding alternative sources for looking at working-class women's lives. There was, moreover, the recognition that economic activity should include the home as well as the workplace, that politics was about the networks embedded in everyday life as much as the public face of political organizations and that power could be embedded within assumptions as well as being directly coercive. The women's movement shared with the black movement and the New Left a refusal to reduce subversive desire to the economic. As Baxandall, Gordon and Reverby argued, '... a focus on women shows that class and class consciousness are formed, in individual cases, by a combination of economic and cultural factors'.[11]

This awareness marked Sarah Eisenstein's work which connected political consciousness and personal aspiration. Eisenstein's pioneering studies of women and class, published after her early death, were very much in accord with the New Left's rejection of a narrow economic perspective. For example, in 1970, in *Bread and roses: working women's consciousness, 1905–1920*, she quoted the trade unionist Rose Schneiderman in 1912: 'What the woman who labors wants is the right to live, not simply exist ... the right to life, and the sun, and music and art. ... The worker must have bread, but she must have roses too.'[12]

This early women's history was very much concerned with 'visibility' and with women's active agency. Women's agency was, moreover sought by looking at the lives of 'ordinary', not just outstanding women.[13] There was also a recognition, following Marx, that individuals did not act upon history in a vacuum but were caught within a web of social relationships. In the introduction to *Radical America* which carried 'Women in American Society', by Ann Gordon, Mari Jo Buhle and Nancy Schrom the editors of the journal asserted this integral connection, '... the most fundamental changes in society have been at all points mediated through changes in social and sexual patterns expressed by different classes, so to misunderstand women's history is to misunderstand American history as a whole'.[14]

Indeed it was not the case that early writers on women's history were content to simply discover women and add them on.[15] We were concerned not just with finding out more about women, although this was exciting in itself, we knew that this meant transforming how history was seen and understood.[16] We were, moreover, convinced that our enquiry would change how social relationships and politics as a whole were seen.

While the small groups of socialist feminists who began writing women's history in Britain and the USA shared many common assumptions and perspectives, the areas of study which were to open up have developed in disparate ways. One reason for this divergence has been the differing relation to the academy. Women's history in the USA during the 1980s became much more securely rooted within academic institutions than in Britain. Courses, publishing and conferences took off and women's history expanded into many areas which had not been part of the early pioneering studies. One offshoot was to be the creation of a large academic market, which in turn has made it possible for work to appear on topics which would have not found publishers in Britain. This process of institutionalization has certainly carried problems we could not have envisaged. One ironic feature of success has been the indirect exclusion of a wider readership. There is, for example, the unhappy confinement of excellent studies of women's labour history to university libraries, simply because marketing mechanisms which require big runs, effectively isolate them as academic commodities. On the other hand, as radical enthusiasm waned, the process of academization was also to secure a vital continuity for women's labour history through a new generation of graduate students.

In Britain the impact of women's history in general on history as an academic discipline was to be on a much smaller scale and the growth in institutional footholds in universities came in the 1990s, rather than the 1980s. By this time the active women's movement had shrunk and inspiration was more likely to come from within women's studies itself. From the late 1980s many new subjects, from colonialism to women's friendship networks have engaged the interest of feminist historians in Britain. However, it often happens, that as new insights become ascendant, older understandings get lost, and, during the conservative years of the 1980s and early 1990s, women's history and labour history in Britain were to cease to have such a close connection. Though some books and articles continued to appear on individual women socialists and on the history of women in socialist and labour organizations as well as on gender and the division of labour, class ceased to be the passionate preoccupation it had been in the 1970s.

This shift reflected a wider cultural ambience within the British intelligentsia. Class inequality was becoming actually more marked; however, class struggle after the miners' strike of 1984–85 was no longer being viewed as heroic. The social perceptions of the 1980s and 1990s were to stimulate interesting enquiries into consensus and popular conservatism but resulted in a turning away from any examination of class or class consciousness. A result of this divorce is that one set of questions now tend to be asked in women's history and cultural history and quite different ones in labour history.

In contrast, in the USA, partly because women's history is a vast field, an interesting space was being hewed out in the 1980s and 1990s by historians who have been attempting to apply some of the insights of the feminist movement, not to maintain a separate sphere, but to redefine the whole territory of labour history. Ruth Milkman, reviewing twelve such studies, in her article 'New Research in Women's Labor History', commented on the paradox: '... despite the current crisis of unionism, research on women's labor history – a field that barely existed twenty years ago – has burgeoned'.[17] Thus, though both countries have seen a weakening of labour organizing and a pronounced cultural conservatism the relation between labour history and women's history has differed considerably.

One contributory factor has been the pervasiveness of feminism within American culture. During the 1970s and early 1980s, socialist feminists did not feel the need to defend feminism against socialism in quite the same way as they have in Britain. For in the USA it was all too evident that socialism and a recognition of the significance of class were the poor relations. One consequence has been very differing attitudes towards the balance between the personal and the public. While the North Americans have shared British feminists' interest in personal and domestic life, there has also been greater interest in reexamining the conventional concerns of labour history, such as class formation, conditions of work and trade unions.

During the 1980s the trade union movement in the USA was to be weakened

14

even more than its counterpart in Britain; on the other hand the unions were to embrace some important feminist demands, such as comparable worth and parental leave. There were also to be high profile campaigns around affirmative action and efforts to gain trade union support for gays and lesbians assailed by Reaganism which helped to maintain links. Moreover, from the late 1970s, the rise of the New Right meant that the public sphere of work was becoming a politically contested terrain because the fundamentalist wing of the New Right persistently presented it as 'unfeminine'. So the conventional subject of traditional labour history began to have an urgent strategic meaning for feminists in the USA which it did not acquire in Britain. A notable example is Alice Kessler-Harris' *Out to Work*, which was published in 1982. Kessler-Harris connected women's long history of paid employment with the changing circumstances of domesticity, technology, the state, and cultural attitudes. She saw the pull into paid work as a crucial dynamic: 'As the notion of more or less permanent wage work for women spreads, it raises twin demands for changes in the family and changes at work. These undermine the reciprocally confirming system of values that has for so long affirmed women's special place'.[18]

Another important factor in making some USA feminist historians look beyond the personal has been the pressure from the 1980s of black feminists, who have mounted a sustained challenge to the power of white middle class feminists to set the terms of 'women's studies'. The result has been a much fiercer questioning of those feminist perspectives which have focused exclusively on gender. To some degree, the greater awareness of race and ethnicity which was to result, has made it possible to continue to raise the question of class within women's studies, even though discussion of 'class' has been banished from the dominant discourse.

By an irony of history the North Americans were to be better prepared psychologically for the transformation in class structure which was to throw the British left into such confusion. It is important to realize that for North American socialist feminists 'class' as a category had been problematic from the beginning of the women's liberation movement. Working-class consciousness and socialism were never a 'given' for the Americans, as they were in Britain, until the dramatic defeats of the late 1980s. Not only were some of the economic and social changes which were to affect all developed countries evident rather earlier in the USA, but 'difference' was already a familiar fact of life. The impact of the McCarthy period on the trade unions and on the left, along with the rise of the black movement, had already stimulated New Left historians to look at the particular history of the American working class and examine the divisions between various sections of the working class. Indeed, when *Radical America* published 'Women in American Society' by Mari Jo Buhle, Ann G. Gordon and Nancy Schrom in 1971, the editors'

15

introduction declared that '... objective differentials in the working class ... are the primary obstacle to social reconstruction in America'.[19]

By looking at the making of the North American working class with an awareness both of American particularity and of women's predicament, feminist historians were to go on to question many orthodox Marxist assumptions about the broader picture of class formation and class consciousness. For instance, Christine Stansell and Mary Blewett's histories of women and work in nineteenth century America indicate how gendered assumptions about who are the 'real' workers and a focus on a male path to proletarianization have obscured the interconnection between the factories and the putting out system in labour historiography.[20] From a different starting point, it is interesting that, like the historians of the New Left such as E.P. and Dorothy Thompson, they were to find themselves rejecting the Marxist teleology of the factory proletariat.

Another concept which derived from the New Left and was to resurface in the work of several feminist historians has been 'community'. From the mid 1970s, Herbert Gutman had already begun to break up 'community' as a homogeneous term by studying ethnic diversity.[21] Several feminist historians were to recast his recognition in relation to gender. For example Susan A. Glenn's *Daughters of the Shtetl* (1990), a study of life as well as labour, showed how traditions of resistance were carried from the old world to the new through East European Jewish women in New York during the early twentieth century garment workers' strike.[22]

Feminist historians, influenced by this broader view of 'class' as a social and material relationship, spanning community and workplace, life and labour, began to ask what might be different in male and female manifestations of class? For instance, Temma Kaplan, writing on a series of mass strikes in the early twentieth century, showed how these workplace rebellions were accompanied and sustained by community uprisings in which women's crowd action played a crucial part.[23] She suggested that this kind of action can be understood as 'female consciousness', exploring how women's activities as housewives and mothers, rather than as waged workers, gave rise to resistance around daily livelihoods in her study of Barcelona.[24]

The effort to integrate different aspects of subordinated experience has tended towards the local study because it is easier to trace the interconnections through a specific geographical context over time. Several feminist historians have adopted this approach. For example, Elizabeth Ewen, who included a tribute to Gutman in her introduction to *Immigrant Women in the Land of Dollars: Life and Culture on the Lower East Side, 1890–1925* (1985), looks at women's community-based resistance around rents and prices, showing how in the immigrant centres in New York this was often connected through families to the rebellions of women wage earners.[25] Another good example is Ardis

Cameron's study of Lawrence, Massachusetts between 1860 and 1912. In *Radicals of the Worst Sort* (1993) she describes women's community networks and workplace militancy in a factory town which included numerous ethnic groups. She is interested in the 'primitive rebels', to use Eric Hobsbawm's phrase, who are outside 'formal political movements',[26] and links the feminist interest in personal networks to public politics.

> Following female activists through their own neighborhoods, especially at the height of labor–capital tensions, suggests an alternative notion of politics – one developed relationally, from neighbor to neighbor and rooted in the material reality of everyday life.[27]

Elizabeth Faue's *Community of Suffering and Struggle: Women, Men, and the Labor Movement in Minneapolis 1915–1945* (1991) looks at how this 'relational' politics at the ground floor levels of workplace and community networks interacted with institutional expressions of labour's power. She traces the 'creation, decline and rebirth of a community-based labour movement during the depression decade'.[28] Faue's study of a particular place over three decades, moreover, demonstrates how there have been varied possibilities for women in different contexts of labour organizing. For instance, during the Second World War more women were in the workplace, but at that time the trade unions' political and social emphasis was to narrow. Faue's history of labour in Minneapolis also uncovers forgotten community-based traditions on the left. She thus places the assumption that production is the key to class militancy, in historical relief, showing that this syndicalist version of left trade unionism, against which the women's liberation groups were to rebel in the early 1970s, has been simply one strand among others.

By looking at the ways in which women became active and by bringing an awareness of gender to the undifferentiated concept of 'community' there now exists a substantial body of work challenging the assumption that class consciousness can be understood simply through the relations of production. These studies of class and community have taken off from the New Left project of the 1960s which, partly through the inspiration of the civil rights movement, was so intent on redefining the existing constitution of politics. In their turn, they are opening up approaches towards the past which suggest innovative social and political perspectives.

Purchasing Power (1994) by Dana Frank is a study of the labour politics of consumption organizing in Seattle between 1919 and 1929, through boycotts, cooperatives and labour-owned businesses. Frank observes, 'The story of consumer organizing by the labor movement offers one way to rethink the nature of class conflict'.[29] Here a gender lens is used to bring back into focus aspects of working-class struggle which have been occluded by the syndicalist-influenced emphasis on rank and file work place militancy which

17

had a creative, yet ultimately restricting influence during the 1970s. In one sense Frank is telling us what the productionist bias temporarily obscured about the general history of labour; the effort to reshape the market and consumption has been as important as the fight for wages and better conditions at work. But she brings a new way of looking at consumer movements by combining class, gender and race.

By showing how the class consciousness expressed by both men and women in the Seattle Labour movement in this period, was shaped not only by definitions of gender but also by race, Dana Frank returns us to one of the original dilemmas of the American New Left – the epic struggle to understand the constraints on class formation in their country. Moreover, *Purchasing Power* also suggests the need for a more nuanced picture of class consciousness, for Frank uncovers quite different kinds of gendered class consciousness among the Seattle women. Her work suggests that in looking at working-class women it is important to have an eye for diversity. Women did act collectively around prices as consumers, asserting traditional housekeeping responsibilities; there was also a cooperative version of making the world 'homelike',[30] a political perspective which they shared with progressive maternalists who believed women had special understandings to bring to politics. However, the attraction of involvement in consumer organizing for working-class housewives who were looking for a broader social existence could also be because of a lack of interest in personal domestic activity. The Seattle study also describes how, for those who were employed outside the home, class awareness as workers, interacted with prevailing notions of womanliness.

If the local study makes it possible to analyse changing dynamics in labour organizing and resistance over time, the individual complexities in gendered forms of class consciousness are depicted by Annelise Orleck with great sensitivity in *Common Sense and a Little Fire*. This is an account of the lives of four women labour organizers, Fannia Cohn, Rose Schneiderman, Pauline Newman and Clara Lemlich. The biographical approach makes it evident that working-class women have been active in different ways and held dissimilar political views. It also provides a personal way of travelling through public large-scale movements and events, such as the clothing workers' strikes between 1905 and 1915, the connection between trade unionism and the suffrage cause, the struggle for labour legislation and workers' education, along with the organization of housewives around consumption. Orleck's focus on individuals means too that sexual choices and desires appear in the story; lesbianism as well as heterosexuality, figure in her account.[31] These personal aspects of working-class women activists' lives have been frequently excluded from the history of labour, partly because they have not been regarded as 'political' and partly because it has been feared that sex would discredit the seriousness of their public commitments. The minority of working-class women who entered the public sphere were thus divested of sexuality.

Yet, of course, sex and appearance have been crucial in the systems of surveillance and control which have restricted women's lives and these have always assumed varying cultural and social manifestations depending on class, race and ethnicity. An interesting change in interpretation has occurred. In contrast to the suspicion of young working-class women's interest in romance and popular culture which appeared in some writing of the 1970s, Stephen Norwood's *Labor's Flaming Youth; Telephone Operators and Worker Militancy, 1878–1923* (1990) shows glamour strengthening the confidence of young women workers, whose strikes became festive occasions.[32] Jacquelyn Dowd Hall has also integrated sexuality as an aspect of resistance in two illuminating essays on women's roles in strikes in the South. In 'Private Eyes, Public Women: Images of Class and Sex in the Urban South, Atlanta, Georgia, 1913–1915' (1991) she describes the sexual tensions and smears which ensued when O. Delight Smith, modern woman, journalist, labour organizer and divorcee, appeared in a dispute at the Fulton Bag and Cotton Mills, in 1914–15.[33] While in 'Disorderly Women' (1993) Dowd Hall tells how, when cotton workers rebelled in Elizabethton, Tennessee in 1929, townsmen and trade unionists alike, believed that, where women were concerned, 'respectability' was 'measured not only by chastity but by nuances of style'.[34] Trixie Perry, who was 28 when she was arrested for taunting the National Guards, broke all the taboos. She appeared in court wearing red, white and blue with the United States flag as a cap. Asked about how she was dressed she replied 'I was born under it, guess I have a right to it'.[35] A fellow striker remembered her sexual defiance and militancy, fifty years later, adding protectively, 'Trixie was not a woman who sold her body for sex ... She just had a big desire for sex ... and when she had a cause to fight for, she'd fight'.[36]

A similar association of the personal with public action is made by Jacqueline Jones in the very different context of the 1860s in Charleston. Here the 'nuances of style' assumed a particular significance because slavery had denied African American women any choice in clothing. She quotes a hostile white observer: 'Negro women dressed in the most outre style, all with veils and parasols for which they have an especial fancy – riding on horseback with negro soldiers and in carriages'.[37] The perception that personal defiance can provide a clue to social resistance in everyday life connects with a growing interest in the visual and symbolic signs of rebellion within social history. By looking at women's personal experience and behaviour in thinking through the meanings of gender historically, feminist historians have been shedding new light, not only on rank and file movements at work and in communities, but also on the terms in which grass roots resistance can be envisaged.

19

However, the lesson of the 1980s was to be that defiance is not the whole story. Living through the Reagan era taught some harsh lessons, among them the need to consider how spontaneous action could be sustained. The shifts in outlook which were to ensue have provided radical historians with some new entry points. Ava Baron notes that from the mid 1980s an effort to reconnect history from below to the structures of power was appearing in American labour history. Community centred workers' movements were being linked with the institutional history of unions and both were being situated in the wider economy and society.[38] An impressive number of trade union histories about women, including some which have drawn on oral history, represent a growing realization that it is not enough to search for alternative sources of rebellion; the existing basis of power has also to be tackled.[39]

By showing how male trade unionists have had diverse and conflicting attitudes to women workers' rights which cannot be read from an existing political script, these studies have begun to present a more graduated assessment than provided either by the syndicalist idealization of the rank and file or by the demonization of male workers in feminist invocations of 'patriarchy' as an abstracted continuum. An early example was Ruth Milkman's *Gender at Work: The Dynamics of Job Segregation by Sex during World War Two* (1985). This shows how post-war union attitudes to women varied between unions and also between particular union locals and leaderships. Milkman demonstrates that the view, popular within some strands of feminism, that male workers are responsible for women's subordination at work is to attribute much greater power to them than they have possessed in actuality. Only in alliance with employers were they able to block women's entry into jobs.[40]

In an essay on 'Gender and Trade Unionism in Historical Perspective'[41] Ruth Milkman traced the differing historical structures of trade union organizing in the USA more generally, examining their contradictory responses to gender. For example, craft unions excluded women but sometimes accepted their contribution in social and cultural spaces which enabled the women to organize. During the 1930s the Congress of Industrial Organizations (CIO) did formally endorse women's equality, and already in the late 1940s there were women trade unionists arguing for what later became known as comparable worth. However these mass unions were predominantly male. Milkman shows that it has been the recent unionization of women in the service and public sector unions, a phenomena closely bound up with the feminist movement, which has really marked a new stage. From the 1970s women workers have tried to combine the pursuit of equality as workers, with a recognition of the particular needs of women, taking this challenge into the mainstream of union policy.

Ruth Milkman thus presents a complex and differentiated overview of specific organizational forms of unionism. This way of looking at unions means it is possible to consider the pros and cons of specific structures for women or for specific groups of women, rather than resorting to an ahistorical and generalized criticism of unions as simply 'male dominated' which produces a literature of complaint rather than analysis. Her conclusion is that there have been both openings for women workers to push their own interests and restrictions on how far these could go.

Milkman's use of the idea of 'gender' to look at trade unionism is part of a broader recognition that it is not just what men have done to women or what women themselves have done which is at issue. 'Women's history' has shared with labour history an obvious snag. In asserting one group which has been neglected, whether this be 'women' or 'workers', there is the danger of distorting the record by extracting a single category from social relationships as a whole. The various uses of the concept of 'gender' have arisen partly out of an awareness of the need for integration. For example, Ava Baron in her collection *Work Engendered*, pointed to the differences in emphasis in many studies of men's and women's work and argued that we needed to be looking at gender also in relation to men in labour history. She stated that the book was not

> ... about women workers, although women, and women's work are central subjects in some of the chapters. Rather this book shows that gender colors a myriad of relations of power and hierarchy, including those between employers and workers, men and boys, and whites and blacks, as well as those between men and women. Gender is continually reconstituted as various groups politically contest multiple forms of masculinity and femininity.[42]

This approach to gender is dynamic, rather than suggesting an abstract structure. For example, Ava Baron has shown how nineteenth-century American male printers and employers invoked differing views of womanliness in relation both to technological changes and in arguments about labour relations. She has also traced the various historical meanings of manliness which have appeared in the printing trade.[43]

There has been a strong tendency in feminist history simply to assume that men and women's experiences of class are opposing rather than shared. Carole Turbin points out in her history of laundresses, *Working Women of Collar City: Gender, Class and Community in Troy, 1864–86* that this can be as misleading as the presumption that no antagonism has existed. As she observes, '... interests based on gender are not necessarily shared by all women, or women of the same class, but reflect differences in household structure, cultural traditions, and political ideologies'.[44] So, rather than seeing women's history as occupying a separate sphere, recognition of gender relations can bring the interconnections between men and women back into view. A historical awareness of gender

21

relations makes it possible to approach the particularities and diversities of their manifestation without prejudgement.

Moreover, the concept of 'gender' provides a means of moving outwards into the masculine public sphere of labour and trade union history with some new insights. It has been employed to break out of camp and take some issues raised by feminism into how labour history itself is conceived and constituted. As Joan Scott has observed, gender can bring a wider perspective to how power is defined, structured and exercised.[45] In the introduction to *Work Engendered*, Ava Baron uses 'gender' in this sense when she points out that women and men's '... participation in the labor movement was shaped by assumptions about gender built into union organization, policies and tactics'.[46] This kind of 'gender lens' has been an important means of exiting from a ghettoized labour history in which men look at male workers and women look at women. Feminist historians consequently have been digging away at many of the broader presuppositions about labour's past – among these has been a rethinking of what Elizabeth Faue has described as the 'paths of unionization'.[47]

Moreover, 'gender' has enabled feminist historians to look critically at how assumptions are embedded, not only in labour institutions, but in state policies – from employment legislation to welfare.[48] Eileen Boris' research into homework, for instance, has demonstrated how the meaning of who could be seen as a 'worker' has been affected by gendered assumptions within state policies, as well as by the differing modernizing discourses about employment favoured by both liberal reformers and the labour movement.[49]

However, like all approaches that foreground a specific aspect of history, disregarded by partial interpretations of a supposedly 'universal' outlook, 'gender' also contains certain problems. Actual women's lives can vanish once again and so can their views and actions, lost in a series of gendered discourses. Conversely the concept of gender can coagulate into an unwieldy block which can make it harder to consider those aspects of women's subordination which are affected by other social factors or recognize that women can conceive their gender needs and interests in dissimilar, sometimes conflicting, ways. Class, ethnicity and race can be subsumed within gender as the theoretical trends go into a new spin of exclusion which simply substitutes gender for class as *the* determining reason for oppression. The result is that the other influences upon women's lives and consciousness are again concealed.

How and why individuals situate themselves in specific social situations in history is always a complex and many faceted process which cannot be neatly encapsulated by explanations which assume a single cause. As Carole Turbin says of the collar laundresses,

> The public statements of collar laundresses reveal a consciousness of themselves as subordinate women who were, at the same time, men's

equals as trade unionists. Identifying themselves squarely within the labor movement, collar laundresses were concerned with women's issues that were directly related to working-class families' daily life and economic goals, not with rights or identities shared by all women.[50]

One corrective to ideological simplification is certainly to interpret and apply 'gender', not as a fixed structure, but as a relationship which is redefined and reshaped by individuals in the particular historical circumstances in which they find themselves. However, an advantage in continuing to look at 'women', is that it is possible to take on board how various forms of subordination can manifest themselves in specific historical contexts. These can be easily missed if the focus is just on 'gender'. For example, *Dishing It Out* (1991), Dorothy Sue Cobble's account of the waitresses' organization as craft workers in all-female local union branches, describes how they did gain male support, but were to exclude black and Asian workers until the 1930s.[51] As Ellen Carol DuBois and Vicki L. Ruiz indicate, in the title of their influential multi-cultural reader in women's history, it has often been a case of 'unequal sisters'.[52] Part of this inequality has been a tendency for the opinions of the privileged to prevail. Jacqueline Jones begins her history of black women since slavery, *Labor of Love, Labor of Sorrow* (1985) with a reminder that the assumption that work is somehow inherently emancipatory, has been challenged by poor black women's experiences of work.[53]

In their somewhat contorted Hegelian prose, the editors of *Radical America* presumed cheerfully in 1971, 'When ... consciousness grows fuller and more self-confident, the particularity of the women's movement will not be abolished but may be linked to the generality of the tasks ahead'.[54] Socialist feminist historians initially saw the emphasis upon women as a temporary remedy for exclusion. Many of us believed, as Linda Gordon stated in 1975, that this would '... throw a wider circle of illumination which takes in men as well'.[55] Our aim was to broaden the understanding of class and race, not to 'eradicate' either.

Moreover, by entering a neglected social experience the intention was to recast the prevailing orientation of historical enquiry rather than establishing a permanently separate camp. Instead, of course, inventing a new discipline of 'women's history' was to prove easier than shifting historical perspectives. This vast body of work was to result in many gains in understanding, however, as time went by the main preoccupation of women's history was to be with what was regarded as peculiar and distinct to women. It was thus to be only a minority of feminist historians who have been attempting to rethink the classic ground of labour history by bringing new ways of looking at the formation of classes, class struggle, work and community as well as trade unionism. However, this minority tradition has been extremely significant, not simply in keeping a bridge open between scholars in the two fields, but in provoking

23

rethinking. As David Montgomery observed in 1981 to Mark Naison and Paul Buhle:

> The work of feminist scholars, indeed the whole *corpus* of recent work on women's history, has been of central importance in getting me to think about what else is involved in class beyond the relations of production. How does a work force overlap with a working class?[56]

In her article 'Women's Labor History' in *Signs* in 1993, Ruth Milkman remarked that, '... recent writings in twentieth-century women's labor history' could have a contemporary application. Milkman suggests that they might reveal the circumstances and structures which have helped or impeded 'women's labor activism', and, 'illuminate the roots of the present impasse facing organized labor'.[57] I think this is indeed true. For, although women's labour history emerged out of the particular circumstances of the 1960s, it has assumed a remarkable relevance for thinking through the new reality of labour in the world today. As the global span and organization of production have been transformed and the forms of class resistance developed after the Second World War have lost much of their effectiveness, it has become evident that class and the labour movement are not fixtures which can be taken for granted. These are far from being parochial concerns. As we look outwards at the conditions of a new working class – many of whom are women – in Vietnam, in China, in Malaysia, in Korea, a much wider class struggle, which requires a new gendered labour history, comes into view.

A new set of questions are being created by a changing present. Questions about who constitutes the working class, about how fragmented and divided groups of workers have organized, issues about workplace and community and the democratization of unions and state policies are assuming centre stage. As the contours of the present shift, it is becoming possible to look back from new perspectives. And North American feminist historians who have been moving the boundary stones between categories such as 'women', 'gender', 'labour' or 'culture', have found new vantage points.

The consequences of historians' researches cannot be predicted – one very good reason to avoid being prescriptive. Take a fascinating and evocative comment by Sherna Berger Gluck in her study of women in the Second World War, *Rosie the Riveter Revisited* (1987):

> ... changes in consciousness are not *necessarily*, or immediately reflected in dramatic alterations in the public world. They may be very quietly played out in the private world of women, yet expressed in a fashion that can both affect future generations and eventually be expressed more openly when the social climate is right.[58]

Gluck is drawing on thoughts and debates in women's history, but her

24

observation is evidently marked by an awareness which comes from living through a right-wing era. Her reflection has a wider bearing on social consciousness for it suggests how historical perceptions can migrate across artificial boundaries. Labour historiography, which has been preoccupied with the heroic moments, could learn from private worlds and quiet times as well. After all some understanding of how periods which seem uneventful can be sources for renewal is in accord with the exigencies of our own times.

Rosalyn Baxandall and Linda Gordon remind us of the shared ambitions which marked the radical origins of both labour and women's history. They conclude their introduction to the revised version of *America's Working Women* by saying, 'We see this book not only as a tool for learning and teaching about working women, but also as a contribution to advancing their living and working conditions, pride in their history, and the respect that they are accorded'.[59] The challenge faced by both feminist and labour historians continues to be how to ensure that the intellectual resources and skills of the academy can be combined with reaching outwards towards a wider community of learning.

One of the lessons of the last three decades is that this aspiration to contest a dominant culture and democratize knowledge is much less straightforward than we envisaged in the late 1960s. Yet it remains vital. One of its most surprising assets has proven to be that remarkable tendency for work pursued with one set of questions in mind to contain revelatory insights for quite different circumstances.

The long term aim is surely a history that takes for granted the whole range of social relationships when looking at their manifestation in any specific situation in the past. In the short term we have much to learn from one another.

Notes

1. Giddings, Paula (1985), *When and Where I Enter: The Impact of Black Women on Race and Sex in America*, Toronto and New York: Bantam Books.
2. Buhle, Paul (1990), *History and the New Left: Madison, Wisconsin 1950–1970*, Philadelphia: Temple University Press, p. 27.
3. MARHO: The Radical Historians' Organization (1984), *Visions of History*, New York: Pantheon, pp. 154, 176.
4. See Buhle, Mari Jo, Gordon, Ann D., Schrom, Nancy (1971), 'Women in American Society: An Historical Contribution', *Radical America*, 4 (5), 3–66 and Anon, (no date circa 1972), *American Labor History: Women in the Working Class*, Boston: Radical America Pamphlet.
5. Rowbotham, Sheila (1983), *Dreams and Dilemmas*, London: Virago, pp. 38–9.
6. Alexander, Sally (1994), *Becoming a Woman and Other Essays in 19th and 20th Century History*, London: Virago, p. xvii.
7. MARHO: The Radical Historians' Organization (eds) (1984), *Visions of History*, New York: Pantheon, pp. 75–6.

8. Baxandall, Rosalyn, Gordon, Linda, Reverby, Susan (eds) (1976), *America's Working Women: A Documentary History 1600 to the Present*, New York: Vintage Books, p. xix.
9. Cluster, Dick, (ed.) (1979), *They Should Have Served That Cup of Coffee: Seven Radicals Remember the Sixties*, Boston: South End Press, p. 7.
10. Breines, Wini, (1982), *The Great Refusal: Community and Organization in the New Left: 1962–1968*, New York: Praeger, pp. 1–8.
11. Baxandall, Gordon, Reverby (eds) (1976) *America's Working Women*, p. xxii.
12. Eisenstein, Sarah (1983), 'Bread and Roses: Working Women's Consciousness, 1905–1920' in *Give Us Bread But Give Us Roses: Working Women's Consciousness in the United States: 1890 to the First World War*, Boston: Routledge and Kegan Paul, p. 32.
13. Scott, Joan Wallach (1988), *Gender and the Politics of History*, New York: Columbia University Press, pp. 17–19.
14. Editors' Introduction (1971), *Radical America*, **5** (4), 1.
15. Lerner, Gerda (1975), 'Placing Women in History: Definitions and Challenges', *Feminist Studies* **3** (1), 5–14.
16. Rowbotham, Sheila (1983), *Dreams and Dilemmas*, London: Virago, pp. 188–9.
17. Milkman, Ruth (1993), 'New Research in Women's Labor History', *Signs* **18** (2), 377.
18. Kessler-Harris, Alice (1982), *Out to Work: A History of Wage-earning Women in the United States*, New York: Oxford University Press, p. xi.
19. Editors' Introduction (1971), *Radical America*, **5** (4), 2.
20. Stansell, Christine (1986), *City of Women: Sex and Class in New York, 1789–1860*, New York: Alfred A. Knopf; and Blewett, Mary (1988), *Men, Women and Work: Class, Gender, and Protest in the New England Shoe Industry 1780–1910*, Urbana and Chicago: University of Chicago Press.
21. Baron, Ava (1991), 'Gender and Labor History: Learning from the Past, Looking to the Future', in Baron, Ava (ed.), *Work Engendered: Toward a New History of American Labor*, Ithaca: Cornell University Press, p. 3.
22. Glenn, Susan A. (1990), *Daughters of the Shtetl: Life and Labor in the Immigrant Generation*, Ithaca, New York: Cornell University Press.
23. Kaplan, Temma (1987), 'Women's Communal Strikes in the Crisis of 1917–1922', in Bridenthal, Renate, Koonz, Claudia, Stuard, Susan, Mosher (eds), *Becoming Visible: Women in European History* (Second edition), Boston: Houghton Mifflin.
24. Kaplan, Temma (1982), 'Female Consciousness and Collective Action: The Case of Barcelona 1910–1918', *Signs*, **7** (3).
25. Ewen, Elizabeth (1985), *Immigrant Women in the Land of Dollars: Life and Culture of the Lower East Side, 1890–1925*, New York: Monthly Review Press.
26. Cameron, Ardis (1993), *Radicals of the Worst Sort: Laboring Women in Lawrence, Massachusetts, 1860–1912*, Urbana and Chicago: University of Illinois Press, p. 4.
27. Ibid., p. 5.
28. Faue, Elizabeth (1991), *Community of Suffering and Struggle: Women, Men and the Labor Movement in Minneapolis, 1915–1945*, Chapel Hill: The University of North Carolina Press, p. 18.
29. Frank, Dana (1994), *Purchasing Power: Consumer Organizing, Gender, and the Seattle Labor Movement 1919–1929*, New York: Cambridge University Press, p. 7.
30. Ibid., p. 60.

31. Orleck, Annelise (1995), *Common Sense and a Little Fire: Women and Working Class Politics in the United States 1900–1965*, Chapel Hill: The University of North Carolina Press.
32. Norwood, Stephen H. (1990), *Labor's Flaming Youth: Telephone Operators and Worker Militancy, 1878–1923*, Urbana and Chicago: University of Illinois Press.
33. Dowd Hall, Jacquelyn (1991), 'Private Eyes, Public Women: Images of Class and Sex in the Urban South, Atlanta, Georgia, 1913–1915', in Baron, *Work Engendered*, pp. 243–72.
34. Dowd Hall, Jacquelyn (1993), 'Disorderly Women: Gender and Labor Militancy in the Appalachian South', in Melosh, Barbara (ed.), *Gender and American History Since 1890*, New York and London: Routledge, p. 259.
35. Dowd Hall, Jacquelyn (1993), 'Disorderly Women', in Melosh, Barbara (ed.), *Gender and American History Since 1890*, p. 257.
36. Ibid., p. 261.
37. Jones, Jacqueline (1985), *Labor of Love, Labor of Sorrow: Black Women and the Family from Slavery to the Present*, New York: Basic Books, p. 259.
38. Baron, Ava (1991), 'Gender and Labor History', in Baron (ed.), *Work Engendered*, pp. 3–4.
39. See for example, Gabin, Nancy F. (1990), *Feminism in the Labor Movement; Women and the United Auto Workers, 1935–1975*, Ithaca, New York: Cornell University Press; Hine, Darlene Clark (1989), *Black Women in White: Racial Conflict and Cooperation in the Nursing Profession, 1890–1950*, Bloomington: Indiana University Press.
40. Milkman, Ruth (1985), *Gender at Work: The Dynamics of Job Segregation by Sex During World War Two*, Urbana and Chicago: University of Illinois Press.
41. Milkman, Ruth (1992), 'Gender and Trade Unionism in Historical Perspective', in Tilly, Louise A. and Gurin, Patricia (eds), *Women, Politics and Change*, New York: Russell Sage Foundation.
42. Baron, (1991), 'Gender and Labor History', in Baron (ed.), *Work Engendered*, p. 1.
43. Baron, Ava (1991), 'An "Other" Side of Gender Antagonism at Work: Men, Boys, and the Remasculinization of Printers' Work, 1830–1920', in Baron (ed.), *Work Engendered*; and Baron, Ava (1987), 'Contested Terrain Revisited; Technology and Gender Definitions of Work in the Printing Industry, 1850–1920', in Wright, Barbara Drygulski (ed.), *Women, Work and Technology: Transformations*, Ann Arbor: University of Michigan.
44. Turbin, Carole (1992), *Working Women of Collar City: Gender, Class, and Community in Troy, 1864–1886*, Urbana and Chicago: University of Illinois Press, p. 218.
45. Scott, Joan (1996), 'Gender: A Useful Category of Historical Analysis', in Scott, Joan (ed.), *Feminism and History*, Oxford and New York: Oxford University Press, pp. 170–5.
46. Baron, Ava (1991), 'Gender and Labor History', in Baron (ed.), *Work Engendered*, p. 39.
47. Faue, Elizabeth (1991), 'Paths of Unionization: Community, Bureaucracy and Gender in the Minneapolis Labor Movement of the 1930s', in Baron (ed.), *Work Engendered*, p. 296.
48. See for example, Kessler-Harris, *Out to Work*; Gordon, Linda (1990), *Women, the State and Welfare* (ed.), Madison: University of Wisconsin Press; Mink, Gwendolyn (1995), *The Wages of Motherhood: Inequality in the Welfare State 1917–1942*, Ithaca: Cornell University Press.

49. Boris, Eileen (1994), *Home to Work: Motherhood and the Politics of Industrial Homework in the United States*, New York and Cambridge: Cambridge University Press, p. 14.
50. Turbin (1992), *Working Women of Collar City*, p. 128.
51. Cobble, Dorothy Sue (1991), *Dishing It Out; Waitresses and Their Unions in the Twentieth Century*, Urbana and Chicago: University of Illinois Press.
52. Du Bois, Ellen Carol and Ruiz, Vicki L. (1990) (eds), *Unequal Sisters: A Multi-Cultural Reader in U.S. Women's History*, New York and London: Routledge.
53. Jones (1985), *Labor of Love, Labor of Sorrow*, p. 7.
54. Editors' Introduction (1971), *Radical America*, **5** (4), 2.
55. Gordon, Linda (1975), 'A Socialist View of Women's Studies: A Reply to the Editorial, Volume 1, Number 1', in *Signs*, **1** (2), 563.
56. 'MARHO: The Radical Historians' Organization' (1984), *Visions of History*, p. 177.
57. Milkman, Ruth (1993), 'New Research in Women's Labor History', *Signs*, **18** (2), 377–8.
58. Gluck, Sherna Berger (ed.) (1987), *Rosie the Riveter Revisited: Women, the War and Social Change*, Boston: Twayne Publishers, p. x.
59. Baxandall, Rosalyn and Gordon, Linda (eds) (1995), *America's Working Women: A Documentary History 1600 to the Present* (second edition, Revised and Updated), New York: W.W.Norton, p. xxvii.

CHAPTER TWO

Gendering Work in Eighteenth-century Towns

Deborah Simonton

Eighteenth-century towns

Many towns and cities of eighteenth-century Europe experienced significant, often rapid, growth. For example Aberdeen expanded from just over 10 000 in 1755 to over 16 000 by the 1790s; Berlin grew from 8000 in 1648 to 170 000 in 1790. The population of Copenhagen quadrupled between 1660 and 1760 and London increased by a third in the second half of the eighteenth century.[1] At the same time towns were at the centre of commercial developments which meant that more goods and services were available to support the urban community. The middle classes were developing an identity and an awareness of their position while the processes of industrial and commercial change meant that there was greater tension between the 'employers' and the 'workers'. Significantly, workplace relations were undergoing important transformations which were neither uniform in effect nor which took the same route in towns across Europe. Demographic change and the increasing use of rural industry outside the control of the corporate structures of many towns, meant that men, particularly artisans, were increasingly aware of their vulnerability in the workplace. This chapter will explore the ways in which the tensions of claiming position in the urban workplace and the struggles to retain status at work were reflected in a gendering of the workplace in new and important ways which had long-standing resonance.

There was a steadily rising female-to-male sex ratio in the growing cities of Europe with an expanding range of jobs open to women. In 1720 the population of Geneva was 55 per cent female; that of Aberdeen 61 per cent.[2] Yet, as Pam Sharpe has written, 'urban history has so far made little of the fact that towns were often areas with populations in which women predominated'.[3] *The Statistical Account for Scotland* stressed the importance of accommodation, employment opportunities and rural emigration in explaining this dominance; points echoed in Sharpe's work on Colchester:

> Befides, the temptations of cheap commodious houfes, of eafy accefs to fuel, and to all the neceffaries and comforts of life, from our vicinity to the port and the market of Aberdeen, and of the high probability of finding

employment from fome of the many manufactures carried on in the neighbourhood, induce many old women, and many of the widows and daughters of farmers and tradefmen, to leave the country and refide in this parifh, while their fons have either fettled as farmers in their native place, or gone abroad, or entered into the army or the navy.[4]

Though the urban economy could be a minefield with the risk of destitution leading to prostitution amongst other dangers, it also represented opportunity for married and unmarried women. Although precarious, furnished rooms, lodging houses and networks of women, not to mention shops and taverns with prepared food meant that women could live alone and survive. Throughout early modern Europe women regularly participated in the urban economy, their economic role was acknowledged, and their status as traders was widely recognized. But they did not take part in the trades on equal terms with men and the character of their work could and did vary radically. Women's status within a trade as well as the status of the trade are central aspects of how their activities related to the urban economy. The notion that women's work was necessarily home-based undervalues the extent to which they operated outside the household, and in towns, the extent to which the street and the market was their milieu. Their role in trading networks was important as was their financial role in keeping household and workshop accounts, and in managing the sale of workshop products. Similarly, the proportion of single and widowed women trading, sometimes temporarily, sometimes permanently, has to be reckoned with.

Status, position and gender

Permeating eighteenth-century society was a belief in the right order of things. Status and one's social position in the rank order of society were paramount in many people's minds. Reminiscent of Pope's 'vast chain of being', Clara Reeve stressed 'in a well regulated state, a right and true subordination is beautiful, where every order is kept in its proper state'.[5] Public identity was defined by birth, property, occupation and, collectively, by rank in the social order. However, 'most women were defined by the honour of their presiding male'.[6]

People did not perceive monolithic or homogenized classes, but groupings of a number of echelons, each represented by a variety of characteristics. Contemporary writers referred to the lower orders or middling orders for just such a reason. King's and Colquhoun's ordering of society based on income lends weight to this assertion as does Defoe's ranking according to consumption. Similarly, examples from the Continent divided the three (and sometimes four) estates into several subdivisions. Within each level, there were a number of minute gradations which were important in creating status differentiation and defining one's place in society. The political economist Antoine de Montchrestien argued that the third estate was composed of three sorts of men: labourers, artisans and merchants.[7] Defoe was at great pains to distinguish tradesmen from manufacturers and artisans on the one hand and peddlers on the other, and 'As there are several degrees of people employed in trade below [tradesmen] ..., such as *workmen*, *labourers*, and servants; so there is a degree of traders above them, which we call *merchants*'.[8]

Along with the sense of industrial and scientific improvement and a feeling of growing prosperity, social aspirations governed the actions of wide sections of society across Europe. As Dorothy Marshall explained, 'class distinctions were important and gave form and order to everyday living, but created no insurmountable barrier to either economic or individual progress'.[9] Thus the belief in improvement often translated into the desire for social advancement, for upward social mobility. Industrial and economic change brought structural changes in occupational relationships which affected social position. Old distinctions between labourer and artisan were blurred by increasing employment of waged labour under skilled foremen instead of journeymen qualified by apprenticeship. Increasing affluence, particularly for sectors of the middling orders, put them in a better position to assume the trappings of those above them in the social hierarchy. For example, better incomes led to a more pretentious social life for many Essex farmers and the smaller professional groups. The falling demand for Essex baize undermined clothiers, while successful artisans began to rise in prominence.[10] In Paris, tension between masters and men, and concern to tie men to their work and place was a recurrent theme. This anxiety resulted in *lettres patentes* in 1749 with the clear purpose of controlling workers' movement.[11] Similar mobility operated for those in the lower orders, both male and female, who were able to 'better themselves' through apprenticeship or movement through the servant hierarchy.[12] The apprehension about social mobility was illustrated by a German writing in 1722, 'it would be better if everyone kept his station'.[13]

At the same time, ideological and social change resulted in a reworking of gender so that women's roles became central to defining social status. New scientific thought and the Enlightenment reshaped the Judeo-Christian tradition that depicted women as evil and dangerous and added new and extremely durable theoretical justifications for legal, economic, social and educational disabilities. The bourgeoisie was significant in creating gender roles defined in terms of public and private spheres and emphasizing domesticity for females. Although the new middle classes shared Enlightenment criticisms of absolutism, 'they adhered to tradition when it came to the role and rights of woman'.[14]

Beginning from the supposedly weaker physical nature of the female, it was possible to exclude them from a range of occupations and activities. Thus, identification of women with an idealized domestic role defined the character of their activities, whilst it appeared to enhance their image, sanctifying as virtues characteristics arising from their 'weakness'. Yet weakness, no matter how gloriously described, meant women required not mates, but protectors. Rousseau's creations of Julie, the perfect woman, and Sophie, Emile's companion, were prominent expressions of the new bourgeois ideal. Thus a key element of the idea of woman was that she was becoming defined by and restricted to domestic pursuits, because her 'acknowledged delicacy and weakness of person' disqualified her from heavy, robust activity.[15]

Linked to sexual protection of women, ideology ultimately subordinated women to men, while women's particular responsibilities as helpmates to husbands or as educators of children defined them in relation to men and family. New attitudes towards children and the identity of childhood as a formative stage in personality development modified perceptions of child and mother. Highlighting the importance of childhood in shaping adult character, many, like Rousseau, gave mothers primary responsibility for childcare and nurture so that 'there will be a reform in morals'.[16] At the same time, women were at the centre of the debate about social mobility because of the role they were expected to fill and the influence they had on future generations. As Reeve complained, 'Every rank and degree of people bring up their children in a way above their station and circumstances: they step over their proper place and set themselves on a higher form'.[17]

The culture of the workshop

Towns tended to be built on a foundation of corporatism and *ancien régime* societies' self-perception stressed corporate identity and organization. In this context the 'profundity of the divide between skill and lack of skill offers a key to understanding the insistent concern of those without skill, or whose skills were at risk, to create or consolidate their own associative structures'.[18] Woolf thus explains the tendency for the endogamous marriage of widows within trades in order to retain an *effective* if not *legal* membership in the corporation. Such practices were reflective of a widespread need to achieve corporate identity. Corporate identity had a number of important implications for control of community and maintenance of custom, and particularly helped protect small masters from the implications of free enterprise. Corporate regulation helped protect trades, maintain quality and regulate the workplace and through it the community.

Sonenscher's discussion of French *compagnonnages* and Darnton's essay 'The Great Cat Massacre' identify the importance of rituals in creating symbolic inequalities in order to establish barriers which protected workers' fragile claims to the work that they did. In a world which relied on relatively homogeneous skills and a range of abilities, rituals and ascription of status or honour were important to defend workers' places, and allowed masters a means of controlling work and journeymen.[19] French, German and English experience of work and the workplace defined an important characteristic of skill, in that it is a linguistic device to claim and maintain control and exclusivity in the workplace. The idea that there was a secret to maintain, that there were rituals to go through, even that strength or size were aspects of the ascription of status and skill is significant to understanding women's position with regard to the workplace. Farge explained that a man's tools represented his patrimony; they signified his 'possession of a personal qualification'. He possessed not only the tools of the trade but the trade itself. 'The implement was the privileged means by which he created his own free space between himself and his master'.[20] Rule has shown how the property of skill was at the centre of workers' self-evaluations, and the notions associated with skill spilled far beyond the workplace to enter the vocabulary of a more generalized labour with its own rights and dignity.[21] As Darnton explained, 'In entering an "estate", Jerome assimilated an ethos. He identified himself with a craft; and as a fully-fledged journeyman compositor, he received a new name. Having gone through a rite of passage in the full, anthropological sense of the term, he became a Monsieur'.[22]

Whilst this image had meaning in the urban community, as Farge says, 'the workshop was not ... a system based on the bond between the master's family and his journeymen where all lived together in blessed intimacy and familiarity'. Neither can we assume the workplace was static. Farge identifies a great deal of mobility with journeymen moving from one master to another in the same town, across country and from one type of work to another. Similarly the idea of a trade for life has to be modified, since it was not unusual to find a journeyman working in a different trade from his apprenticeship, either through shortage of work or the means to carry out the trade. Such insecurity was another factor promoting dissension in the ranks of custom and practice of the workshop.[23]

Custom and control in the workshop, divisions of labour and the political and economic life of many towns inhibited women's access to certain trades and occupations. The extent of such restrictions depended on the ability of male power structures to limit women's work, which in turn depended on the corporate structure of the town. Thus those towns which were not governed by guilds and corporate regulations might have provided women with more opportunities than those which were. Yet, despite regional and national differences, the working experiences of urban women throughout Europe were strikingly alike. Changes in institutional structures, methods of production, ideologies and conditions of labour supply influenced them in similar ways and shaped the character of their work.

Most European city economies were dominated by guilds and the corporate structures and controls which came with them. The effect was to link economic, social and political roles in explicit and implicit ways which had important ramifications for rank and status, but which also had particular meaning for women's role in urban society. Although there were female guilds, notably in Cologne, Paris and Rouen, and women gained admission to some male guilds, they were essentially masculine organizations which paralleled the male life cycle, reflecting in their structure and rules aspects of male rites of passage. Guild regulation of the workplace, and of access to it through apprenticeship and mastership rules, helped embed masculinity into artisanal work and to define as male, work which was perceived as skilled. These regulations were about control and exclusion. Whilst they existed to maintain standards of production, they were equally intended to hold up prices and prevent unskilled labour from undermining their position.

Ostensibly apprenticeship was about training in a craft or trade, and the literature and documentary evidence is full of references to training, carrying with it to modern eyes the notion of ability, skill and expertise. Rule refers to skilled workers seeking to preserve the apprenticeship sections of the English Statute of Artificers and Apprentices, while Behagg links 'skilled' with 'artisan' when discussing workers who had served apprenticeships and who argued to preserve the custom of the trade. In France, whenever a woman attempted to do a skilled job without serving an apprenticeship and passing through the guild structure, male members of the guild asserted their exclusive right to skilled work.[24] However, the language of apprenticeship included 'mysteries', 'arts' and 'practices' of trades, and represented the need to pass on behavioural patterns expected of one who conducted a trade. The use of the word 'mystery' conveyed a sense of value or rank which apprenticeship gained for a young man; it operated as an induction into a hierarchy which had social meaning. The word 'trade' as opposed to 'occupation' implied much the same sense. In this way apprenticeship marked a rite of passage, not only from youth into manhood, but also into a recognized status or position. He became one of them. While this had always been important, in eighteenth-century Europe, as notions of social rank and order intensified, regulation of social mobility became a central feature of economic life.

The period of apprenticeship was a period when the male apprentice moved from lad to man; it was a transitional period which meant far more than 'learning a skill'. The close identification of apprenticeship with sexual development helps to identify the role of the institution in defining masculinity and conversely femininity and in excluding females from the system. As Sheridan explained, 'The exclusion of women from apprenticeship contracts was therefore an integral part of a closed guild system which ensured that the transfer of property and power remained within a privileged group'.[25] Skill and status which boys could achieve through apprenticeship were simply not options for girls. While girls might learn technical ability, they did not acquire the quality of 'skill'. They might learn a trade or get a job, but they did not become skilled. Underlying girls' apprenticeships were the values which society placed on status and the meaning of skill. They did not gain the attributes which went with skill and which had by the end of the eighteenth century, become clearly part of masculine qualities. Skill and training were not the root cause of exclusion in the workplace, but notions about masculinity and femininity and their relationship to the meanings of work were.[26]

Challenges to corporatism

During the century, workplace tensions were exacerbated by a fundamental split over protection of the workplace and retention of the property of skill on one hand and pressures for unregulated free enterprise on the other. At the same time, the occupational controls of guilds and apprenticeship seemed to loosen, because many workers lay outside that structure. Additionally, the hierarchy of trades underwent disorientation in the fluid economic situation where time-honoured occupations declined and new ones rose to take their place. This situation created uncertainty about status and heightened a concern for maintaining social distinctions. It was often a very fine job for craft guilds and civil authorities to establish and maintain equity between masters and men and between small and large masters, especially in the fluid market of the eighteenth century. Each expected their position to be protected and their rights not to be abused. As Farge explained, three opposing concepts operated: the desire of authorities to see that the power of masters was not undone, thus guaranteeing the policing of the realm; political economists arguing for suppression of corporations which held back industrialization, and wage earners using an alliance with masters to gain the right to set up on their own, whilst also undermining the system by breaking contracts to take on more advantageous ones.[27]

Economic opinion which favoured removal of trade restrictions was aggressively opposed to apprenticeship. Adam Smith's classical statement of this position gave theoretical force to views which were already widely held across Europe. He built his case for abolition of apprenticeship on what he saw as the fallacy that apprenticeship produced a skilled and industrious workforce. The thrust of his attack was precisely that few trades required extensive skills to practise them. If skill were the most important aspect of apprenticeship, most apprentices' terms could have been far shorter. He argued that apprenticeship restricted entrance to employment, by limiting the number of apprentices allowed each master. Lengthy training, which increased the expense of

35

education, restrained it indirectly. Similarly apprenticeship obstructed the free circulation of labour from one employment to another, by requiring seven years' training in any craft or trade before it could be practised. Smith saw apprenticeship as a deliberate attempt by craftsmen to restrain competition and protect their own position and earnings. In the climate of free ebullient competition, with the abolition of apprenticeship 'the publick [sic] would be a gainer, the work of all artificers coming in this way much cheaper to market'.[28] The same approach lay behind Turgot's short-lived edict of 1776 banning guilds and masterships, making the exercise of all trades free.[29]

In opposition to the forces of free trade stood skilled workers who wished to protect their position within a trade and the trade's position within the economic and social structure. Smith argued that apprenticeship regulations offended against the property each worker had in his own labour. In contrast, skilled workers maintained that apprenticeship conferred a particular property right to the exclusive exercise of their trade. Their seven-year service was thought to have purchased this right for them, enhanced in better trades by sizeable premiums which guaranteed admission to a trade with status and prospects. In addition to providing a 'closed shop', the right to control numbers of apprentices helped to prevent dilution of the trade thus maintaining price and wage levels. The fundamental issue was that craftsmen believed they had earned an exclusive property right to exercise their trade, while economic pressures backed by ideology pressed for the individual's natural right to employ his labour. The number of disputes involving untrained workmen or inadequately prepared apprentices suggests that adherence to formal apprenticeship increasingly was challenged by employers and that the challenge was resisted by their artisanal workforce.[30]

As pressures grew on guilds from competition by merchants putting work out to unincorporated areas, from new unregulated trades, from governments which reflected laissez faire attitudes, and from shifts in the economic structure of Europe which undermined many older trades, guild members became ever more assiduous in asserting their right to control labour and production. The challenge to guild structures and long-standing working practices meant that men had to fight to retain their place in the labour market.

Gendering labour

In protecting their position, men frequently redefined skilled work as male and low status work as female. Significantly, they more explicitly defined work practices with respect to masculinity. Indeed they often defined work which they wished to preserve for men as skilled in order to exclude women. As shifting definitions of status came together with re-evaluations of femininity, women were more frequently perceived as unsuited for work, particularly skilled work. Quataert has argued that such views drew on the importance of the distinction between 'honourable' and 'dishonourable' work, so that disesteemed and 'unskilled' rural industry was redefined as 'women's work' during the period. Equally important was the assurance that persons who learned the trade in a household would not be admitted to guilds. By denigrating the productive strength of the rural household, guildsmen came to equate village work with women's work. Previously rural work had been deprecated because it was non-guild, but after the mid-seventeenth century, such disesteemed work came to be identified as women's. Thus the increasingly closed world of the guild began to use gender as a fundamental determinant of work roles and their valuation. In this way, artisanal practice identified productive work as properly male and domestic activities in households as properly female. Significant was the association of women with dishonourable non-guild work and thus work which was perceived as 'unskilled'.[31]

At the same time, the widely held notion that status attached to the worker and not the work was explicit in the identity of male workers in the *compagnonnages* and implicit in reworking notions of skill when gender was at stake. Thus 'skilled' work was increasingly defined as men's work and craft mysteries as something not to be shared with women. However, the reasons for male exclusivity went beyond the notions of proper sphere and esteemed work. Wiesner has shown how to work with women could, in itself, dishonour a male worker, and argues that guild honour was the primary reason. In other words, 'women were to be kept out of guild shops not only because they had not been formally trained or would work more cheaply, but simply because they were women'.[32] Honour was an important commodity to journeymen as it protected their right to work. When prevented from attaining masterships they could become obsessed with the 'symbolic capital of honour'. As Lis and Soly have said, 'Afterall, honour and dishonour were not only moral categories but qualifications that affected someone's material status'.[33] How people spoke about each other was of considerable importance. They would feel themselves particularly vulnerable to dishonour, and to reiterate Woolf's view, the 'profundity of the divide between skill and lack of skill offers a key to understanding the insistent concern of those without skill, or whose skills were at risk, to create or consolidate their own associative structures'.[34] Wiesner demonstrates how not working next to women became an important part of a journeyman's notion of honour. Thus 'skilled work in guild shops was increasingly defined as men's work, and the "mystery" of any "craft", the "secrets of the trade" as something which should not be shared with women.'[35] The guild concept that the strongest bonds were those between men had implications far beyond the realm of economics and went hand in hand with other developments in the eighteenth century which operated to redefine male and female roles.

By the eighteenth century, important changes had taken place in women's guild position which undermined their status and right to trade. Guild response to the challenges which they perceived was to further restrict membership and to remove women from independent artisanship. First, guilds became more restrictive and protective of what they saw as their own interests. This was not explicitly gender-based, but had a detrimental effect on women's role within guilds. Second, identification of women with dishonourable work such as domestic production, and the recurrent notion of women as casual labour, as housewives and mothers, and a growing hostility to women's work contributed to specific restrictions levied against them. Thus urban guildsmen articulated the issues of competition arising from domestic industry by adopting a gender order that reserved to guildsmen sole control over production for exchange, and inextricably linked household production, now defined as dishonourable work, with women's work.[36]

Women were generally denied access to political institutions and civic life; their exclusion from the right to pass on guild privileges was limited in the same way. Eighteenth-century France provides one example of the impact on women's position. Admission to guilds usually depended on their relationship to the master, and women operated without full rights. Widows were allowed to continue a shop and retain journeymen, but could not themselves begin a new piece of work nor take on new apprentices, though apprentices indentured to late husbands could finish their time. Women also did not participate in the *compagnonnage*, except in the symbolic role of the *mère* who welcomed and housed journeymen during their stay in the city. Although girls were admitted as apprentices to the London booktrade, they were not in France, despite no specific prohibition by the *Compagnie des libraires*. Daughters could not gain entrance by patrimony, although they could confer rights upon suitably qualified husbands, similar to those which widows could confer on remarriage, but daughters had no legal right to enter a trade. It was argued that they had not served an apprenticeship, but of course, they were prohibited from doing so. Widows were permitted to continue in a 'private' capacity as 'relicts' of their husbands, because it gained them a livelihood and precisely because authorities preferred that they work than receive charity.[37] The situation was similar in English towns. No women were enrolled as mistresses in eighteenth-century Kingston upon Thames, though a handful took 'tolerations' allowing them to trade as 'not being free of the town'. Kingston, Southampton and Oxford limited trading women to widows, and allowed apprentices to serve the master's widow as long as she remained unmarried and continued to practise her husband's trade only. No widows took apprentices in their own right and girls were not apprenticed. There are no instances of married women trading in

38

their own right in Oxford between 1500 and 1800, though they certainly worked alongside husbands. Neither daughters nor spinsters had a right to trade.[38]

Some towns, however, provided openings for women. London clockmakers received girls as apprentices, and the Goldsmith's Company continued to admit women upon completion of apprenticeship, while other guild trades allowed women, not only widows, to enrol and take apprentices. Similarly, girls were apprenticed to the retail trades and women admitted to the Merchant Company of Edinburgh.[39] Genevan corporate structure provided advantages for anyone with citizen status while business opportunities for non-citizens, male and female alike, were restricted. Equal inheritance laws and female citizenship, carrying with it political power, could enable enterprising women to build up wealth, standing and 'clout'. However, women participated only marginally in the guild system. In two key areas, *passementerie* and watchmaking, girls were increasingly restricted from apprenticeship. In 1696 when a group of masters petitioned magistrates to permit girls to learn 'small tasks of gilding', the majority of masters, journeymen and masters' daughters opposed them, because 'decency and honesty never wished that the two sexes be mixed together to learn the same trade', thus reflecting the interplay of economics and ideology. Thus, as Monter says, guild regulation handicapped female artisans more effectively than social customs impeded businesswomen.[40]

These restrictions clearly were part of a campaign to restrain competition within the trade and to maintain an elite group of tradesmen. They also ensured that women's association with high status trades was mediated by men and was contained within the patriarchal structure. Trades comprised both the manufacture and selling of a product in the sense that goldsmiths, for example, both made and sold their goods. Therefore, while usually we think of the smith as a 'maker' of something, the whole activity is implied. Also, women who worked in a shop usually were occupied with menial tasks, finishing and selling. This activity was frequently ignored by the artisan community, but a woman selling such 'controlled' artisanal goods in her own right would have been restrained as not having been apprenticed to do so. A good example is women in Kingston upon Thames who were required to apply for 'tolerations' in order to be allowed to trade in the town, even to sell goods, as in the case of Sarah Ford between March and June of 1776. The Borough required that she take a toleration and pay a fine of £5 'to keep an open Shop there to sell by Retail Snuff, Toys and other Merchandizes within the said Town she not being free of the said Town ...'. In fact she refused the toleration 'to be granted to her as she intended leaving off businefs'.[41] Furthermore, women were prohibited from learning new processes or using new tools or machinery. Such controls made it more difficult for them to retain any position of importance within a shop, because not only were they contending with the ideological restraint which the changes represented, but they would have been unable to work as well or as fast as men.[42]

Another feature to the gendering of urban labour, however, was that domestic industries were practised in the towns of Europe, and indeed contributed to the change of many towns into the cities of Europe. Although proto-industry and the putting-out system are most closely identified with the countryside, it may be more accurate to think in terms of areas where corporate structures had little control. However, Ogilvie's work on Württemberg and Whyte's on Scotland demonstrate how simplistic such a distinction can be, in their exploration of the extension of corporate control to the countryside itself and the interplay of urban and rural structures.[43] Nevertheless, in less regulated sectors of work and regions of Europe and in processes which had not become coded as male, women were able to interject their presence more prominently.

In cloth centres like Augsburg, Ulm or Strasbourg both urban and rural women were kept busy spinning, as they were in Rouen and Aberdeen, and in Paris, one of the biggest female guilds was the guild of *filassières* and *fileuses*. Lace and silk industries often took place in towns like Lyon, Antwerp, Caen, Geneva and London, with women providing the bulk of the work force. The terrific increase of women in Aberdeen was partly attributed to the prevalence of hand knitting and linen spinning, which a woman was brought in to teach to other women shortly after the Battle of Culloden. In such trades women frequently were able to operate independently, either because of weak regulation, because they were closely identified as women's crafts or because the level of demand was such to allow them the freedom to trade. Such was the case for the spinners of Rouen and Augsberg, where large numbers worked directly for merchants rather than for weavers. In the same way, women were active in the hardware trades of Birmingham, as wage earners, independent traders and as members of family workshops. In the French booktrade, when there was a shortage of family help, non-kin females were employed, many of whom came from outwith the trade and without skills. Many low-profit items had never been regulated, such as brushes, combs, candles, soap, thimbles, brooms, needles and pins, wooden bowls and spoons, and women making them were not seen as a threat to the status of a craftsman.[44] As more towns grew up without ancient guild regulations, and as proto-industry tended to loosen their hold in other towns, women could maintain a sense of mobility and independence. Clearly, demographic trends indicate that significant numbers of single women operated in the urban economy. Indeed, official concern with unbridled women was partly a result of the visibility of the independent female trader, working outwith the control of a male, exacerbating the hostility to women who did not assume the natural state.

Patriarchy and worker identity

There is widespread evidence that European society attempted to rigidly control single women, with efforts made to keep them within a male-headed household, further underpinning patriarchal control. European society was suspicious of masterless persons, particularly women who were not controlled by a man: father, husband, or employer. Regulations, work practices and legal restrictions reinforced powers of husbands and fathers and were used to try to force females into households headed by men. Often unsuccessful, these attempts remain a reminder that what women did was not dependent solely on economic factors. The notion of a masterless woman applied equally to young single females, who were effectively between masters, that is between father and husband, and independent single women who by choice or accident were unmarried, working in their own right. Economic change and fears of a breakdown in public order combined with views of women's proper place and emergent notions of domesticity to increase suspicion of masterless women. Contemporaries explicitly tried to control their sexuality and blamed women for any perceived sexual laxity in society. French administrators sought to direct 'disorderly' single women into the discipline of royal manufactures, new factories and *ateliers de charité*. Such attitudes encouraged perceptions of female work as a 'stop-gap' until they attained a 'proper' married place, and helped to keep female wages low, further pressuring women into male-headed households. Married *femmes sole* were tolerated, if they adhered to the normative view of women's role. In Württemberg, they could be squeezed out of lucrative sectors, but sanctioned when working in a male-headed household or substituting for a husband. In urban Scotland, also heavily governed by corporate institutions, legal and institutional constraints buttressed economic disadvantages of being single in much the same way.[45] Most women remained in a patriarchal structure in households, mills and workshops which limited their freedom of action. Even where women gained or retained economic rights, custom still dictated forms of service and subservience.

Women could be seen as *de facto* joint partners in an establishment, a position gained through marriage, and built on their dowry and skills. But throughout much of Europe because law merged the married woman's legal identity with her husband's, as a *feme coverte*, she could be restrained from independent trading. In most instances, 'the man governed and the women assisted. ... Custom and law combined to promote asymmetrical relations between men and women within the family, but whatever the subordination of the wife, the work of both partners remained essential to success'.[46] Often the master's wife was a key member of the urban firm who

> had to feed and clothe not only her own family but also the apprentices, journeymen and any domestic servants that lived in. She also worked in the

shop and often sold the products her husband had made, ... She was often responsible for keeping records and collecting debts and for purchasing raw materials. If her husband was away, she ran the shop in his absence, directing the journeymen and apprentices.[47]

The significance of her contribution was recognized by guild regulations which often specified that masters had to be married and is attested to by a variety of sources, including police records of wives arrested or questioned about trading violations, and treated as equally responsible for the business.[48] Nevertheless, she was expected to respect accepted hierarchy and patriarchal control. Campbell's guide for apprentices and parents advised against a master whose wife ruled him, 'if the woman rules her Husband, it is generally remarked, the Master is incapable to teach his Apprentice; ... Such a woman who has got the better of her Husband, in the management of her Domestic Concerns, must of course rule his Apprentice'.[49] Farge cites examples from Paris which show journeymen complaining of the violation of order where the wife ruled the shop instead of the husband or 'master'. The master's wife was also particularly vulnerable to slurs on her reputation, and she was often the central figure when others wished to cast aspersions on the reputation of a business couple.[50]

At the same time women appear regularly with husbands in legal documents, such as apprenticeship indentures, often when girls were involved. Almost all documents signed by merchants consulted by Abensour for Paris and the Ile de France were countersigned by their wives.[51] Port books of late seventeenth-century Scotland also contain a sprinkling of wives signing for consignments in lieu of their husbands.[52] Earle argued for an 'extreme gender division of labour in London, and ... the work of women was almost entirely divorced from the men's work'; 'there was very little partnership between husband and wife'. However, others such as Davidoff and Hall, Barker on English printing trades, Darrow for Montaubon, Abensour and Sheridan for France argue strongly that women's activity in business was as a de facto if not de jure partner.[53]

Women's trading identity was often weak because they did not share in the comradely activities and rituals which permeated urban crafts. Because the transition from one life-cycle stage to another occurred at different points in women's lives, they generally did not develop a strong sense of kinship with women of their age group. Life-cycle changes also could mark shifts in their occupation, so that although a woman might have sold workshop products as daughter and wife, the product itself might have changed when she married. Thus women developed transferable skills, but did not necessarily develop a strong sense of occupational identity. However, through the esteem in which female traders were held by husbands, kin, neighbours, clients, and other women in the trade, they could gain and maintain a sense of craft and status. Groups of women sometimes evolved their own internal discipline and usages, such as the *crieuses de vieux chapeaux*, trading in old clothes and furniture, who developed their own extensive hierarchy and 'apprenticeship' system. In Lyon, as Davis shows, identity was noted by feminization of names, such as Estiennette Cappin, a tavernkeeper, becoming Estiennette Cappine, and by attribution of nicknames or titles of respect such as Dame. Such women's positions might be recognized by their frequency as godmother, by small loans to neighbours or gifts to needy women. Thus women gained a sense of achievement less through the identity of skill and more through establishing position in the neighbourhood.[54]

Conclusion

Demographic trends meant that most regions in Europe experienced population growth which put pressure on available jobs, such that those in positions to defend their work and status did so, both against women and against untrained men. Women's work often came to be seen as casual and untrained and associated with the homework which guildsmen saw as undercutting their position. Ideological pressures operating in society exacerbated gendered attitudes to women's work, and heightened women's responsibility for childcare. Many women who could afford to may have adopted the new model of womanhood willingly, although in many cases they continued to fulfil a role in the marriage market which helped to establish business ties and trade cohesion.

Various forms of gender-based division of labour had always existed. In towns women's trading role was always restricted by guilds, corporations and patriarchal officialdom. Women continued to operate in defiance of such restrictions, either by taking up new trades, or working in parallel with them. The increase in the kinds of industrial activities in the eighteenth-century through the development of domestic industries, especially in textiles, but also in auxiliary trades and metal trades, provided opportunities for unqualified men and women to insert themselves into the workplace in new and different ways. Specifically male honour became more important as definitions of work changed, and as men sought to protect their position relative to changes in the economic structure that meant that many men's independent work status was threatened and with it their personal status and value. Thus it became important not only to define skill and status *vis-à-vis* men who were seen as poachers, but against women. Men became the artisans, while women were relegated to low-status activities. On one level debates were not about gender but about position. But capitalistic challenges as well as shifting attitudes toward women meant that women came to be targets of specific interdictions and redefinitions of work. In fact, the need to define skill and redefine work probably contributed to the reshaping of femininity that was taking place.

Notes

1. Sinclair, Sir John (ed.) (1791–1799), *The Statistical Account of Scotland*, Witherington, Donald J. and Grant, Ian R. (eds) (1982), Wakefield: EP Publishing Limited, **xiv**, 285. Hereafter referred to as OSA; George, Dorothy (1931), *England in Transition* (reprint), Harmondsworth: Penguin Books Ltd., p. 318.
2. Monter, E. William (1980),'Women in Calvinist Geneva (1550–1800)', *Signs*, **6** (2), 189; OSA, **xiv**, 285.
3. Sharpe, Pamela (1994), 'De-industrialization and Re-industrialization: Women's Employment and the Changing Character of Colchester 1700–1850', *Urban History*, **21** (1), April, 78.
4. OSA, **xiv**, 293–4.
5. Reeve, Clara (1792), *Plans of Education; with Remarks on the Systems of Other Writers*, London: J. Johnson, p. 70.
6. Porter, Roy (1982), *English Society in the Eighteenth Century*, Harmondsworth: Penguin Books Ltd, p. 63.
7. George, *England in Transition*, pp. 150–5; Porter, *English Society*, pp. 63–112, 386–9; Earle, Peter (1976), *The World of Defoe*, London: Weidenfeld and Nicholson, p. 164; Burke, Peter, 'The Language of Orders in Early Modern Europe', in Bush, M. L. (ed.) (1992), *Social Order and Social Classes in Europe since 1500*, London: Longman, p. 6.
8. Defoe, Daniel (1727), *The Complete English Tradesman in Familiar Letters* (reprint), New York: Augustus M. Kelley Publishers, 1969, **I**, 2.
9. Marshall, Dorothy (1962), *Eighteenth-century England*, New York: David Mackay Company Inc., p. 39.
10. Brown, A. F. J. (1969), *Essex at Work, 1700–1815*, Chelmsford: Essex Record Office, pp. 138, 158–9, 163.
11. Farge, Arlette (1993), *Fragile Lives, Violence, Power and Solidarity in Eighteenth-century Paris*, London: Polity Press, p. 126.
12. See Hecht, J-Jean (1980), *The Domestic Servant in Eighteenth-century England*, London and Boston: Routledge and Kegan Paul, pp. 35–70.
13. Quoted in Treasure, Geoffrey (1985), *The Making of Modern Europe, 1648–1780*, London and New York: Methuen and Co. Ltd, p. 18.
14. Frevert, Ute (1988), *Women in German History, from Bourgeois Emancipation to Sexual Liberation*, Oxford: Berg Publishers Limited, p. 12.
15. Brown, John (1765), *On the Female Character and Education*, London: a sermon preached at the anniversary meeting of the Guardians of the Asylum for deserted Female orphans, p. 6.
16. Rousseau quoted in Pope, Barbara Corrado (1987), 'The Influence of Rousseau's Ideology of Domesticity', in Boxer, Marilyn and Quataert, Jean (eds), *Connecting Spheres*, Oxford: Oxford University Press, p. 140.
17. Reeve, *Plans of Education*, p. 60.
18. Woolf, Stuart (1992), 'Order, Class and the Urban Poor', in Bush (ed.), *Social Order and Social Classes*, p. 189, *see also* p. 190.
19. Sonenscher, Michael (1989), 'Mythical Work: Workshop Production and the *Compagnonnages* of Eighteenth-century France', in Joyce, Patrick (ed.), *The Historical Meanings of Work*, New York and Cambridge: Cambridge University Press, p. 50; Darnton, Robert (1991), *The Great Cat Massacre and Other Episodes in French Cultural History*, London: Penguin Books.
20. Farge, *Fragile Lives*, p. 125.

21. See Rule, John (1989), 'The Property of Skill in the Period of Manufacture', in Joyce (ed.), *Historical meanings of work*, pp. 99–118.
22. Darnton, *The Great Cat Massacre*, p. 91.
23. Farge, *Fragile Lives*, pp. 108–9.
24. See Dunlop O. J. and Denman, R. D. (1912), *English Apprenticeship and Child Labour – A History*, London: Fisher Unwin; Merson, A. L. (1968), 'Apprenticeship at Southampton in the Seventeenth Century', *A Calendar of Southampton Apprenticeship Registers, 1609–1740*, Southampton Records Series, **XII**, Southampton: Southampton University Press; Rule, John (1981), *Experience of Labour in Eighteenth-century Industry*, London: Croom Helm; Behagg, Clive (1979), 'Custom, Class and Change: the Trade Societies of Birmingham', *Social History*, **4** (3), October, 455–80; Simonton, Deborah (1988), 'The Education and Training of Eighteenth-century English Girls with Special Reference to the Working Classes', PhD Thesis, University of Essex, and (1998), *A History of European Women's Work, 1700 to the present*, London: Routledge; Farge, *Fragile Lives*, pp. 117–21; Abensour, Léon (1923), *La Femme et la Féminisme en France avant la Révolution* (reprint 1966), Geneva: Slatkine-Maganotis, p. 196.
25. Sheridan, Geraldine (1992), 'Women in the Booktrade in Eighteenth-century France', *British Journal for Eighteenth-century Studies*, **15** (1), Spring, 52.
26. Simonton, 'Education and Training', Ch. 5.
27. Farge, *Fragile Lives*, p. 126.
28. Smith, Adam (1776), *An Inquiry into the Nature and Causes of the Wealth of Nations* (reprint, 1976), Oxford: Oxford University Press, pp. 135–40, 151–2.
29. Abensour, *La Femme*, p. 197.
30. See Rule, *Experience of Labour*, pp. 106–7; Thompson, E. P. (1968), *Making of the English Working Class*, Harmondsworth: Penguin Books Ltd., p. 279; Dobson, C. R. (1980), *Masters and Journeymen: A Prehistory of Industrial Relations, 1717–1800*, London: Croom Helm, pp. 56, 114, 134; and George, Dorothy (1925), *London Life in the Eighteenth Century* (reprint 1965), Harmondsworth: Penguin Books, pp. 233–4.
31. Quataert, Jean (1985), 'The Shaping of Women's Work in Manufacturing Guilds, Households and the State in Central Europe, 1648–1870', *American Historical Review*, **90**, 1126–7, 1134–5.
32. Wiesner, Merry (1989), 'Guilds, Male Bonding and Women's Work in Germany', *Gender and History*, **1** (2), Summer, 127.
33. Lis, Catharina and Soly, Hugo (1993), 'Neighbourhood Social Change in Western European Cities, Sixteenth to Nineteenth Centuries', *International Review of Social History*, **38**, 16
34. Woolf, 'Order, Class and the Urban Poor', p. 189, see also p. 190.
35. Wiesner, 'Guilds, Male Bonding and Women's Work in Germany', p. 131.
36. Ibid., *passim*; Quataert, 'Shaping of Women's Work', p. 1124.
37. Fox-Genovese, Elizabeth (1984), 'Women and Work', in Samia Spencer (ed.), *French Women and the Age of Enlightenment*, Bloomington: Indiana University Press, p. 117; Abensour, *La Femme*, p. 187; Sheridan, 'Women in the Booktrade', pp. 51–2; Wiesner, Merry (1987), 'Women's Work in the Changing City Economy, 1500–1650', in Boxer and Quataert (eds), *Connecting Spheres*, p. 67; Prior, Mary (1985), 'Women and the Urban Economy, Oxford 1500–1800', in Prior, Mary (ed.), *Women in English Society 1500–1800*, London and New York: Methuen and Co., p. 103.
38. Kingston Upon Thames, Roll of Admission to the Freedom of ... Companies, 1746–1835, KB 11/1/4, Court of Assembly Minutes, 1725–1776, KB 1/2;

Kingston Upon Thames, *Ordinances of the Corporation Governing the Trading Companies*, KB 8/1/3; Daly, Ann (ed.) (1974), *Kingston upon Thames Register of Apprentices*, 1563–1713, XXVIII Guildford: Surrey Record Society, pp. ix, 165; Prior, 'Women and the Urban Economy', pp. 103, 108–10; Merson, 'Apprenticeship at Southampton in the Seventeenth Century', p. xxviii.

39. Dunlop and Denman, *English Apprenticeship*; Pinchbeck, *Women Workers*, p. 293; Hill, Bridget (1989), *Women, Work and Sexual Politics in Eighteenth-century England*, Oxford: Basil Blackwell, p. 94; Snell, Keith (1985), *Annals of the Labouring Poor, Social Change and Agrarian England, 1660–1900*, Cambridge: Cambridge University Press, p. 299; Sanderson, Elizabeth C. (1996), *Women and Work in Eighteenth-century Edinburgh*, London: Macmillan Press Ltd.

40. Monter, 'Women in Calvinist Geneva', pp. 201–4.

41. Kingston Borough Archives, Court of Assembly Minutes, 1725–1776, KB 1/2 folio 221–3.

42. Wiesner, 'Women's Work in the Changing City Economy', p. 67.

43. Ogilvie, Shelagh (1990), 'Women and Proto-industrialisation in a Corporate Society: Württemberg Woollen Weaving, 1590–1760', in Hudson, Pat and Lee, W. R. (eds), *Women's Work and the Family in Historical Perspective*, Manchester and New York: Manchester University Press; Whyte, Ian (1989), 'Proto-industrialisation in Scotland', in Hudson, Pat (ed.), *Regions and Industries: A Perspective on the Industrial Revolution in Britain*, Cambridge: Cambridge University Press.

44. Wiesner, 'Women's Work in the Changing City Economy', pp. 68–9; Reddy, William (1984), *The Rise of Market Culture, The Textile Trade and French Society, 1750–1900*, Cambridge: Cambridge University Press, pp. 24, 31–2; Abensour, *La Femme*, p. 192; Hufton, Olwen (1975), 'Women and the Family Economy in Eighteenth-century France', *French Historical Studies*, **9**, 14–16 and (1981), 'Women, Work and Marriage in Eighteenth-century France', in Outhwaite, R. B. (ed.), *Marriage and Society, Studies in the Social History of Marriage*, London: Europa, pp. 191–2; Lown, Judy (1990), *Women and Industrialization, Gender at Work in Nineteenth-century England*, London: Polity Press, pp. 9–15; Lis, Catharina and Soly, Hugo, (1979), *Poverty and Capitalism in pre-industrial Europe*, Atlantic Highlands, NJ: Humanities, p. 170; OSA, pp. 315–16; Sheridan, 'Women in the Booktrade', p. 55.

45. Sharpe, Pamela (1991), 'Literally Spinsters; a New Interpretation of the Local economy and Demography in Colyton in the Seventeenth and Eighteenth Centuries', *Economic History Review*, **VLIV** (1), 68–9; Ogilvie, 'Women and Proto-industrialisation', pp. 86–97; Houston, Rab (1989), 'Women in the Economy and Society of Scotland', in Houston, R. A. and Whyte, I. A. (eds), *Scottish Society, 1500–1800*, Cambridge: Cambridge University Press, pp. 132–3; Fox-Genovese, 'Women and Work', p. 114.

46. Fox-Genovese, 'Women and Work', p. 116.

47. Wiesner, 'Women's Work in the Changing City Economy', p. 66.

48. Ibid.; Ogilvie, 'Women and Proto-industrialisation', p. 84; Sheridan, 'Women in the Booktrade', pp. 54–5.

49. Campbell, Robert (1747), *The London Tradesman* (reprint 1969), Newton Abbot: David and Charles (Publishers) Ltd., pp. 22–3.

50. Farge, *Fragile Lives*, pp. 114–15.

51. Abensour, *La Femme*, p. 168.

52. Houston, 'Women in the Economy and Society', p. 122.

53. Earle, Peter (1994), *A City Full of People, Men and Women of London, 1650–1750*, London: Methuen, pp. 120–22; Barker, Hannah (1997), 'Women, Work and the Industrial Revolution: Female Involvement in the English Printing Trades', in Barker, Hannah and Chalus, Elaine (eds), *Gender in Eighteenth-century England, Roles, Representations and Responsibilities*, London and New York: Addison, Wesley, Longman, p. 88; Davidoff, Leonore and Hall, Catherine (1987), *Family Fortunes, Men and Women of the English Middle Class, 1780–1850*, London: Hutchinson, pp. 52–8; Darrow, Margaret (1989), *Revolution in the House, Family, Class and Inheritance in Southern France, 1775–1825*, Princeton: Princeton University Press, pp. 150, 169, 117–18; Simonton, *History of Women's Work*, pp. 54–7.
54. Davis, Natalie Zemon (1986), 'Women in the Crafts in Sixteenth-century Lyon', in Hanawalt, Barbara (ed.), *Women and Work in Preindustrial Europe*, Bloomington: Indiana University Press, pp. 183–4.

CHAPTER THREE

Age and Gender at the Workplace: The Historical Experiences of Young People in Western Europe and North America[1]

Colin Heywood

From the day we are born, the influence of gender looms large in our lives. On the maternity ward, we might still be given a pink wristband if we are a girl, and a blue one if we are a boy. Our families will probably choose a forthrightly masculine or feminine name for us, rather than a slightly ambiguous one such as Leslie or Marion. And our parents will often fall back on traditional stereotypes when interpreting our actions: daughters will be described as beautiful and cute, sons as strong and well co-ordinated.[2] These are but the first steps in a lifelong process of gender socialization, defined by the sociologist Marlene Mackie as learning to become feminine and masculine according to the expectations current in our society. The primary phase of this process takes place during childhood and adolescence, while we are developing a language and an individual identity, learning cognitive skills and self-control, and internalizing both moral standards and appropriate attitudes and forms of interaction.[3] Social scientists tell us that today the family and the peer group take most of the responsibility for gender socialization, though schools, churches, the mass media and language itself also have a role to play.[4] Historians in their turn have begun to explore the gender dimension to childhood at various periods and places in the past.[5]

What is largely missing from these accounts is the impact of the workplace on the primary stage of gender socialization. The marginal position of child labour in the economies of the 'developed' world, and the decline of the family as a unit of production, explain why sociologists and psychologists have not included its influence in their work. Within the historical literature, it has tended, rather curiously, to fall between two stools. On the one hand, specialists in child labour have often focused on the age dimension to the exclusion of gender, particularly if they are concerned with the passing of protective legislation for children or with representations of childhood. On the other hand, scholars interested in the division of labour by sex have quite naturally devoted most of their attention to adults. However, an increasing gender consciousness among historians, combined with an interest in writing history from the 'bottom up' to recapture the day-to-day experiences of children and adolescents, has helped to throw some light on the subject of age and gender in the workplace. The time is surely ripe, then, for a preliminary synthesis of research on the ways that the experience of work and the workplace might have influenced the acquisition of gender identities during childhood and youth.

One can take it as axiomatic that even in an isolated peasant household there will be some division of labour within the family, based on age and gender. The immediate issue is how these two criteria intersect. Was it a matter of families or employers allocating 'children's work' to both boys and girls? Ester Boserup notes that in low-income societies some particularly light tasks around the farms, such as shepherding and scaring away wild animals from the crops, were left to children and old people.[6] If this was generally the case, then the implications for gender socialization would have been minimal – though the children might have been observing and modelling themselves on adult men and women engaged in very different types of work.[7] Alternatively, were boys and girls more commonly assigned to different jobs around the farms and workshops? Examples of this form of segregation are easy to find. On the northern French coalfield, at Anzin, the censuses of the late nineteenth century reveal that sons could readily follow their fathers or other adult males into the pits or the foundries, while daughters were likely to remain at home with their mothers, in some cases helping with the running of a shop or dressmaking.[8] This implies that the two sexes were taught different skills and attitudes, by means of apprenticeships, or, less formally, by helping adults around the home and the workshop. These contrasting experiences could hardly fail to affect the formation of separate gender identities. Either way, Ernestine Friedl is surely right in proposing that the tasks assigned to young boys and girls depended on three considerations: the nature of work done by adults of each sex, the preoccupations of the children's mothers and the labour requirements of society.[9]

The two questions for this chapter are therefore how and why this differential socialization of children and adolescents at the workplace varied in the past. Cross-cultural and cross-time comparisons suggest some answers, but initially some insights from anthropology, the one discipline that has systematically confronted the issues raised here, are required.

Anthropological perspectives on gender socialization

An early, 'biosocial' approach to the study of sex differences in socialization, published during the 1950s by Barry, Bacon and Child, can be summarized in three propositions.[10] First, it asserted that 'there are certain universal tendencies in the differentiation of adult sex role'. Here the authors were influenced by the work of George Murdock, who drew on ethnographic studies to contrast 'strictly masculine activities' such as hunting, mining and metalworking, with 'quasi-feminine' tasks, which revolved around the all-too-familiar routines of cooking and cleaning.[11] Second, they argued that 'biological differences between the sexes strongly predispose the distinction of role' along these lines. Again they echoed Murdock and his assumption that the superior strength of men directed them towards strenuous work, while the 'handicap' of pregnancy and nursing directed women to lighter tasks around the home.[12] Third, they proposed that everywhere there existed clear differences between the sexes in the 'systems of behaviour' fostered between the ages of four or five and puberty. In their own words, 'pressure towards nurturance, obedience and responsibility is most often stronger for girls, whereas pressure toward achievement and self-reliance is most often stronger for boys'. They concluded that this pattern of training was far from arbitrary, because it prepared boys and girls, in their different ways, for the type of work expected of them as adults. In this way, the culture generally manages to adapt to the 'biological substratum of human life'.

Since the 1950s, however, feminist and 'postmodern' influences have undermined this approach to gender socialization. Revisionists now question the assumption that there is a universal pattern of task specialization between the sexes. No one disputes the division of labour by sex in all societies, but it is the variety of gender relations that is emphasized, rather than the similarities.[13] The 'biosocial' approach to gender relations, with biological differences between the sexes pointing men and women to different tasks, is also thought to be simplistic. Most tellingly, opponents of this view dispute the extent to which childbearing and childrearing necessarily limit the other activities of women. Friedl, for example, suggests that it is better to think about how child-tending is accommodated to women's economic tasks, rather than vice versa. She believes that social and cultural influences on gender are predominant. In similar vein, Peggy Reeves Sanday proposes that 'plans for the sexual division of labor ... are formed from a people's adaptation to their environment'. As such, she argues that they must be seen in the context of a more general cultural environment.[14] Finally, given considerable diversity in the 'theatre of life' where children are socialized, the polarization of 'systems of behaviour' for girls and boys begins to look suspect. Yet, as Armstrong and Armstrong note, there is a danger of replacing some form of biological determinism with a cultural one, where individuals are the hapless victims of expectations of 'masculine' and 'feminine' behaviour imposed by some abstract 'culture' or 'society'.[15] The upshot is a theoretical perspective on gender socialization far removed from the relatively solid 'biological' framework provided by some among an earlier generation. Increasingly, the revisionist emphasis is on the variety of options taken in the sexual division of labour, the social construction of gender roles according to local circumstances, the complexity of the learning process, and the scope for contesting and redefining established norms.[16]

If the general approach taken by Barry, Bacon and Child now looks dated, their work remains helpful when considering variations in the degree of sex differentiation in the socialization of the young. They formulated two hypotheses: first, that a pronounced difference in socialization is correlated with a large family group, and second, that it is associated with an economy which places a high premium on the superior strength of the male.[17] These at least provide a starting point for analysis. It may indeed be useful to think in terms of the environment for children being influenced by family size, though surely in combination with other localized factors such as the scale of production, the tightness of the labour market, and relative affluence or poverty. As for male strength, this hypothesis would become less and less plausible as one moves towards a 'mechanized economy' from the eighteenth century onwards. A generation of feminist historiography has also exposed the shaky foundations to the 'strength' and 'skill' which groups of male workers have insisted are their preserve in order to exclude women from certain well-paid jobs.[18] The next two sections of this chapter will pursue these insights by looking across Europe and North America in the eighteenth and nineteenth centuries. Have historians found 'an amazing variety of gender relations', as an enthusiastic revisionist put it, rather than a universal pattern in the division of labour?[19] And precisely how important was family size and the prominence of 'masculine' work in explaining sex differences in socialization?

A cross-cultural survey: large versus small families

Evidence from the agricultural sector does tend to show that large-scale farms, with an abundance of hired labour, could observe a rigid division of labour by age and sex. Conversely, on the smaller farms and landholdings, the hard-pressed family labour force was obliged to turn its hand to anything, without paying much attention to such conventions. Arthur Young was much impressed by the way smallholders in northern England sometimes turned out their wives or daughters to drive a plough in the depths of winter.[20] Similarly visitors to the northern part of the USA during the early nineteenth century noted the flexibility of labour on the family farms: men and boys, for example, taking on 'women's work' in the dairies and gardens when female members of the household became overburdened with work.[21] Later in the century, the contrasting experiences of American families as they moved from the settled farming communities of the Midwest to the far western frontier provide a slightly different perspective.

In the Midwest, 'men and women worked in different areas, skilled at different tasks, prepared and trained for their work in different ways'.[22] Young children of both sexes shared little tasks around the farms, fetching water, feeding animals, milking cows, collecting eggs, weeding and so on. However, from around the age of ten, boys joined their fathers in the fields, harrowing and weeding before the harvest, binding the wheat, and looking after hogs and sheep. They also learned to hunt, an activity central to a man's image of himself as 'keystone of the hearth, defender of the household, and main provider'. Girls meanwhile learned to sew, their worth being judged by their ability to manage the most elaborate appliqué and quilt stitching. They continued with their earlier routines around the farm, 'apprenticed to the housewife's craft', thereby acquiring a generally caring and nurturing role within the family.[23] Further west, by contrast, the acute scarcity of labour during the late nineteenth century and the relative isolation of families obliged children to take on all sorts of responsibilities unthinkable in the more settled east.[24] Sons undertook women's work, and, more commonly, daughters became involved in such unfamiliar tasks as herding, harvesting and hunting. Fifteen-year-old Luna Walker, newly arrived in Kansas in 1871, boasted in her diary of bringing home rabbits, ducks and turkeys, and even of attempting to ambush buffalo, while out hunting with her brother. Teams of children, boys and girls alike, might occasionally take on such 'adult' work as ploughing and planting. They also became adept at herding sheep and cattle, and at making a quick profit selling food to the men in the new mining towns. As a visitor to Nebraska wrote, 'It has been a novel sight to watch a little girl about ten years old herding sheep near town, handling her pony with a masterly hand, galloping around the herd if they begin to scatter out, and driving them into a corral'.[25]

The small, family workshops found in areas of proto-industrialization provide further examples of this kind of diversity of experience. In the South Oberlausitz region of Saxony, during the nineteenth century, large property-owning peasant families maintained a clear separation of tasks by gender. The poorer weaving households, by contrast, could not afford such a marked gender division: in this milieu, flexibility was the order of the day.[26] Early in the century, an observer recorded that: 'In the so-called weaver-villages, men and women, sons and daughters weave. The oldest and the children sit near the looms and wind the bobbins and prepare the spools. All are interdependent and rely on one another ...'[27] While the husband was on the road, hawking the family's wares, the wife continued to weave; and when the wife took her turn peddling goods, the husband took care of the home and the children. Young people started to make themselves useful in the workshops from the age of five or six, and gradually learned their trade by a process of 'training through practice'. Any lad or girl could take a short apprenticeship with a weaver and then start work as a 'master'. In the cities, too, small family enterprises in the 'sweated' trades expected children of both sexes to turn their hand to various tasks. In London, for example, Anna Davin cites cases of children helping with laundering, wood chopping, and the running of shops and street stalls during the late nineteenth century.[28]

Further cross-cultural comparisons: strength and 'masculine' work

What light does a historiographical survey throw on the 'biological' explanation of the sexual division of labour, and its implications for gender socialization? To return first to the farm sector, it would be unwise to dismiss biological influences entirely: as Olwen Hufton pointedly remarked, in early modern Europe 'no one, for example, could plough a five-inch furrow in a condition of advanced or even early pregnancy'.[29] During early childhood, gender differences at work were at their minimum. A common pattern on the land was for children of both sexes to start their working life with light tasks such as looking after younger siblings, bird scaring, stone picking, collecting dung and guarding animals.[30] Young shepherds and shepherdesses were not taxed physically by their work, though their self-reliance and courage might well be tested in a crisis. For the young Roussel, in the Limousin region of France during the 1840s, it was a matter of facing down a wolf by banging together his clogs and shouting at the beast. For Joe Pearce in Arizona it meant humouring a notorious murderer at his sheep camp: 'an ominous, smooth-faced Apache man and his woman companion'.[31]

On reaching adolescence, girls became increasingly caught up in the routines of women around the home, the garden and the dairy, while boys joined the men in the heavier work in the fields and stables. Doubtless contemporaries thought that this divergence was perfectly 'natural', resting on different aptitudes. As a peasant in the Auvergne obligingly observed, 'I have always heard it said that a man knew enough when he was capable of digging a hole big enough to bury a donkey in'.[32] None the less, it is doubtful whether differences between the strength of the average male and the average female will go far in explaining the pronounced division of labour between the sexes found in many regions: the role of custom and patriarchy must also come into play. Young women on the farms had to be strong enough to cope with strenuous jobs, such as the mowing with a sickle, the stacking of hay and corn, and the threshing expected of female servants in Bavaria.[33] Indeed, middle-class contemporaries in England often compared girls brought up to work in the fields unfavourably with those confined to domestic duties. Too much of the masculine had rubbed off on those allegedly 'coarsened' by their work and the mixed company they had kept.[34] There were, in addition, considerable variations in the work expected of the two sexes according to region and type of agriculture. For example, tasks considered men's work in south-east England by the mid nineteenth century, such as harvesting with a sickle or loading manure on to a cart, were still routinely taken on by women in the north and west.[35]

In the manufacturing and service sectors, the workplace once again tended to differentiate between the sexes: at the extremes, boys were channelled into 'virile' trades such as stonemasonry and iron making, while girls went their separate ways into, say, embroidery, lace making and domestic service. In a centre for heavy industry such as Bochum, by 1907, as at Anzin, the coal mines and foundries had become almost entirely male territory, leaving food, clothing and the service sector as the only areas for young women to find employment. Even in the small metal trades there was a degree of specialization along gender lines: in Birmingham girls took on jobs requiring 'nimble fingers and artistic ability', such as japanning and fine gold-chain making, while boys went into the rolling mills and brass-casting shops.[36] However, this type of polarization based on physical strength needs some qualification, given the example of, say, 'pit-brow lassies' in Lancashire, or the small boys employed around Nottingham as lace embroiderers. In other words, girls in certain labour markets would have to develop some muscles, and boys might find themselves drawn into needlework by their mothers.[37]

But what of that vast grey area in between which Murdock and Provost classified as 'swing activities'? These were tasks assigned predominantly to males in some regions but predominantly to females in others, such as weaving, clothesmaking and pottery.[38] Such a pattern implies that gender socialization would remain highly differentiated. Children of both sexes might do the same work, but their future careers would inevitably diverge. In the Pays de Caux region of Normandy, for example, mothers taught both their sons and their daughters to spin cotton, but during adulthood in the late eighteenth century, the convention generally held that only women did the spinning, while men concentrated on weaving. Across the Channel, in Essex, Samuel Courtauld employed boys as well as girls to wind silk at his Halstead mill during the early nineteenth century. For most of the males it was a dead-end job: there was even a notice in the mill reminding them that they would have to leave at the age of fifteen. A fortunate few would remain to be trained as overseers or mechanics. For the females, meanwhile, winding was a straightforward preliminary to joining the main body of the workforce, around the age of seventeen, weaving on the power looms.[39] In retrospect, contrasts between regions in the organization of different types of labour were sometimes startling. Would it be the boys among the piecers who became spinners on the hand mules, as in Lancashire and Ghent during the early nineteenth century, or the girls – on short mules – as in the country mills around Glasgow? Would men train young lads to operate the big Cotton's-patent type of knitting machine, as in the East

Midlands and the lower Champagne region of France? Or would it be a matter of women training girls, as happened on the other side of the Atlantic, in Ontario?[40]

A peculiar form of organization, which, incidentally, involved a large sex difference in socialization, occurred when employers chose to rely almost exclusively on the daughters of local farming families for their labour force. With factory work generally considered 'degrading' and 'immoral' by the population at large, they found it essential to reassure parents that the girls – teenagers and young women in their twenties for the most part – would be in safe hands. The 'convent workshops' of south-eastern France, in the Lyonnais, the Vivarais and the Cévennes, provide a ruthlessly efficient example. The manufacturers employed nuns to supervise the youthful silk throwers and weavers in their dormitories, refectories, infirmaries and schools. In cases such as the Jujurieux mill, founded by Joseph Bonnet in 1835, the nuns also took responsibility for running the workshops. The girls were made acutely aware of the respect they owed to the Divine and to the factory hierarchy; they were taught sewing and cooking as well as the 3Rs; and they were helped to find husbands when they left. (Apparently they were regarded as a good catch by the local peasants.[41]) In the case of those cotton mills in New England which were run on the 'Waltham' system during the 1820s and 1830s, the manufacturers had to placate puritan Yankee hill farmers, and the instruments they chose were 'matrons of tried character' who ran company boarding houses. A 73-hour working week operating spinning machinery or power looms did not leave much scope for the corrupting influence of the outside world to intrude, but in any case the girls had to be in by 10 p.m., were not allowed to smoke or drink on the premises and were expected to attend church on Sundays. Caroline Ware described the atmosphere as closer to a girls' boarding school than a factory for the operatives. The more intelligent ones at least read magazines, played the piano, formed an improvement circle and wrote stories for their own journal, *The Lowell Offering*.[42]

Sometimes men and women worked beside each other on similar jobs, or at least proved willing to bend the conventional division of labour by age and sex, as already noted in the case of the Saxon handloom weavers. The light metal working trades provide many such examples. In the Ardennes region of France, boys and girls alike started a long life of nail making around the age of nine or ten, while their counterparts in the Auvergne began polishing and sharpening cutlery. Powerloom weaving was an another area where both boys and girls could work their way up from assistant to minder – though females were far more common. Such arrangements would appear to have minimized gender differences among young people on the shop floor. However, it must be said that women were generally restricted to the lightest, coarsest or plainest work, allowing men to trumpet their superior strength and skill. Knitting on the stocking frame in the East Midlands hosiery industry was by custom an adult male occupation, leaving the ancillary work of winding to boys, and seaming and stitching to women and girls. It seems likely that wives and daughters had occasionally taken over work on the frame when necessary, and during the early nineteenth century this became increasingly common. A Parliamentary Commissioner reported in 1845 that:

> vast numbers of women and children are working side by side with men, often employed in the same description of frames, making the same fabrics, and at the same rate of wages; the only advantage over them which the man possesses being his superior strength, whereby he can undergo the fatigues of labour for longer hours than the weaker physical energies of women and children enable them to bear.[43]

However, when wide frames were introduced into specialized workshops, men monopolized this branch of the industry. Nancy Grey Osterud explains that this was partly because of the heaviness of the physical labour involved: 'while this definition was primarily an ideological one, it had just enough basis in immediate experience to give it added power at this juncture; strength was at least as important as sex, for neither young nor ageing men were employed in wide frames'.[44]

To conclude, there was considerable diversity of practice in the division of labour by age and gender in modern Europe and North America, though it was far from random: the imprint of customary notions of 'men's' and 'women's' work lingered in the background. 'Biological' influences on this pattern should not be ignored, but there was above all a massive 'encrustation of cultural meanings upon biological facts'.[45] It follows that the learning process during the early years was of major importance in moulding gender identities. There is a wealth of evidence to show that, in some contexts, working girls were encouraged towards nurturing and obedient behaviour, and boys towards self-reliance and achievement: it was the males, after all, who had a better chance of taking the higher-paid and responsible jobs. Again, however, in some circumstances girls as well as boys were thrust into situations requiring considerable self-reliance and competitiveness. If some girls spent much of their time looking after siblings or cocooned in a convent-type of atmosphere, others were sent out with their flocks alone, hawked their wares on the streets or joined their brothers down coal mines. The intrepid girls raised in the far west of America were an extreme case – and it cost them dear. Elliott West highlights the 'sad paradox' of the pioneer childhood, which 'offered the most liberating possibilities to young girls, only to snatch them back as they reached their adult years'.[46]

Some cross-time comparisons

Historians are, by the very nature of their discipline, interested in changing patterns of gender socialization over time as well as across space. Bringing the chronological dimension to the fore provokes a number of important questions. Was the socialization of boys and girls increasingly differentiated during the nineteenth century, and if so, why? How did traditional apprenticeships fare in modern Europe? What was the influence of technical progress on age and gender relations in the workshops? Did the notion of 'separate spheres' for men and women have much of an impact on young workers? And how did social legislation affect different categories of labour? The general drift of the argument here will be that there was considerable turbulence in gender relations affecting young people over the short term, within a tight framework of long-term stability.

Historians have often depicted a series of radical transformations of age and gender relations in the workplace since the eighteenth century. Hans Medick famously asserted that the need for members of the proto-industrial family to cooperate in order to survive meant that 'under certain market conditions and within certain branches of production this imperative could go so far as to erase the traditional division of labour between the sexes and the age groups'. Children, instead of spending their adolescent years as servants with other families, remained in the parental home to become spinners, weavers or knitters. Women neglected their household 'duties' for industrial work, while men came in from the fields to take over the cooking and milking of cows.[47] A compelling number of local studies have documented this phenomenon, particularly in the textile and metal working trades during the first half of the nineteenth century. By the 1840s in the Leicestershire village of Shepshed, boys of ten or slightly older were starting work on the stocking frames, and in a short time earning almost as much as their fathers. Girls too became accustomed to knitting, or, in the case of the Pays de Caux and the Oberlausitz, handloom weaving, having yielded their traditional role as spinners to the new mills of the Industrial Revolution.[48]

In these same mills, the classic view argues that steam power and mechanization allowed women and children to take over the work of adult males. The power loom provided the most dramatic example, with the quintessentially male handloom weaver of the eighteenth century being largely superseded everywhere from the 1820s onwards by the young female 'minder'.[49] The large numbers of children employed on the early spinning technology in the late eighteenth century also struck contemporaries – though, strictly speaking, this was a matter of young people taking over from adult females. The earliest spinning mill in the USA used Arkwright's invention to employ 100 children aged between four and ten in 1801. In Britain, one fifth of all cotton workers in 1818 were under 13. Manufacturers pressed their case for favours from the state by emphasizing their ability to generate employment among poor women and children – and the parish apprentices were on hand in Britain, or the *enfants assistés* in France, as a source of cheap, docile labour. The Quarry Bank Mill at Styal was giving work to 90 such apprentices (60 girls and 30 boys) around 1800 – approximately half of its total labour force.[50]

Technical progress in another form, revolving around an elaborate division of labour, allowed the 'sweating' of various trades, and the partial replacement of skilled males by cheaper female labour. The garment trades of major cities such as Paris, Berlin and Hamburg employed a few skilled men and women, plus armies of semi-skilled females of all ages, using their supposedly 'natural' aptitude for needlework.[51] The long-term decline of the apprenticeship system encouraged this increased flexibility on the labour market. Males in particular were affected: although girls as well as boys had been apprenticed to certain trades during the early modern period, they were a minority. In any case, the training of girls may have been concentrated more on the values and behaviour expected of them than on industrial skills.[52] The upshot was that young people had to prepare for a degree of disruption of the established family hierarchy, still largely intact in the eighteenth century, in which the father/master was assisted by his wife and children. Girls had to start learning skills and attitudes previously reserved for males, provoking concern in some quarters about the new-found independence of young women.

Yet by the end of the nineteenth century various counter-currents were in evidence which meant that on balance it was the continuities in gender socialization that were most in evidence. One should never lose sight of the long-term stability in the sex-typing of jobs, and the subordination of women to men. Women's work continued to be largely restricted to a few occupations, notably in farming, textiles and domestic service. In the agricultural sector, some historians have argued that the eighteenth and nineteenth centuries saw an 'intensified sexual specialization' in certain regions. Keith Snell linked this development to a growing concentration on grain production in southern England, which limited women's work to weeding corn, haymaking and gleaning, and excluded them from a 'traditionally fuller and more sexually equal participation in agriculture'. Similarly, in the Magdeburg region Hainer Plaul asserted that the shift to large-scale sugar-beet production made agriculture an increasingly seasonal activity, causing local female farm workers to lose out to seasonal workers from further east. Snell has perhaps exaggerated the sharing of tasks between men and women in the early modern period. None the less, in the long term, the shift towards a larger scale of farming in some regions, and the increasing resort to science and technology in agriculture, militated against the employment of females. In the early modern period, the female farm servant had been an adolescent, learning her work beside her male counterpart. By the middle of the nineteenth century, in south-east England at least, she was more likely to start early on a life of casual, unskilled labour.[53]

In the manufacturing sector, the gradual decline of proto-industrial workshops in the countryside and the corresponding rise of the factory system tended to firm up the 'traditional' division of labour between the sexes and age groups. In addition to the greater predisposition of large-scale units of production to such a move, there was an effort by adult males to restore the old family hierarchies. The introduction of complex machinery gave men the opportunity to assert the need for 'skill' and strength to operate it. The invention of the Cotton's-patent type of machine, for example, ended the temporary incursions of women into knitting – in Europe at least. From the 1860s onwards in Troyes, the young *rebrousseurs* who assisted the knitters, and around the age of sixteen became apprentices to them, would be exclusively males. Meanwhile young girls reverted to training for simple jobs in the preparatory and finishing processes.[54] Perhaps most blatant of all was the campaign by males in the Lancashire cotton industry to exclude females from mule spinning, even after the introduction of the self-actor had supposedly eliminated the need for employers to rely on skilled adult males. In 1886, when confronted by an attempt to introduce women as minders on fine-spinning self-actors in Bolton, the local Spinners Union voted almost unanimously that 'members in the future decline to teach or cause to be taught the trade of piecing to any female child'.[55]

In the background during the second half of the century was a campaign for a 'family wage': in other words, the notion that a husband should be able to earn enough to support his wife and children, without them having to work for wages. This of course implied that girls should be prepared for a caring and nurturing role in the home, boys for the competitive world of the labour market. A delegate to the Socialist Workers' Congress at Marseille in 1879 asserted that 'woman's place is in the home, where so many daily concerns call her, and not in a factory or workshop ... The young girl should never learn any trade except those which, later, when she has become a wife and a mother, she can carry out in the home'.[56] How far the mass of workers accepted the 'domestic ideology' implied here is not clear, and needless to say, even if they did, few outside the ranks of the highly-skilled had much hope of earning sufficiently high wages to realize it.[57] More potent was the influence of 'protective' legislation to restrict the employment of women (as well as children) in certain types of work – again underpinned by the idea current in middle-class reforming circles of separate spheres for men and women.[58] The effects of the 1842 Mines and Collieries Act in Britain have been well documented. In excluding females from underground work, the Act helped to kill off a system of family labour, and to make mining an exclusively masculine occupation.[59]

Conclusion

Much work around the home and the workplace was common to boys and girls, as they gradually matured through their childhood. Defenders of child labour in the nineteenth century constantly referred to the need for young people to become accustomed to the discipline of work as early as possible, and to acquire the skills needed later in life. The custom was for the children of the poor to take on a host of little tasks which were suitable for their small size and lack of experience. Hence the 'apprenticeship' they went through, more often informal than formal, involved such jobs as running errands, looking after siblings, shepherding, piecing, winding, carrying, hawking – and generally watching and helping adults. To some extent, children and youths could hardly avoid the influence of the marked division of labour between the sexes among adults. The world of work resembled that of the church and the school in its tendency to encourage the values of nurturance, responsibility and obedience among females, and competitiveness and self-reliance among males. Even when very young, boys were reluctant to become involved with caring for siblings or cleaning the house, while girls had less freedom to seek employment outside the home. During their teens, divergences between the sexes at the workplace became more apparent. Young women would continue to help their mothers with housework, were likely to learn 'feminine' skills such as dairying and needlework, and prepare for a subordinate role in the family hierarchy. Meanwhile young men would be more likely to have the opportunity to enter a variety of skilled trades, and to anticipate ruling the roost in their own home at least.

Yet this contrast can easily be exaggerated, given the considerable variations in gender relations at work in modern Europe and North America, not to mention the way in which individual relations between husbands and wives panned out in practice. The various influences of poverty, labour shortages, recruitment strategies of employers, family size and location, and varying expectations of what was 'men's' and 'women's' work ensured that traditional gender stereotypes were often subverted. What emerges from the historical evidence assembled here is that differences in gender socialization were minimized on family farms and in small 'proto-industrial' workshops, and maximized in large-scale enterprises and among families of skilled artisans whose wives did not take on paid work. In short, this chapter has followed the well-established trend of playing down the biological origins of the sexual division of labour, and attempted to put some shape on the 'amazing diversity' of experience in the workplace.

Notes

1. The author would like to thank Olena Heywood and Margaret Walsh for comments on an earlier version of this chapter.
2. Robinson, B.W. and Salamon, E.D. (1987), 'Gender Role Socialization: A Review of the Literature', in Salamon, E.D. and Robinson, B.W., *Gender Roles: Doing What Comes Naturally?*, Toronto: Methuen, pp. 123–4.
3. Mackie, Marlene (1991), *Gender Relations in Canada: Further Explorations*, Toronto: Butterworths, p. 75.
4. Robinson and Salamon, 'Gender Role Socialization', pp. 123–42.
5. Recent works include: Strumingher, Laura (1983), *What Were Little Girls and Boys Made Of? Primary Education in Rural France, 1830–1880*, Albany: State University of New York Press; Jacobi-Dittrich, Juliane (1984), 'Growing Up Female in the Nineteenth Century', in Fout, J.C. (ed.), *German Women in the Nineteenth Century*, New York: Holmes and Meier, pp. 197–217; Clark, Linda L. (1984), *Schooling the Daughters of Marianne: Textbooks and the Socialization of Girls in Modern French Primary Schools*, Albany: State University of New York Press; Heywood, Colin (1991), 'On Learning Gender Roles during Childhood in Nineteenth-Century France', *French History*, 5 (4), December, 451–66; Maynes, Mary Jo (1995), *Taking the Hard Road: Life Course in French and German Workers' Autobiographies in the Era of Industrialization*, Chapel Hill: University of North Carolina Press; Hufton, Olwen (1995), *The Prospect Before Her*, London: HarperCollins; Cox, Roger (1996), *Shaping Childhood*, London: Routledge.
6. Boserup, Ester (1970), *Woman's Role in Economic Development*, London: Allen and Unwin, p. 15.
7. For the controversies surrounding this issue, see Mackie, *Gender Relations*, ch. 4.
8. Tilly, Louise A. (1978), 'Structure d'emploi, travail des femmes et changement démographique dans deux villes industrielles: Anzin et Roubaix, 1872–1906', *Le Mouvement Social*, 105, November–December, 33–58.
9. Friedl, Ernestine (1975), *Women and Men: An Anthropologist's View*, New York: Holt, Rinehart and Winston, p. 82. Her discussion of 'age as modifier of sex roles' was in the context of horticultural societies.
10. Barry, Herbert, Bacon, Margaret K. and Child, Irvin L. (1957), 'A Cross-Cultural Survey of Some Sex Differences in Socialization', *Journal of Abnormal and Social Psychology*, 55, November, 327–32.
11. Murdock, George P. (1937), 'Comparative Data on the Division of Labor by Sex', *Social Forces*, 15 (4), May, 551–3. The quotations are from a later elaboration of the original material in Murdock, George P. and Provost, Caterina (1973), 'Factors in the Division of Labor by Sex: A Cross-Cultural Analysis', *Ethnology*, 12, 206–10.
12. Murdock, George P. (1949), *Social Structure*, New York, Macmillan, p. 7.
13. Oakley, Ann, (1972), *Sex, Gender and Society*, London: Temple Smith, pp. 128–57; Aronoff, Joel and Crano, William D. (1975), 'A Re-examination of the Cross-cultural Principles of Task Segregation and Sex Role Differentiation in the Family', *American Sociological Review*, 40, February, 12–20; Friedl, *Women and Men*, pp. 6, 13.
14. Friedl, *Women and Men*, p. 8; Sanday, Peggy Reeves (1981), *Female Power and Male Dominance*, Cambridge: Cambridge University Press, p. 76.
15. Armstrong, Pat and Armstrong, Hugh (1990), *Theorizing Women's Work*, Toronto: Garamond Press, ch. 2.

16. Mackie, *Gender Relations, passim*; Dirks, Nicholas B., Eley, Geoff and Ortner, Sherry B. (eds) (1994), *Culture/Power/History*, Princeton: Princeton University Press, Introduction.
17. Barry, Bacon and Child, 'A Cross-cultural Survey', pp. 330–1.
18. Recent studies include Murgatroyd, Linda (1985), 'Occupational Stratification and Gender', in The Lancaster Regionalism Group, *Localities, Class, and Gender*, London: Pion; Rose, Sonya O. (1986), '"Gender at Work": Sex, Class and Industrial Capitalism', *History Workshop Journal*, **21**, 113–31; Bradley, Harriet (1989), *Men's Work, Women's Work*, Cambridge: Polity Press; Frader, Laura L. and Rose, Sonya O. (eds) (1996), *Gender and Class in Modern Europe*, Ithaca: Cornell University Press.
19. Quataert, Jean (1986), 'Teamwork in Saxon Homeweaving Families in the Nineteenth Century', in Joeres, Ruth-Ellen B. and Maynes, Mary Jo (eds), *German Women in the Eighteenth and Nineteenth Centuries*, Bloomington: Indiana University Press, p. 3.
20. Hill, Bridget (1989), *Women, Work and Sexual Politics in Eighteenth-century England*, Oxford: Blackwell, p. 35. See also Sharpe, Pamela (1996), *Adapting to Capitalism: Working Women in the English Economy, 1700–1850*, Basingstoke: Macmillan, p. 81; Schulte, Regina (1985), 'Peasants and Farmers' Maids: Female Farm Servants in Bavaria at the End of the Nineteenth Century', in Evans, R.J. and Lee, W.R. (eds), *The German Peasantry*, London: Croom Helm, pp. 165–6.
21. Craig, Lee A. (1993), *To Sow One Acre More*, Baltimore: Johns Hopkins University Press, chs 2–3.
22. Faragher, John (1979), *Women and Men on the Overland Trail*, New Haven: Yale University Press, p. 47.
23. Ibid., pp. 45–59.
24. The following section relies on West, Elliott (1989), *Growing Up with the Country: Childhood on the Far West Frontier*, Albuquerque: University of New Mexico Press, chs 4 and 6.
25. Fulton, F.I.S. (1884), *To and Through Nebraska*, Lincoln: Journal Co., p. 42, cited by West, *Growing Up*, p. 88.
26. See Quataert, Jean H. (1985), 'Combining Agrarian and Industrial Livelihood: Rural Households in the Saxon Oberlausitz in the Nineteenth Century', *Journal of Family History*, **10**, Summer, 145–62; *idem*, 'Teamwork', *passim*.
27. Pescheck, Christian (1852), 'Geschichte der Industrie und des Handels in der Oberlausitz', *Neues Lausitzisches Magazin*, **29**, 8, cited by Quataert, 'Teamwork', p. 11.
28. Davin, *Growing Up*, ch. 10.
29. Hufton, *The Prospect*, p. 5.
30. The process can be traced in Mitterauer, M. and Seider, R. (1982), *The European Family*, Oxford: Blackwell, ch. 5; Heywood, Colin (1988), *Childhood in Nineteenth-century France*, Cambridge: Cambridge University Press, ch. 2; Hopkins, Eric (1994), *Childhood Transformed: Working-class Children in Nineteenth-century England*, Manchester: Manchester University Press, pp. 11–22.
31. Chaulanges, Martial (1972), *La Terre des autres*, vol. 2, *Le Roussel*, Paris: Delagrave, p. 7 (this is a novel based on the reminiscences of the author's grandfather); West, *Growing Up*, pp. 126–7.
32. Sylvère, Antoine (1980), *Toinou: le cri d'un enfant auvergnat*, Paris: Plon, p. 52.
33. Schulte, 'Farm Servants in Bavaria', pp. 164–5.
34. Kitteringham, Jennie (1975), 'Country Work Girls in Nineteenth-century

England', in Samuel, Raphael (ed.), *Village Life and Labour*, London: Routledge and Kegan Paul, p. 97.

35. Bradley, *Men's Work*, ch. 4; Sharpe, *Adapting to Capitalism*, ch. 4.
36. Crew, David F. (1979), *Town in the Ruhr: A Social History of Bochum, 1860–1914*, New York: Columbia University Press, ch. 1; Heward, Christine (1981), 'Growing Up in a Birmingham Community, 1851–1871: Some Preliminary Findings', in Hurt, J. (ed.), *Childhood, Youth and Education in the Late Nineteenth Century*, London: History of Education Society, p. 40.
37. Medick, Hans (1976), 'The Proto-Industrial Family Economy', *Social History*, **3**, October, 312; Pinchbeck, Ivy (1930), *Women Workers and the Industrial Revolution, 1750–1850*, London: Frank Cass, ch. 11; John, Angela V. (1980), *By the Sweat of their Brow*, London: Croom Helm; Bradley, *Men's Work*, ch. 6; Sharpe, Pamela and Chapman, Stanley D. (1996), 'Women's Employment and Industrial Organization: Commercial Lace Embroidery in Early Nineteenth-century Ireland and England', *Women's History Review*, **5** (3), 328.
38. Murdock and Provost, 'Division of Labor by Sex', p. 209.
39. Gullickson, Gay (1986), *Spinners and Weavers of Auffay*, Cambridge: Cambridge University Press, p. 74; Lown, Judy (1990), *Women and Industrialization*, Cambridge: Polity Press, ch. 2.
40. Bolin-Hort, Per (1989), *Work, Family and the State*, Lund: Lund University Press, ch. 2; Scholliers, Peter (1995), 'Grown-ups, boys and girls in the Ghent Cotton Industry: The Voortman mills, 1835–1914', *Social History*, **20** (2), May, 204; Parr, Joy (1988), 'Disaggregating the Sexual Division of Labour: A Transatlantic Case Study', *Comparative Studies in Society and History*, **30**, July, 511–33; Chenut, Helen Harden, 'The Gendering of Skill as Historical Process: The Case of French Knitters in Industrial Troyes, 1880–1939', in Frader and Rose, *Gender and Class*, pp. 77–107.
41. Vanoli, D. (1976), 'Les Ouvrières enfermées: les couvents soyeux', *Les Révoltes logiques*, **2**, Spring–Summer, 19–39; Heywood, Colin (1989), 'The Catholic Church and the Formation of the Industrial Labour Force in Nineteenth-century France', *European History Quarterly*, **19** (4), October, 509–33.
42. Ware, Caroline F. (1931), *The Early New England Cotton Manufacture*, Boston: Houghton Mifflin, especially p. 221; and Dublin, Thomas (1979), *Women at Work: The Transformation of Work and Community in Lowell, Massachusetts, 1826–1860*, New York: Columbia University Press, *passim*.
43. Cited in Levine, David (1977), *Family Formation in an Age of Nascent Capitalism*, New York: Academic Press, p. 27.
44. Osterud, Nancy Grey (1986), 'Gender Divisions and the Organization of work in the Leicester Hosiery Industry', in John, Angela V. (ed.), *Unequal Opportunities: Women's Employment in England, 1800–1918*, Oxford: Blackwell, p. 50. See also Rose, Sonya O. (1988), 'Proto-Industry, Women's Work and the Household Economy in the Transition to Industrial Capitalism', *Journal of Family History*, **13** (2), 181–93.
45. Mackie, *Gender Relations*, p. 57.
46. West, *Growing Up*, p. 143.
47. Medick, 'Family Economy', pp. 302, 310–12.
48. Levine, *Family Formation*, p. 28; Gullickson, *Spinners of Auffay*, *passim*; Quataert, 'Teamwork', *passim*.
49. See, for example, Hall, Catherine (1989), 'The Home Turned Upside Down? The Working-class Family in Cotton Textiles, 1780–1850', in Whitelegg, Elizabeth, et al. (eds), *The Changing Experience of Women*, Oxford: Blackwell, pp. 17–29;

and Cammarosano, S.O. (1991), 'Labouring Women in Northern and Central Italy in the Nineteenth Century', in Davis, J. and Ginsborg, P. (eds), *Society and Politics in the Age of the Risorgimento*, Cambridge: Cambridge University Press, pp. 103–4.

50. Ware, *New England Cotton*, p. 23; Freudenberger, Herman, Mather, Frances J. and Nardinelli, Clark (1984), 'A New Look at the Early Factory Labor Force', *Journal of Economic History*, **44** (4), December, 1087; Bolin-Hort, *Work, Family*, p. 35; Berg, Maxine (1994), *The Age of Manufactures, 1700–1820*, London: Routledge, ch. 7; Heywood, *Childhood*, pp. 121–2; Rose, Mary B. (1986), *The Gregs of Quarry Bank Mill*, Cambridge: Cambridge University Press, p. 31.

51. Recent surveys include Robyn Dasey, 'Women's Work and the Family: Women Garment workers in Berlin and Hamburg before the First World War', in Evans, R.J. and Lee, W.R. (eds), *The German Family*, London: Croom Helm, 1981, pp. 221–55; and Coffin, Judith, *The Politics of Women's Work: The Paris Garment Trades, 1750–1915*, Princeton: Princeton University Press, 1996, *passim*.

52. The English case is the most intensively studied from the gender perspective. See Dunlop, O. Jocelyn and Denman, Richard D. (1912), *English Apprenticeship and Child Labour: A History*, London: Fisher Unwin, ch. 9; Snell, K.D.M. (1985), *Annals of the Labouring Poor*, Cambridge: Cambridge University Press, ch. 6; Simonton, Deborah (1991), 'Apprenticeship: Training and Gender in Eighteenth-century England', in Berg, Maxine (ed.), *Markets and Manufactures in Early Industrial Europe*, London: Routledge, pp. 227–58; Ben-Amos, Ilana Krausman (1994), *Adolescence and Youth in Early Modern England*, New Haven: Yale University Press, ch. 6; Lane, Joan (1996), *Apprenticeship in England, 1600–1914*, London: UCL Press, *passim*.

53. Snell, *Labouring Poor*, ch. 1; Plaul, Hainer (1985), 'The Rural Proletariat: The Everyday Life of Rural Labourers in the Magdeburg Region, 1830–80', in Evans and Lee, *German Peasantry*, pp. 102–28; Sharpe, *Adapting to Capitalism*, ch. 4; Horrell, Sara and Humphries, Jane (1995), '"The Exploitation of Little Children": Child Labor and the Family Economy in the Industrial Revolution', *Explorations in Economic History*, **32** (4), October, 502; Kussmaul, Ann (1981), *Servants in Husbandry in Early Modern England*, Cambridge: Cambridge University Press, *passim*.

54. Chenut, 'Gendering of Skill', pp. 89–92.

55. Lazonick, William (1979), 'Industrial Relations and Technical Change: The Case of the Self-Acting Mule', *Cambridge Journal of Economics*, **3** (3), September, 249.

56. Secombe, Wally (1986), 'Patriarchy Stabilized: The Construction of the Male Breadwinner Wage Norm in Nineteenth-century Britain', *Social History*, **11** (1), January, 53–76; Perrot, Michelle (1976), 'L'Eloge de la ménagère dans le discours des ouvriers français au XIXe siècle', in *Mythes et représentations de la femme au dix-neuvième siècle*, Paris: Champion, p. 119.

57. See, for example, Honeyman, Katrina and Goodman, Jordan (1991), 'Women's Work, Gender Conflict, and Labour Markets in Europe, 1500–1900', *Economic History Review*, **44** (4), November, 608–28; and Vickery, Amanda (1993), 'Golden Age to Separate Spheres? A Review of the Categories and Chronology of English Women's History', *Historical Journal*, **36** (2), 383–414.

58. The literature here is now voluminous. See, for example, Boxer, Marilyn J. (1986), 'Protective Legislation and Home Industry: The Marginalization of

Women Workers in Late Nineteenth- Early Twentieth-century France', *Journal of Social History*, **20**, 45–65; Gordon, Linda (ed.) (1990), *Women, the State, and Welfare*, Madison: University of Wisconsin Press; Accampo, Elinor A., Fuchs, Rachel G. and Stewart, Mary Lynn (eds), *Gender and the Politics of Social Reform in France, 1870–1914*, Baltimore: Johns Hopkins Press; Rose, Sonya O. (1996), 'Protective Labor Legislation in Nineteenth-century Britain: Gender, Class, and the Liberal State', in Frader and Rose, *Gender and Class*, pp. 193–210.

59. For the debates in this area, see John, *By the Sweat, passim*; Humphries, Jane (1981), 'Protective Legislation, The Capitalist State, and Working Class Men: The Case of the 1842 Mines Regulation Act', *Feminist Review*, **7**, Spring, 1–33; Mark-Lawson, Jane and Witz, Anne (1988), 'From "Family Labour" to "Family Wage"? The Case Of Women's Labour in Nineteenth-century Coalmining', *Social History*, **13** (2), May, 151–74; Bradley, *Men's Work*, ch. 6.

CHAPTER FOUR

The Making of Men: Masculinities in Interwar Liverpool

Pat Ayers

Notions of masculinity and womanhood lie at the heart of gender relations. In particular, masculinity has functioned as a powerful tool of patriachy. Work which has stressed the idea of masculinity as something which is socially constructed rather than biologically determined[1] has fuelled research and discussion in this area.[2] It is argued that the elements relevant to the construction of masculinity are historically, geographically and culturally specific.[3] This assertion comprises the starting point for what follows – a micro study which explores some of the factors and mechanisms which informed male identity in interwar dockland Liverpool.

This chapter arises out of a much larger study investigating working class economies in Liverpool in the years between 1918 and 1939.[4] Men and women in Liverpool had sharply differentiated parts to play in the multi-faceted, intricate mesh of needs, desires, priorities, limitations, responsibilities and relationships which made up the economics of daily life. In particular, irrespective of their actual role in and contribution to the family economy, men were granted status and privilege within the household simply by virtue of being men. The larger study explores the rationale and dynamics of working-class economy within a framework which stresses gender distinctive assumptions and expectations and the implications of these for power relations between men and women. Notions of masculinity and womanhood were fundamental features of household and community economics during the period. The consideration of masculinity offered, is necessarily selective and concentrates attention on employment, family and religion as prominent sites in its construction. As a consequence, there are absences. For example, male identities were constructed and played out relative to other social identities. These 'others' were often women but might, just as easily be Chinese seamen, police officers or employers. Moreover, women themselves played an important role in the reproduction of masculinities which evolved – something there is no space here to explore.

The Liverpool docklands were made up of chains of individual residential areas which stretched for six miles along the waterfront. Although linked to each other by their common association with the port economy and by the movement of workers among the riverside industries, each was essentially a closed neighbourhood. Individual localities encompassed a multitude of communities. Occasionally, the boundaries which defined each could be physical[5] but more usually they were less immediately visible and associated, for example, with a particular parish or industry. It is the North End docklands which provide the focus for this chapter. The people who populated this area of Liverpool were, for the most part, white, Roman Catholic and of Irish origin.

Although social, environmental and economic factors conspired to produce appallingly low standards of living for much of the waterfront population, it was the structure of employment that provided the most intractable problem for local families. From the early years of the twentieth century, the system of casualism endemic to the local labour market, was consistently identified as the culprit in terms of the level and extent of poverty.[6] Port employment – the persistence of casual labour and the experience of seafaring – constituted a bridge which linked the life, work and culture of nineteenth-century Liverpudlians with that of subsequent generations right up to the outbreak of the Second World War.

Making men in interwar Liverpool

Social scientists across a range of disciplines, have stressed the cultural significance of work in relation to the construction of masculinity.[7] Local historiography has similarly focused on the labour market as the space within which masculine identity is most visible and best understood. With respect to Liverpool, Linda Grant has emphasized the importance of the work process in developing local men's understanding of what 'being a man' actually meant. She argues that casual dock work generated a culture which enabled the men who worked in a 'degrading and dehumanizing' system to salvage some measure of self-esteem. In this way a sense of manliness which was equated with heavy dangerous work and images of powerful men who possessed particular skills, informed local notions of masculinity.[8] Tony Lane also stresses a construction of local masculinity rooted in the workplace:

> It is hard to exaggerate the influence of seamen in Liverpool life. All those stories – of gambling and illicit trading, of womanising and drinking in foreign ports ... produced an image and an ideal of a highly desirable freewheeling life of adventure and independence. Of course the *practice* contained only the merest fraction of the colourful promise ... What mattered was that the *message* of the stories represented an account of the 'sort of people we are'. The meaning of the stories was not in any actual event described but in the contribution every 'event' made to an overall picture of a 'man's life'.[9]

67

If the work process and the workplace were central to the evolution of concepts of masculinity, neither provided the boundaries within which it was played out. Both writers argue that notions of what made men 'men', crossed over the high dock walls, into those communities where dock workers and seafarers lived.[10]

Valerie Burton has challenged both the imagery of seafarers as feckless, hard-drinking, womanizers and the conceptualization of masculinity as rooted mainly in port work. She suggests, rather, that for the late nineteenth and early twentieth centuries, notions of masculinity, in this sector of the labour force, were increasingly informed by understandings of men as providers. The rise of the male breadwinner norm in the nineteenth century,[11] increasingly meant that, 'The acquisition of a wife and the fathering of children were key reference points in the definition of masculinity'.[12] Burton argues that the desire of seamen to be recognized as responsible husbands and fathers was made explicit in formal wage bargaining. However, men coveted the title of breadwinner only in so far as this did not challenge their rights, as men, to decide on the destiny of the wage they secured. It seems, then, that an understanding of masculinity which emphasizes men's perception of themselves as fathers and husbands can only be partial. Setting aside the rhetoric of the formal labour movement and the value of the male breadwinner model as a lever in wage bargaining, this dimension of male self-image served other non-altruistic purposes. Most obviously, it conferred domestic privileges even in situations where men could not or did not actually fulfil the role of family financier.[13]

However, either/or analysis of this sort is not very helpful. Burton's defence of seafarers does little to challenge Tony Lane's notion of the *imagery* of seafaring as crucial. The masculinities which Lane, Grant and Burton identify are all evident in the behaviour of men in interwar Liverpool. Local under-standings of masculinity were to a large extent informed by the roles men played. Men were 'real' men by virtue of their positions as workers, husbands and fathers. However, these were not the only identities which forged and reinforced notions of manhood in the North End docklands. What follows explores the complexity of male identity in Liverpool, suggests additional arenas within which dockland masculinities were constructed and played out, and argues that the demands attached to the fulfilment of particular notions of manhood, could be contradictory. For individual men, the consequent tensions were, in part, resolved by regarding their respective responsibilities as fluid.

Employment and masculinity

The starting point for this exploration of North End masculinities has to be the dominant employment structure – casualism. In the context of the Liverpool labour market, work-based conceptions of manhood were inseparable from class position. Moreover, class identity was, in large measure, articulated via the strategies workers used to create some sense of autonomy and control in situations where they actually had very little.

Male solidarity was an essential element in many different aspects of dock labour. Men worked in gangs and the productivity of all depended on everybody pulling their weight or, alternately, participating in 'skives'[14] when this was possible. In addition, work could be hazardous and trust in the reliability, alertness and reactions of workmates was a necessary corollary. More tangibly, workplace theft implied a high degree of mutual fidelity and a universal view of entitlement. Stealing from work was not simply about getting goods but represented also, workers' assertion of their right to do so. The notion of the 'moral economy' is not pertinent only to the eighteenth and nineteenth centuries. The working class struggle to maintain traditional social and economic control over their lives persisted well into the twentieth century, and is particularly visible in labour markets where casualism was dominant.[15] Justifications for workplace theft are sometimes articulated in an explicitly class conscious framework. A ship repairer, who began work in 1914, argues:

> There's been thieving of materials ever since the world was built, from the ship owners down to the working man. That's why sometimes the bosses knew the working man was doing it but they couldn't do anything because they were doing it themselves, only they were doing it with stuff of more value. The workman was only stealing shillings, they were stealing pounds. ... They'd have 150 men listed working on that ship and there's not 50. For every man who goes to work the firm gets a fixed price for him. But if he goes aboard the ship, up the gangway and down the other one, he's not there, is he? But the firm still gets their money. All firms did it.[16]

Crucially, what mattered was the *principle*. Opportunities for theft were circumscribed by employer strategies and the activities of dock police. Over and above this, individual workers out of moral conviction and/or through terror of getting caught, might choose not to be involved or to 'turn a blind eye' to the theft of others but refuse themselves to benefit from it. It was the *meaning* attached to notions of workplace theft which mattered. Skiving, thieving, and the perception of choosing when and when not to compete for work, can be interpreted as attempts to maintain some degree of personal control over a system of employment which both demanded and emphasized powerlessness. Men's identities as workers and as 'men' were mutually reinforcing.

The practical demonstration of men's commitment to each other did, however, run against the flow of a stream controlled by the structure of the local labour market. In particular, the recruitment practices associated with much port employment during this period, which put men in competition with each other, militated against collective male solidarity along the length of the waterfront. Amongst the white, Roman Catholic, casually employed port workers of North Liverpool, trade unionism (that traditional measure of male class consciousness) was relatively weak. Eric Taplin has argued that in the period before 1922:

> Dock workers were notoriously difficult to organise on a permanent basis. Employers could ignore trade unions, confident in the knowledge that deprivation, sectional jealousies and the debilitating effects of casualism would render most strikes short-lived and ineffective.[17]

During the 1920s and 1930s, economic depression increased competition for limited work and further militated against effective industrial action. This does not imply, however, an absence of a generic political identity, although what there was, necessarily emphasized different forms of agency at different times and in different situations. Workplace resistance and a sense, no matter how ill-founded in practice, that they could always choose not to give their labour if they so desired, were key elements in the way in which men asserted themselves as workers and as men. The collectivities which evolved out of the structured situation of port workers, can only be understood by reference to the immediate work space and immediate workmates, at any one time. These could, and often did, change from day-to-day. The central determining factor was the nature of the local labour market. It imposed a mutability on social and economic relationships in order to accommodate loyalties and allegiances, alongside rivalries and contests, in a system which made 'adversary' and 'comrade' one and the same thing.[18]

The realities of the labour market demanded some sort of global sense of identity which reconciled the necessary social relations of the workplace with the existence of recognized demarcations between men and the daily contest for what work there was. This was particularly so, when those who were rivals at stands one day and workmates the next could also be kin, friends or neighbours: the day-to-day shifts in worksites, workmates and between employment and unemployment, were reconciled in masculinity. Dock workers, shipbuilders, seafarers and other port workers, constructed a corporate identity which unified them as men. Male solidarities evolved and emerged within and outside the workplace; male bonding was underpinned by a generalized understanding of a male community of interest. This provided bridges across the various fissures which divided them. However, this collectivity[19] of men was exclusive as well as inclusive. Most obviously, in the context of the North End docklands, it was almost universally white.

In the North End labour market, where trade unionism was relatively weak and where individualized, open defiance would simply ensure future exclusion, workers' self-assertion adopted a different mantle. Counteractive strategies such as, thieving, skiving and not offering themselves for hire were significant factors in terms of how men measured their own worth and that of others. To a large extent such strategies were illusionary, offered only a semblance of control and were not necessarily universally participated in.[20] What mattered, however, was attitude and intent; maintenance of self respect was rooted in men's understanding of themselves as men. Implicitly, this was a masculinity which delineated the only real power of men, as a collectivity, in terms of gender. It was made formal in the local sexual division of labour and played out, on a daily basis, in the home. In this way the nature of the labour market and the particular work processes associated with port employment, effectively froze men into gender-focused identities which remained meaningful despite other personal or structural dynamics such as getting married, becoming a father, moving away or being without work for most of the time. However, although the local labour market provided the context within which all docklanders lived their lives, the work situation was not the only place where notions of masculinity were constructed.

Family and masculinity

The concept of masculinity which emphasized the domestic role of men was, though, just as complex as that related to work.[21] Marriage and fatherhood offered evidence of manhood which was substantiated by the acceptance of responsibility for the maintenance of wives and children and was encapsulated in the title of breadwinner. That title, however, was often a hollow one; it carried status but implied no automatic right of families to support from the bearer of it. This breadwinning notion of masculinity incorporated elements which appear contradictory. The support of families was regarded as a duty but not an obligation. The money men earned, or received in the form of benefits, was their own to give over or withhold as they so wished – a factor which, itself, represented a further component in the complex embodiment of male identity.[22]

The role of breadwinner gave men status and privileges but implied no necessary self-sacrifice. Indeed, the right of individual men to a proportion of what they earned for personal spending was implicit. Although some men did not take advantage of this 'right' and others only insofar as it did not impact too heavily on the living standards of the rest of the family, they risked being called 'hen-pecked' as a consequence. Most family systems of household income allocation included provision for breadwinners' spends. Clearly, given the extremes of economic distress occasioned by the dislocations in the formal economy during the interwar years, the men's portion was frequently only token but what counted, in terms of male identity, was the *right* of men to have money for personal spending.[23] In addition, irrespective of what proportion of their income they handed over for housekeeping, no matter how nebulous the

71

meaning of the title of provider, men expected and were given, certain services and resources in return for being named as such. It is by reference to the entitlement of men to dispense or withhold income, that this construct of masculinity can be understood.

The power of income control was both born from, and was a component of, male identities which evolved within the framework of a local labour market which denied men the role of breadwinner, in the truest sense of the word, but which demanded recognition of their responsibilities in this respect. In the framework of a port economy the concept of provider could seldom be anything other than symbolic. Irregularity, low earnings and unemployment conspired to make it very difficult for men to earn enough money to assure the subsistence of their families. Definitions of the role of provider were fluid enough to accommodate this fact without challenging the masculinity of dockland men. Indeed, recognition as provider was not dependent on the monetary support men were able to bring in, but was found in the domestic prerogatives it afforded them, irrespective of the contribution they made.

> In our family, dads were kings and sons were princes [laughing]. Don't get me wrong, our dad was lovely but he had his own throne and his own great big mug for his tea and he was waited on hand and foot. Even when he'd retired and we'd go there for our dinner, the minute he'd finished – didn't matter if my mum had finished hers – she'd get up and take his plate out and bring in his pudding.[24]

Given the realities of the port economy, few men could earn a family wage; what they did earn they would share but this was always contingent on the co-operation of the rest of their families in giving them precedence. This sort of rationalization of men's position within the family was, then, particularly pragmatic and offered public acknowledgement of their masculinity in circumstances where, objectively, it could be called into doubt. In addition, it brought personal satisfaction and status as a counter to the oppressive forces of the labour market to which men were subject outside the home. Eleanor Rathbone argued that 'man', albeit in his 'unconscious mind', was only too aware of the power over wives and children which his role as breadwinner gave him; that the dependency of his family added measurably to the authority and self-esteem of husbands.[25]

A man's position in the labour market and his role as family provider implied both demands and entitlements. The two were united in male patterns of consumption. In addition to the favoured position granted to men with regard to scarce subsistence resources, such as food, notions of men's rights as men gave them the right to prioritize other consumption desires, if they so chose. Conspicuous consumption by men was most clearly visible in relation to expenditure on alcohol.[26] Yet, when assessing drinking habits, factors other than male self-interest should be weighed. Alcohol dependency must provide at least a partial explanation of the centrality of drinking to the lives of some men. Then, participation in the web of association which crisscrossed the area between the fixed points of home, stand, workplace, street corner and pub offered access to the conduits of information which circulated around each. For casual workers knowledge about ships due in or companies taking men on could be crucial. Friendships also had to be created and maintained to maximize the possibility of someone 'speaking for you' when job opportunities did come up. Furthermore, dockland understandings of the workings of the casual system, assigned importance to the ability of men to buy favour and the chance of being selected for work, by purchasing drinks for, or otherwise bribing, corrupt foremen.[27] Stories of such incidents abound, although it seems clear that while sometimes carrying validity, much of the evidence which emphasizes the widespread nature of the practice is apocryphal.[28]

Even setting aside such practical considerations, though, consolidation of relationships through the mechanism of socializing and drinking together was especially important in economies where there were high degrees of informality.[29] This was particularly so in situations where kin, friends and neighbours were in competition for a limited number of jobs. Social contact in arenas outside of home and workplace offered a mechanism by which men could partition off those parts of their lives which made them adversaries of each other or where objective criteria, such as the ability to provide for their families, might call their masculinity into question. The reciprocity inherent to male networking, manifest in treating and 'standing your round', comprised a key element in masculine affirmation.

Not all men participated in this bonding process. Although seafarers were expected to treat on a generalized basis[30] in regular, everyday situations men would not accept being taken for a pint unless they could buy one back. Reciprocity did not have to be immediate but there had to be at least some realistic prospect of doing so in the very near future, if men were to maintain their self-respect in relation to pub custom and practice. An alternative was to buy only for yourself. However, even in an economy where income getting and retaining was as circumscribed as it was locally, drinking 'alone' could be regarded as suspect. Rather than risk being targeted as such, men who were unable or unwilling to participate fully in pub culture and male bonding of this sort, simply stayed away.

Yet, 'staying away' might be a positive choice. Pat M's father was 'a saver' who 'didn't drink' and took one of his children on holiday to Ireland each summer.[31] Gerry B. was a 'lovely, lovely man' who worked tirelessly for the St Vincent de Paul Society and 'would give you the bread out of his mouth'.[32] Although poverty and the realities of dockland life made notions of working-class respectability necessarily mutable, some men defined their own standards of behaviour on the basis of criteria more usually associated with other parts of the city. Sobriety, thrift and the embracing of family and community responsibility were not synonymous with a lack of manliness. They, nevertheless, did imply a degree of self-confidence which enabled men who possessed these qualities to set themselves apart from peer pressures about what made a 'man'. The evidence suggests also that these men had a higher degree of independence in such matters, because of factors which distinguished them from the mass of those who competed for work on the casual labour market. Pat M's father, for example, was a senior foreman in a cattle food mill; a job which gave him access to regular wages and paid holidays. Gerry B. also had full time employment. Other individuals who were respected but who did not conform to expected norms of masculine behaviour, often derived their status on the basis of other manly criteria – as successful sportsmen or as prominent local figures such as teachers or owners of small businesses. One man who grew up in the area recalled that:

> ... the most highly regarded person in our neighbourhood was Jim Clarke [a black man who had been brought up in a white Irish Catholic family]. He was certainly regarded as a 'man's man' because of what he did in the neighbourhood, his natural friendliness and his close family relationships.[33]

Clearly, such attributes engendered respect but Jim Clarke's additional status as a champion swimmer and a brave man who rescued several people from the canal, also served to put his masculinity beyond question.

Notions of masculine behaviour relative to consumption patterns were complex. The crucial factor, however, was that the choice, almost universally, was held in male hands. However rational the reasons, whatever the social, psychological and cultural motivations which underpinned male consumption, this prioritization of men's collective and individual psyche had profound implications for the material and emotional well-being of women and their families.[34] Capitalism and patriarchy interacted with individualized male self-interest to create and support a concept of masculinity which men embraced and used to their advantage. Masculinity bolstered self-image and ensured that low and irregular earnings and unemployment were primarily a problem for those women whose credibility was dependent on their being perceived to manage on what they were given. Local notions of masculinity allowed men the status and privileges of 'provider' without any necessary fulfilment of that role.

It is possible, then, to identify two prominent forms of masculinity constructed around male identities in respect of the separate but related spheres of male employment and the household. Both reflected the powerlessness of men relative to their subsidiary place in the labour market and their inability to secure the life course subsistence needs of their families. Both empowered men

74

by investing them with a semblance of self-governance in the workplace and authority within their homes. Both implied the exertion of control over women and emphasized the precedence of men. They did so by virtue of the sexual division of labour in the workplace and the primacy of male privilege in the home. They met and overlapped in arenas of male bonding such as pubs, cocoa houses and street corners and were strengthened by leisure pursuits. Enrolment in the Territorial Army, for example, offered a temporary escape from the responsibilities of daily life and an opportunity to reinforce the ties of male allegiance.

Sport also served this dual purpose. Regardless of whether or not men could actually afford to attend professional football matches during the period – and many could not[35] – virtually all supported one or other of the two local football teams. In addition, men played football in local amateur street leagues while boxing and billiards offered other outlets for both spectators and participants. As today, for many working-class men, the winning of trophies gave evidence of personal achievement and gained the respect of other men. In addition, success in sport offered one of the very few opportunities for upward social mobility and escape from the futures otherwise mapped out for dockland boys. Dreams and aspirations, were not extinguished by the limited possibilities of fulfilling them. Participation in 'men's' sports, football talk, bandinage and 'in' jokes gave men areas of common ground which, allied to other elements of male bonding such as drinking, playing cards gambling or hanging round street corners, served to reinforce notions of a subliminal male self.

Religion and masculinity

The Roman Catholic church was an additional focal point for the male solidarities and understandings of manhood which were woven into the complex tapestry of local male identity. Although Roman Catholicism stressed the equality of church members in the sight of God, in practice, it designated very different roles for men and women in the furtherance of God's work. Essentially, Catholic women fulfilled their services to the church through marriage and the bearing of children who were reared in the faith. Whilst not condoning ill-treatment of wives, there is little evidence that the church explicitly challenged the right of husbands to do so, albeit some individual priests could be more sympathetic towards women than others. 'Cappy M. used to follow Everton. If his team lost, Mrs. M. used to get to know before Cappy came home and she had to wait in the Presbytery until he cooled off.'[36] A woman explained:

> He took the football so serious that when the team lost he'd come home and beat ten kinds of 'you know what' out of his wife. To avoid the beating,

she'd take refuge in the Priest's house. He used to hide her 'til Cappy had got over it. Just when Everton lost, you could do no good with him.[37]

The concept of womanliness evident in church teaching set women in a subservient role and prioritized the place of men. This was perhaps made most explicit in the exclusively male church hierarchy and particularly so in the figure of the local parish priest. The church insisted that the greatest glory a family could aspire to was to have one of their sons join the priesthood – implicit within this was the value of boy children over girl.

Men and women were organized separately in the various lay bodies and confraternities attached to each parish. In all the feasts and celebrations of the church calendar and the public display of faith and defiance visible in parish, local and city wide parades, men were grouped or walked separately. In a city where sectarianism was a crucial element in working-class identity, public manifestations of faith were likely to attract verbal and physical abuse. Bloody confrontations were common around particular occasions and although these involved both men and women, and all who took part seem to have welcomed the justification for a scrap, it was men – and particularly young men – who were most often involved in (as attackers or attacked) ferocious battles. Furthermore, even those who only nominally regarded themselves as Roman Catholic – who did not attend mass regularly nor belonged to formal church organizations – identified as such when religious loyalties took on a more public form. One contemporary wrote that both Catholic and Protestant marchers were 'flaunting, their allegiance ... rather than their belief'.[38] Religious identity comprised a complex amalgam of different parts:

> Liverpool exhibited sectarian fervour without widespread religious observance. Other antagonisms were involved. Residual religion, patriotic assertion and the clannish camaraderie of slum neighbourhoods were knotted together.[39]

Men's perception of themselves as Roman Catholic men was integral to notions of masculinity associated with other areas of their lives, each being mutually reinforcing. A local priest captured this sense of male solidarity when recording his involvement in a public display of sectarian identification:

> Last Sunday, the feast of Christus Rex, the Archbishop held a monster demonstration in St. George's Hall. Although the night was wild and wet, in the company of about 6,000 men from the Scotland Road area, [the North End of Liverpool] I marched down from Cranmer Street to the Hall, to the accompaniment of cheers, clapping and multifarious forms of salute.[40]

For men who carried little intrinsic status in other areas of their lives, marching through streets to the acclaim of those who lined them, could clearly be a positive experience. Added to that, the sense of male pride evident in this brief account, offered affirmation of manhood. However, there are visible contradictions in the messages given to men who participated in the procession. The expression of male Roman Catholic solidarity at least implied acceptance of the preaching of the church against communism and, what were regarded as, the related scourges of socialism and trades unionism – all of which were condemned from the pulpit. Men who converged on St George's Hall, from parishes throughout the city, listened to speakers who denounced communism and gave thanks for the presence of General Franco, who had so recently 'delivered' Spain from the communist threat. For those Catholic men whose personal points of identity included an empathy with left wing perspectives of one sort or another, this affirmation of masculinity could prove problematic. The diarist went on:

> Inside the Hall I heard a stirring address on Communism by Archbishop McDonald of Edinburgh ... Alderman Hogan, the City Labour Leader, ... introduced the only discordant note of the evening. He said he didn't agree with everything that had been said, – an obvious reference to Blundell's speech on Spain. It was the first time I had seen the said Hogan, but the impression I got was not favourable. He adopts the superior attitude of the Socialist intelligentsia (God knows why), and trusts that a certain superficial cleverness and elephantine wit pass muster as profound thought or oratorical brilliancy. The more I see and hear and read of these labourites and Socialists, the more shallow they appear. Politics is a mania with them. The dirty, mean game of party politics has become a disease with these half-educated men; they are completely blind to wider issues, they eat drink and sleep politics, they continually mouth their threadbare slogans and party cliches and, I believe, would sacrifice cheerfully every ideal of religion, honour or justice to attain their ends. The purging of public life, even in this country, is fast becoming necessary.[41]

Luke Hogan attended the meeting as a Roman Catholic and despite his obvious sympathies refrained from outright condemnation of the attitudes expressed by some of the other speakers. Of course, accord with anti-communist sentiment was perfectly compatible with socialism. However, even in relation to views he felt strongly about, Hogan clearly thought that the meeting was not an appropriate place to challenge church authority too vehemently. In part, this was perhaps politic and a reflection of his desire not to alienate potential voters, who might themselves have been convinced by the church's message on this issue. Such discretion had not always been evident; he was criticized from within his own party when, during the 1931 elections, he threatened to fly the Red flag over the Town Hall and to pack the magistrates' bench with socialists. It is important to remember that Hogan was on the platform at St George's Hall because of his status as a City councillor, but attended the meeting because he was a Catholic man who, in 1935, had opposed (on religious grounds) the decision by the City Council to give a grant to a local birth control clinic.[42]

Such contradictions seem to have been incorporated into the social identities of local men during these decades. In the summer of 1939, parishioners from St Albans joined a Pilgrimage to Lourdes. One evening, one of the group, a member of the local branch of the Labour Party, was chosen to lead the British contingent in one of the nightly international processions, around the grotto. His disconcertion was relished by the priest who accompanied them, '... and John F. who, to his everlasting credit or ignominy (his Labour political complexion could not decide which) carried the Union Jack in the procession'.[43]

The church was very important to the lives of many local men. However, Waller argues that the influence of the church on interwar politics in Liverpool, can be best understood by an analogy with the role of the clergy in nineteenth century Ireland:

> ... the clergy could tap a large stock of affection which might result in a candidate whom they supported polling better than he would otherwise have done; but mostly they could lead their people only in the direction they wanted to go.[44]

This analysis is applicable to other areas of influence and suggests a context within which to locate affiliations and loyalties which were, at one and the same time, equally complex and pragmatic. In many areas of daily life, the norms, beliefs, practices and standards of local people were necessarily flexible. They evolved in a manner which could accommodate aspirations, yet which were both underpinned and divided by factors cutting across political affiliation, gender, age, religion and ethnicity. They could incorporate a large variety of achievements and principles without compromising individual and collective values and concepts of respectability. This is evident with respect to the notion of breadwinner; standards shifted when breadwinning was not achievable or when men chose not to fulfil the role, without necessarily implying any loss of title or status. Similarly, the church could be and often was a powerful influence in men's lives. However, for the most part, individual decisions about such issues as political affiliation, were made on the basis of factors other than blind acceptance of dogma and/or rhetoric.

For men, identification as a Catholic implied a broad spectrum of meaning and experience. At one end there were those for whom Roman Catholicism was the central defining factor in lives which were structured by the church calendar. At the other extreme, Catholicism was a mantle which men could don and parade as a symbol of provocative sectarian allegiance but which they could shed on Sunday mornings when the pull of a bed proved stronger than the obligation to attend Mass. Ethnic identity might also be significant.

Catholicism and Irishness sat side by side in the North End docklands but Irish nationalism could lead to communal protection of individual activists, without this necessarily revealing anything about political affiliation.[45] It was common at festival times to see the Union Jack – that powerful symbol of Britishness and Protestantism – billowing side by side with the Irish Tricolour and the Papal Flag. This might have represented some personal or street statement of the Roman Catholic Irish–British nature of the area, but could as easily depend on the content of local lofts and the desire to put on as good a show of colourful bunting as possible. It is important not to assign meaning where none exists or in a manner which edits out the pragmatism which underlay so much of dockland behaviour.

Nevertheless in localities where parish was synonymous with community, the church was important in a secular as well as a religious sense and provided local men and boys with a place to fraternize, offering the only real alternative to pubs. The church made available separate spaces where men could engage with other men in leisure pursuits. The upstairs rooms of one parish 'club' were given over to the playing of billiards, 'the girls used to go crackers, they were never allowed upstairs. Oh my God ... What? A woman in there! [laughs]'.[46]

In such ways, Roman Catholicism was a key factor in the construction of a particular masculinity which interacted with masculinities formed in other arenas to produce a sense of manhood that was specific historically, spatially, structurally and culturally.

Conclusion

In the North End of Liverpool between the wars, the components which came together, to form a collective masculine identity were fluid, could be contradictory, and were not, in an individual sense, necessarily subscribed to by all men. They could vary over time, spatially and within particular labour market contexts.[47] Nevertheless, the understanding of what comprised masculinity was in any one locality or situation or at any one moment in time, universal. More importantly, the privileges which attached to ownership of a male identity were, for the most part, immutable. They were not dependent on the extent to which men, as individuals, fulfilled the multitude of roles upon which the concept of masculinity was implicitly constructed. Notions of masculinity constantly reinforced the expectations of men and their favoured position in the home, in the labour market and all the key areas of daily life.

Masculinity is a dynamic construct which offers historians the opportunity of exploring the key features of male identity in a framework which allows for variation in its construction and practice. Threads of continuity and change run parallel but at different speeds in different social contexts. This chapter untangles some of the key elements in the constantly shifting masculinities which were evident in one area of dockland Liverpool during the years between the World Wars. However, despite the emphasis put on gender differentiation both in terms of the formation and practice of masculinity, knowledge of the production and reproduction of masculinities only offers one factor to assist understanding of the immensely complex world of gender relations. Nevertheless, masculinity is clearly a valuable concept but it is one which historians can only investigate by exploring practices which were and are historically and spatially specific.

Notes

I am grateful to Maggie Walsh for her comments on this paper. I also thank Valerie Burton, Keith McClelland and Frank Boyce for their comments on an earlier draft and to Alan Johnson for his comments and his generosity in sharing his analysis of Liverpool politics in the twentieth century.

1. For a useful summary see Brittan, Arthur (1989), *Masculinity and Power*, Oxford: Basil Blackwell Ltd., pp. 6–11.
2. See, for example, Hearn, Jeff and Morgan, David (eds) (1990), *Men, Masculinity and Social Theory*, London: Unwin Hyman Ltd.; Roper, Michael and Tosh, John (eds) (1991), *Manful Assertions: Masculinities in Britain Since 1800*, London: Routledge; Morgan, David H. (1992), *Discovering Men*, London: Routledge. Doreen Massey emphasizes the importance of 'geographical variations in the construction of masculinity and femininity and the relationship between the two', Massey, D. (ed.) (1994), *Space, Place and Gender*, London: Polity Press.
3. See Roper and Tosh (eds), *Manful*.
4. Ayers, Pat, 'The Economics of Daily Life: Gender, Household and Community in Interwar Liverpool' (work in progress).
5. Ayers, Pat (1986), *The Liverpool Docklands: Life and Work in Athol Street*, Liverpool: Docklands History Books, p. 2.
6. Liverpool Joint Research Committee on the Domestic Conditions and Expenditure of the Families of Certain Liverpool Labourers (1909), *How the Casual Labourer Lives*, Liverpool: Northern Publishing Co.; Lord Mayor of Liverpool's Conference on Casual Labour, *Report*, 31 December, 1930; Ayers, Pat (1991), 'The Hidden Economy of Dockland Families: Liverpool in the 1930s', in Hudson, Pat and Lee, W.R. (eds), *Women's Work and the Family Economy in Historical Perspective*, Manchester: Manchester University Press.
7. See, for example, Dennis, Norman, Henriques, Fernando and Slaughter, Clifford (1956), *Coal is Our Life*, London: Eyre and Spottiswode (Publishers) Ltd.; Morgan, *Discovering Men*, pp. 72–98
8. Grant, Linda May (1987), 'Women Workers and the Sexual Division of Labour in Liverpool: Liverpool – 1890–1939', PhD, University of Liverpool, pp. 88–94.
9. Lane, Tony (1987), *Liverpool: Gateway of Empire*, London: Lawrence and Wishart, p.109.
10. Lane, *Liverpool*, p.109; Grant, 'Women'; Dennis et al., *Coal*, argued that the notion of masculinity which derived from men's experience of coal mining

spilled over into daily life. Attitudes which evolved over time in the workplace, penetrated leisure and family.

11. Seccombe, Wally (1986), 'Patriarchy Stabilized: The Construction of the Male Breadwinner Wage Norm in Nineteenth-century Britain', *Social History*, **11** (1), 53–76.
12. Burton, Valerie (1991), 'The Myth of Bachelor Jack: Masculinity, Patriarchy and Seafaring Labour', in Howell, Colin and Twomey, Richard (eds), *Seafaring Worlds: Essays in the History of Maritime Life and Labour*, Halifax: Acadiensis Press, p. 187. Burton is, however, writing about seafarers who worked on liners, and these predominantly sailed out of Southampton. Nevertheless, oral testimony would seem to support the notion that, at least by the early part of the twentieth century, Liverpool-based seafarers were establishing households. However, in the absence of detailed work, conclusions about the motivation for this must remain speculative. See also, Mahler, E. and Rathbone, E.F. (1911), *Payment of Seamen. The Present System. How the Wives Suffer*, Liverpool: Liverpool Women's Industrial Council.
13. Burton, 'The Myth', pp. 187–98.
14. 'Skives' were/are informal strategies to, for example, reduce work loads or extend the time necessary to complete a job.
15. Thompson, E.P. (1971), 'The Moral Economy of the English Crowd in the Eighteenth Century', *Past and Present*, **50** (1), 76–136; See also, Ditton, J. (1977), *Part-Time Crime: An Ethnography of Fiddling and Pilferage*, London: Macmillan; Henry, S. (1978), *The Hidden Economy: The Context and Control of Borderline Crime*, London: Martin Robertson; Mars, G. (1982), *Cheats at Work; An Anthropology of Workplace Crime*, London: Unwin Paperbacks. For a short discussion of workplace theft in relation to the formation of masculinity, see Morgan, *Discovering*, p. 89.
16. Moore, Kevin (1987), *The Mersey Ship Repairers: Life and Work in a Port Industry*, Liverpool: Docklands History Books, pp. 55–6.
17. Taplin, Eric (1986), *The Dockers' Union. A Study of the National Union of Dock Labourers, 1889–1922*, Leicester: Leicester University Press, p. 3.
18. Casually employed men were united by their common subsidiary relationship to employers and hirers and the strategies they devised in response to a hostile employment system, whilst simultaneously being divided out from each other by competition for work.
19. I am not happy with the word 'collectivity' but 'corporate' of men is equally problematic and more awkward whilst 'fraternity' has associations with the formal labour movement.
20. The reality for most men was to be without work for most of the time. 'Throughout the 1920s and 1930s male unemployment on Merseyside was consistently above 20 per cent and in some years one in three men were out of work', Merseyside Socialist Research Group (1980), *Merseyside in Crisis*, Liverpool: Merseyside Socialist Research Group, p. 32.
21. See Burton, 'The Myth'. Although Valerie Burton draws on evidence relating to seafaring, it is feasible to extrapolate from this to include men engaged in other port employment. Tony Lane writes, 'A combination of high labour turnover and a large number of men serving as seamen at any one time meant ... an extraordinary number of men had been away to sea at one time or another': Lane, *Liverpool*, p. 99.
22. See Ayers, Pat and Lambertz, Jan (1986), 'Marriage, Money and Domestic Violence in Working-class Liverpool, 1919–1939', in Lewis, Jane (ed.), *Labour*

and Love: Women's Experience of Home and Family, 1850–1940, Oxford: Basil Blackwell Ltd.; Ayers, 'The Hidden'. This was not something particular to Liverpool. See, for example, Burton, 'The Myth'; Davies, Andrew (1992), *Leisure, Gender and Poverty. Working-class Cultures in Salford and Manchester 1900–1939*, Buckingham: Open University Press, pp. 30–1; Ross, Ellen (1993), *Love and Toil: Motherhood in Outcast London, 1870–1918*, New York: Oxford University Press.

23. See Davies, *Leisure*, pp. 43–54 for a discussion of the impact of poverty on men's spending patterns in Salford during the interwar years.

24. Interview, September 1982 with RM (woman born 1922). Interview testimony used in this chapter is drawn from two sources. References marked DHP are taken from interviews conducted by the team of the Docklands History Project which was located jointly in the Departments of History and of Sociology, University of Liverpool, 1996–1990. Other references are taken from interviews conducted by Pat Ayers as part of personal ongoing research.

25. Rathbone, E.R. (1924), *The Disinherited Family: A Plea for the Endowment of the Family*, London: Edward Arnold, pp. 270–3.

26. Ayers, *The Liverpool*, pp. 38–40.

27. Moore, *The Mersey*, p. 49.

28. Hanham, F.G. (1930), *Report of Enquiry into Casual Labour in the Merseyside Area*, Liverpool: Liverpool City Council; Lane, *Liverpool*, p. 94.

29. Medick, H. (1983), 'Plebian Culture and the Transition to Capitalism', in Samuel, R.S. and Stedman, Jones G. (eds), *Culture, Ideology and Politics*, London: Routledge and Kegan Paul.

30. I suspect that this was, at least partly, a route to re-embedding themselves in local male networks, for all the reasons suggested above, rather than altruistic sharing.

31. DHP Interview with PMG (man born 1909).

32. Interview, May 1985 with MB (woman born 1921).

33. Letter from FB commenting on earlier draft of this paper, August 1995.

34. For an analysis of this, see Ayers, 'Survivalist Consumption in Interwar Liverpool', unpublished paper presented at Manchester Metropolitan University, June, 1994 (from work in progress, 'The Economics').

35. See Middleton, T. (1931), 'An Enquiry into the Use of Leisure Amongst the Working Classes of Liverpool', unpublished MA Thesis, University of Liverpool; Davies, *Leisure*, pp. 43–8.

36. DHP. Interview with BG (man born 1909).

37. DHP. Interview with MD (woman born 1912).

38. O'Mara, Pat (1934), *The Autobiography of a Liverpool Irish Slummy*, Liverpool, p. 80.

39. Waller, P.J. (1981), *Democracy and Sectarianism. A Political and Social History of Liverpool 1868–1939*, Liverpool: Liverpool University Press, p. 26.

40. Diary of Fr. D. 30 October 1936. (Fr. D. was then serving in a dockland parish in the North End of Liverpool.)

41. Diary of Fr. D. 30 October 1936. Luke Hogan had been Chairman of Liverpool Council of Action during the General Strike and led the Liverpool Labour Party from 1930–1948. He resigned from the Labour Party in 1950 and subsequently sat as an Independent Catholic Councillor (Waller, *Democracy*, p. 494).

42. Waller, *Democracy*, pp. 340–1, 494. See also, Keeling, Dorothy (1961), *The Crowded Stairs: Recollections of Social Work in Liverpool*, Liverpool: National Council of Social Services.

43. Diary of Fr. D. 26 July 1939.

44. Whyte, J.H. (1960), 'The Influence of the Catholic Clergy on Elections in Nineteenth Century Ireland', *English Historical Review*, **LXXV** (295), April, 239–59, quoted by Waller, *Democracy*, p. 326.
45. Ayers, Pat, *The Liverpool*, p. 55.
46. DHP. Interview with WD (woman born 1936).
47. Even in dockland Liverpool, notions of masculinity and appropriate roles for men could vary. For example, in Garston, to the far south of the city's chain of waterside communities, the relocation of Wilson's Bobbin Works from Yorkshire at the turn of the century, created demand for women's labour. A tradition of married women working was introduced by the large numbers of Yorkshire families which followed. By the interwar period, unlike the North End, there was a clear acceptance of formal paid work for women which did not challenge the masculinity of local men. Alongside this, there is some evidence of greater degrees of shared domestic work between husbands and wives.

CHAPTER FIVE

'Whoring, Drinking Sailors': Reflections on Masculinity from the Labour History of Nineteenth-century British Shipping[1]

Valerie Burton

The primary concern of merchant seafarers in going to sea was to make a living, but the labour historian who treats seafaring only in its potential for wage-earning misses much which is important about the activity.[2] The societies which have seen many hundreds of thousands of individuals regularly departing to sea have rarely done so without placing larger meanings in their comings and goings.[3] Throughout history few women have worked on ships and the sea has been known as a place to which men ventured.[4] Images and narratives of sea-going have afforded powerful ways of representing maleness. They have entered into the world which men shared with women ashore in ways which reflect upon its social arrangements. If maritime historians have rarely stopped to consider these things what is more surprising is that the authors of two, more ambitious, studies of seafaring published in recent years did not incorporate any of this into their understandings.[5] It is true that in the 1980s gender mobilized fewer analytical claims in respect of labour and working-class history than it was to do in the 1990s. Gender was relatively contained so long as the point of its reference was women, but making men the subject of gender analysis confirmed what gender-advocates had always suspected: that joining work and the workplace only through class perspectives was a failure of the historian's political understanding.[6]

By the late 1990s historians can begin to measure the challenge which gender has set; and not simply in augmenting and reinforcing what was already known about the past of working men and women.[7] Work and the workplace still retain their importance, but gender sensitivities point to new links between production, consumption and reproduction. Investigations of the connections between power and the use and distribution of resources are potentially richer for making these links. The analytical tools developed by feminist and gay historians suggest that there were multiple sites differentiating the activities and sensibilities of men and women and bearing upon their capacity to exercise agency. If the price of these new departures has been the unsettling of historians trained to recognize class as a fixed structure and to observe it as a shared identity shaped in common material interests, something important has been gained in return: the freedom to explore processes of social formation and economic relations in their diversity and with reference to the subjectivities which contribute to the sense of things material.

Recent work both departs from and challenges the conventions of explaining working-class formation as a single narrative of proletarianization.[8] It proposes there are differences in work organization and experience which are not accounted for in the narratives which concentrate on the growth of waged labour and workers' progressive loss of control at the point of production. It makes the case for understanding the impact of capitalist work relations on household arrangements, family and community structures and political groupings, giving attention to how those processes worked by producing inequalities of gender, race and class. Particularly important to the theme of this paper are the reservations expressed by Sonya Rose and Alice Kessler-Harris. They criticize the tendency to generalize about these issues from the perspective of the 'representative' artisan and suggest that the 'otherness' of masculinity is now the appropriate place to concentrate attention.[9]

This chapter addresses a need to know more about what are variously called unrespectable manhoods or rough work cultures as distinct from artisanal work cultures embracing respectability and male breadwinning. Regular work habits, family breadwinning and sexual restraint defined only one way of being a man in nineteenth-century Britain and, though they have been made central in analyses of changes to the family with the shift in its material base from a locus of production to one of reproduction and consumption, curiosity grows about the place of scripts and images antithetical to male breadwinning.[10] How were these 'other' scripts and images related to the definition of gender spheres in an industrial society forging new understandings of the organization of productivity and power? The literature which treats the kinds of workers who freighted nineteenth century beliefs about masculinity with unrespectable 'otherness' is dated. It is rendered worthless by adherence to the same civilizing presumptions that their 'betters' in nineteenth-century society assumed when they made navvies, miners and 'sailors' the subject of a prurient interest.[11] Historians are better served by embarking on a new study wherein the civilizing process of industrial capitalism is itself addressed and nineteenth-century concepts of modernization and progress are joined analytically to a discussion of the representation of manhood. Here, I concentrate upon seafarers. In part what follows is a discussion of the more objectively observed ways in which changes in the capitalist organization of shipping affected seafarers during the nineteenth century. But, since my chief purpose is to treat the mythology of the whoring, drinking sailor, this discussion has a further layer of significance, and it is there that I spell out the saliency of ideas which were integral to the reorganization of work and of productivity and power in the period.

'I felt myself a lion among the stay-at-homes ...'
William Alleyn's undated journal entry (c.1887); Brocklebank Collection, Maritime Records Centre, Merseyside Maritime Museum.

In western nations, by the eighteenth century, mastery of nature was conceived of as civilized society's destiny. The Enlightenment understood that humanity's well-being was secured in the organized exploitation of natural resources. Post-Enlightenment definitions of economic rationality privileged entrepreneurial agency in the endeavour, while liberal political economy advanced its capitalist forms. Command of the seas was long the subject of xenophobic ideas of mastery, and in Britain, in the nineteenth century, commerce eclipsed military matters in these concerns.[12] One of the functions of an office of the state, newly created in the middle of the century, was to generate statistics of British-registered tonnage. The Office of the Registrar General of Shipping and Seamen did more, however, than measure the progress of the merchant fleet.[13] By furthering comparison with competitors who retained protection for shipping and trade it illuminated the success of free market capitalism. At a rather later date the office could show the advance of steam in British tonnage concurrent with an increase in the nation's share of world commodity trade. Its statistics were then taken to validate the understandings of economic individualism on which the reorganization of the industry had taken place following the repeal of the Navigation Laws, in 1849. The ingenuity of British inventors and the enterprise of its entrepreneurs were observed and celebrated in the world-wide deployment of its merchant fleet.[14]

When mastery of the oceans was acclaimed as a technical and entrepreneurial achievement this undermined workers' claims to the importance of their own, unaided, efforts to wrest a living from the sea. The battle to overcome the elements had long given a heroic colouring to the job of seafaring. Generations of seafarers under sail used its discursive properties to illuminate the collective and time-honoured character of their endeavour, particularly as it was seen to make men of boys in each generation. William Alleyn, a late nineteenth-century seafarer, still used the terms in which seafarers made their experience explicable to themselves and landsmen as emboldening and strengthening. Yet his personal history was indicative of a change which arrived first in the British merchant marine. At the time when he wrote in his journal that a first voyage made him feel a 'lion among the stay-at-homes' he was an officer apprentice. In the late nineteenth century officer apprentices were some of the few seafarers who spent time under sail, and in Alleyn's case it was with the expectation that he would move to better things: the command of a large steam vessel and its sizeable crew.[15] A sail training did not impart the practicable, marketable, skills of vessel management in the predominantly steam merchant marine of Alleyn's day. Instead the sail training given to premium-paying apprentices used the hard-knock pedagogy of the public

86

school to turn out men who could assume command of occupationally heterogeneous and, sometimes, ethnically distinct, crews by way of the values and attitudes of a class which took control by right of birth.[16]

The shifting technology base of the industry has its place in explaining how heroic myths of sailoring were in some senses lost to ordinary seafaring men. Still, in so far as this change turned on a managerial initiative aimed at the casualization of the greater part of the workforce and the professionalization of its officers, its origins are pre-steam and were initiated under other technological forms. The possibilities of enhancing returns on capital by economies in labour were explored by shipowners in connection with their organization of new markets not long after the conclusion of the Napoleonic wars. When shipowners lobbied for the ending of statutory seamen's apprenticeship in the 1830s and 1840s (some forty to fifty years before the point at which the majority of the workforce was in steam) they framed their arguments for a more limited system to train up masters and mates in respect of the deficiencies of the existing provisions. Those provisions, they argued, brought an undesirable class to sea whose maintenance at the shipowner's expense was detrimental to their ability to compete internationally. The ending of statutory apprenticeship came in 1849 as a significant concession to the advocates of the free market. In turn, state examinations for masters, mates and, later, engineers were initiated.

Professional certification set in train developments which are best described as *embourgeoisement*. They made the shipmasters' and engineers' occupations into desirable middle-class occupations. Its bearing upon my theme is best identified in William Alleyn's pretensions to be a man more manly than the 'stay-at-homes'. His formula involved the subjectivities of class and gender. The manliness of seafaring was, for Alleyn and his counterparts, an expression of their superior class. With the attenuation of seafarers' contact with sailing vessels the context which lent itself best to presenting seafaring as a heroic and noble activity was, in an immediate sense, closed to the rank-and-file. Yet reference to the sailing craft and its traditions was not precluded to this group. It was in no small part a measure of their sensibilities to the new polarities in the industry that many seafarers sought, vicariously, in those traditions a character who described the opposite of the gentlemanly officer. They found it in the rough and tough sailor who free-wheeled around the world and who, when he turned into port, distinguished himself among the 'stay-at-homes' by drinking and whoring on a scale which outdid them all.

In recent years sociologists and ethnographers of seafarers have equated seafaring to incarceration on the basis that to go to sea meant forfeiting all regular social contact and turning, inward, to the ship's company.[17] It had seemed this way even before functionalism and total institution theory shaped scholars' views. More than two hundred years ago Samuel Johnson arrived at a similar conclusion in the aftermath of an uncongenial sea voyage.[18] It made him compare the merchant vessel with a gaol and led him to observe that going to sea rendered men useless for anything else in life once they were accustomed to seafaring. That historians are not better informed historically about seafarers' sea-shore transitions is unfortunate for further research would surely show that the lengthy voyages and life-long commitment which the sociologist's model presupposes were temporally limited, and when they did typify sailing ship employment it was long after Johnson's day.[19] The forces of market capitalism pressed heavily on a segment of the labour force in the declining days of sail. Their marginalization stemmed from a labour market position in which their chances of employment were limited and where their opportunities of settled social contact were constrained.

I shall return to the fate of late nineteenth-century sailing-ship men later, but for the present the concept of seafarers' 'apartness' is paramount. For it was not in disabusing land-dwellers of the notion of their estrangement that seafarers turned the tables on their detractors, but rather by extending the concept of the 'misfit' sailor until he assumed larger-than-life significance in landward society. Behind him was the homosocial world of the fo'c's'l where male norms were unchallenged and supreme. That world was recreated on shore in the brothels, lodging houses and public houses of port towns which were patronized by a seafaring clientele and by other working men. It was there that the tale of Jack's progress through sailortown was told.[20] He consumed drink and availed himself of women to the limits of what his wages could buy and he returned to sea once spent up. The tale explained sailortown binges in terms of seafarers' needs for sex and drink. It suggested that indulging those needs was the legitimate end and reward of wage-earners whose money was earned under extreme peril and privation: it was their let-up in the hardships of going to sea. Since the lives of the sober-living and sexually reticent respectable working class were not given to these displays, there was, in the largely imaginary life of the sailor, a possibility of drawing a fuller distinction from the 'stay-at-homes'. It was the difference of a man who commanded resources and put them to womanizing and drinking knowing that virility and prowess were still measured in these things.[21]

'[Merchant seafarers] have been deprived of the same inducements to self-denial in prosperous times which have exercised a potent influence in elevating and strengthening the character of the operative and industrial classes'
Thomas Brassey (1875), *The Advance Note: What it is and Why it Ought to be Abolished*, London: Longman, p. 55.

As a discourse of work and wages the sailortown legend differs from those more familiar to nineteenth-century labour historians: those which descend from an artisanal tradition and which reference skill to value added in manufacturing. Their usefulness to workers has long been discerned as bringing the possession of skill to bear against the expropriative intent of the capitalist wage-relation. More recently, increased sensitivity to the gendering of work identities has also made us aware that the artisanal definition of skill-possession extended even further into social relations via the one-wage male-breadwinner family ideal.[22] The sailortown legend, however, came from an industry where a producer ideology was weak and where industrial circumstances militated against the domestic arrangements associated with male breadwinning.[23] As an influence upon wages it applied leverage through the worker's right to compensation for workplace deprivation, but its most important feature was in focusing attention on the worker's rights to his pay. Unencumbered as he was in the legend, the sailor secured the fruits of his labour in wages which were his, independent of the competing claims of family. The dangers and isolation of work at sea played into the characterization, but the character was only fully realized when it described a privileged spender in the consumer relations of shore society.

The legend launched a character into popular culture who was known for his recklessness and prioritization of individual needs. With this the sailor became a byword for a disposition to live in and for the moment.[24] He has been acclaimed by workers who see their work as similarly patterned in the twentieth century.[25] Dating this development is difficult, and there are difficulties too in authenticating the seafaring authorship of sailortown songs and tales. It is, therefore, problematic to interpret them as a commentary on the contemporary realities of seafaring: and should analysts attempt their interpretation as narratives of resistance to specific ways that capitalism was re-shaping the shipping industry, the problems are greater still. Yet, more can be done with extracting meaning from the mythology and in understanding how the whoring, drinking sailor was bound up with changing notions of masculinity.

Cohate political formulations were not part of the myth-makers' stock-in-trade; politically important ideas were involved in myth-making however. Sailortown Jack spoke to the politics of men's access to and control of resources. This fact has an important bearing upon why sailors, for so long the subject of land-dwellers' equivocal regard, became prominent in the second half of the nineteenth century, in this more daring characterization. An oppositional modality is key and it is best seen in the prescriptive discourses of the institutions which presumed to modernize manhood by winning the working classes to more 'progressive' ways. They commonly contrasted the whoring, drinking sailor with the soberly inclined, fastidious and sexually reticent artisan or factory-worker.[26] The latter was seen to harness his energies to work and devote the proceeds of his labour to the support of his family. By prudent expenditure he would secure his own and his family's future. Living for the day, the sailor was the perfect foil to this character, but his characterization cut two ways: the unanticipated consequence of proselytizing by way of the sailor was to give him even greater sway. Prescriptions to sobriety, domesticity and thrift made the transgressive nature of his sailortown shenanigans plainer still. Since those activities were tied to male prowess, the sailor grew bigger, bolder and stronger in the laudatory scheme of these songs and tales.

The second half of the nineteenth century was not the first time sobriety and sexual reticence were joined to the imperatives of a domestic regime.[27] What was new was that habits of enterprise and resourcefulness were urged upon working men as part of the culture of economic individualism inspired by political economy.[28] The increase of male workers' wage levels caused the second generation of neo-classical economists to reflect on working-class spending and its relationship to economic growth. They were of the opinion that the economic utility of labour was best served by arrangements which brought men into the workplace serviced from their homes.[29] They identified female and child dependency as a financial burden properly borne by men, and accordingly, when surplus resources were available from the breadwinner-wage, they suggested prudent investment for the family's future.[30] In a further initiative which had implications for men's independent spending, political economists re-defined the boundaries of the productive economy of exchange. Suggesting that resources spent in irregular transactions in brothels and public houses went to no productive ends, they gave a new complexion to existing prejudices against the wastefulness to the nation of 'bachelor' leisure pursuits.

This was a formidable set of understandings to bring to bear upon male workers' consumption habits. Late nineteenth-century institutions took their lead from its distinction between rational and irrational spending. They held men culpable by their wasteful habits for family indigence. The spectre of seafarers' families in poverty had a particularly instructive potential. In a period when libidinal energies were thought to be more properly harnessed to profit-making, seafarers were counselled to avoid sailortown prostitutes and were advised they would be 'safe' within their homes.[31] There is no convincing evidence that seafarers, more than any other working men, did neglect and abandon wives and children.[32] In its absence it would seem that their vilification served the purpose of diminishing their status as popular heroes because bachelor freedoms were symbolized in the imagined life of men who escaped to sea.

Male spending prerogatives were, after all, jeopardized in male-breadwinner family arrangements and scarcely a male breadwinner was not concerned to keep some discretionary spending power.[33] Maintaining the notion that the wage was handed over at their choosing was important to the family provider and myths such as that of sailortown Jack suggested there were other ways that the money could be spent. It was especially important that these options were linked with male needs and drives. The myth of the home-coming sailor mobilized some powerful ideas about male prerogatives which transcended the prohibitions of a civilizing society. When Jack elicited approval for his legendary feats of drinking and womanizing, the rehabilitationist intent of a narrowly conceived reform discourse was easily overturned. Its terms of reference were unstable, for a dual-standard morality extended men freedoms to be men in what were considered natural ways. When the seafarers of the legend came ashore as transgressors of the rules of sobriety, prudence and sexual restraint, they did so with a confidence which spoke of men whose daily battle with the elements left them unitimidated by man-made things. Jack's predilections were indulged as belonging to men in a pre-ordained, natural state.

Ideas rooted in Enlightenment thinking gave a specific form of validity to the expression of 'natural' needs and desires.[34] The sailortown legend set out an essentialist masculinity and identified privileges which belonged to men by virtue of their sex. It accessed a privileged arena within the beliefs of industrial society: one in which libidinal energies could be reclaimed for individual pleasure and enjoyment against the persuasion of political economy to harness them to work.

'he could not speak without a string of oaths; he could not come ashore and walk quietly down the street; he wore a hat and a costume very much like that of a Dutch fishwoman. ...'
Thomas Gray in evidence to the 'Royal Commission Appointed to Inquire into the Alleged Unseaworthiness of British Registered Ships', British Parliamentary Papers 1873, XXXVI, p. 277.

For two decades in the 1870s and 1880s Thomas Gray, Assistant Secretary at the Board of Trade and the highest ranking official in its Marine Department, presided over the most comprehensive system of labour regulation that any nineteenth-century industry knew.[35] Each man employed on a British merchant vessel needed to provide an official reference from his previous voyage before he was engaged; and each had to follow a statutory procedure for signing on and off every time he worked on board ship.[36] In such a system the characterization of the free-wheeling sailor is questionable. There were surely those who held to an itinerant pattern of work; yet trusting to fortune to bring them a berth took men out of line for the best paid jobs. These went to men who worked with some regularity in specific trades and from particular ports. The reference system provided employers with the kind of controls on experience and suitability which were otherwise inconceivable in a casually contracted labour force deployed across the world.[37] The state was engaged in this system because of the importance of shipping to international trade. To maintain a strong merchant marine pragmatism supervened over the niceties of *laissez-faire*.[38] Still, from the mid-nineteenth century the state exercised its regulatory role with every concern for shipowners' freedoms and never, for example, prescribed manning levels. The new labour market structures were built up from an existing institutional presence, originally put in place for the purpose of ensuring the supply of seamen to the military.[39] Now in the post-mercantilist period officials conceived its usefulness as the rehabilitation of an antediluvian workforce to conditions compatible with a modern merchant marine. Thus Thomas Gray used the trope of modernization when he conjured a man from a distant seafaring past. Gray's seafarer was as picaresque as he was primitive.

The significant features of the labour market in the period of industrial capitalism were attained first by the abandonment of regulations which bound shipowners to a permanency of labour. Laying off crews was the preferred retrenchment strategy in a tonnage market which, ever volatile, was now more so as the cycles of the industrial economy came increasingly to affect demand. In the second quarter of the nineteenth century, as tariff protection was removed, shipowners lobbied to end their commitment to training up workers who were not self-financing. With the ending of statutory apprenticeship, quality controls became a major concern. At this point the government-regulated system of formal qualifications for masters, mates and engineers and of references for non-officers provided a vital tool to the employers in their ability to select for skill, experience and reliability. The necessity of all three qualities in men employed in even the most humble capacities increasingly surfaced in shipowners' comments. Rarely had shipowners held back from criticizing the men available to them, but now, in the latter part of the century, they named the short-comings of the workforce and identified their insobriety and insubordination as a commercial liability.[40] These concerns were raised especially by the operators of regular (liner) services, particularly when the costliness of overheads in steam meant that the premium these services commanded for reliability was thought to be imperilled by disruptions to services caused by the irregular habits of crew.

Steam made a great deal of difference to the composition of the workforce. It brought a whole new class of workers to sea. Their work in the stokehold was only grudgingly accepted as seafaring by deck seamen and, because they were strangers to the traditions of seafaring, employers tended to look upon them as a new factor in labour recalcitrancy. No significant alterations in the system of shipboard discipline were, however, attempted by employers. They exacted more work from crew by applying manning reductions, resorting to the older traditions of seafaring as an instrument in labour discipline. The 'gentrification' of an officer corps was one such example. The key initiatives in labour management were, however, institutional and it was here, where the Board of Trade regulated the contractual conditions of labour, that constructs of modernization were joined to issues of recruitment and supply.

When Gray described the 'personal peculiarity that once bespoke the seaman' he conjured the rough-hewn seafarer of an earlier generation into a context where a capitalist order and the primacy given to market forces which that entailed had given rise to a new hierarchy of proprietors, producers and non-producers. He rendered the seafarer sottish and unmanly and spelled out effeminacy in his clothes. Gray was intent on reversing the lionization of the sailor: in everything the character represented, Gray conceived him as ill-adapted to the conditions of a modern industry. Gray was not alone in taking this position, nor was its sense shared only by government bureaucrats. The path to institutional modernity was one which offered organized labour a way to consolidate its position.

The first trade union to attempt the large-scale organization of seafarers emerged in the latter part of the nineteenth century.[41] Officials of this embryonic union were surprisingly vigorous in their criticism of 'old time' sailors.[42] Their rules meanwhile bound their own members to sobriety.[43] This had a practical end of reconciling employers to the union as a source of sober and upright workers. Additionally, it served to advance internal discipline in a union which was, and remained, uncertain of grass-roots support.[44]

There were, already, agents in sailortown who supplied shipowners with men: now in the latter part of the nineteenth century, these agents (or crimps) were subject to an official invective which labelled them freebooters and worse. Government and trade union efforts to vanquish them from sailortown were part of the initiative to regularize the workings of the labour market by eliminating unwanted intermediaries. The very fabric of sailortown was itself under attack as local authorities, equipped with slum clearance powers, demolished the areas of ports which housed brothels and lodging houses, sending them further underground. There is evidence as well that evangelical and temperance reformers redoubled their efforts at converting seafarers. Missionaries' reminiscences, published in the latter part of the nineteenth century, indicated that sailortowns were already 'much altered'.[45] The circulation of such writings piqued interest in the goings-on which were said to have taken place, but they clouded its reality by projecting the existence of sailortown back to another time. And so it was, by the same kind of obfuscation, that Gray's observation worked: by placing the sailor at one end of a continuum he marked out progress to modern manhood along a path of adaptation to the conditions of modern labour.

Wage payment at mercantile marine offices where seafarers were subject to the supervision of the Board of Trade offered officials a rare time and place for addressing the relations of men to their families. Thus a hand-bill prepared in 1885 for distribution in this context admonished seafarers: 'When you come back to port after a long voyage and have to receive wages amounting to £3 or more it is a pity and it is your own fault if you and your wife, children, mother or sister or whoever may be keeping your home together do not have the use of your money. If you stop in a strange port, you may get into debt, lose your well-earned money [and] get disease into the bargain. ...'[46] Its advice emanated from official concern to stabilize the industry's labour in the social relations of the idealized family.[47] Yet it is also clear from this communication that the sailor's life supported a set of references to male practices which were held to be corrosive of family life. The fullness of the connection was realized in the impoverishment of families caused by the 'bachelor' spending spree. For all their apparent coherence the institutional narratives of modernization, too, were built upon a mythology.

'[The meaning] of a prime A.B. was a man who could hand, reef, steer, drink, f__k and fight'. [He would not consider himself a real sailor] 'until he had rounded the horn three times and had seven doses of the pox.'
Stan Hugill (1976), *Sailortown* London: Routledge and Kegan Paul, p. 207.

Stan Hugill was a former seaman and a practised yarn-spinner. He missed no opportunity to promote seafarers in the way which has become familiar to social observers: by enlarging their reputation through representing them tougher, rougher and lustier than the 'stay-at-homes'. Hugill's observations are worth considering. They imply that seafarers made a ready association between manual skills and sexual propensities, between physical adversity and sexual adventurism. Hugill, writing after sail had vanished, captured anecdotally some of the sense of how seafarers looked at their world and represented it to others. The temporality of these references is important however. The experience of work was different for men under sail at the turn of the century, and there is the matter too of the changes in sailortown. In this generation sailors intersected with shore society in quite different ways from their contemporaries in steamship employment; and still more important was the difference from earlier generations in sail. Anthropologists, ethnologists and folklorists were especially energetic about collecting seafaring songs and tales when they knew sail and its 'traditions' were almost vanished: even then they had to look to countries which retained sailing ship fleets later than the British merchant marine.[48]

Much knowledge of the culture of the forecastle in sailing vessels comes from the period of the collection of songs and tales as late as the interwar period and is coloured by the golden glow of the last 'romantic age' of sail.[49] Sometimes historians have used this material without discrimination to period, on occasion projecting its sense back into the eighteenth century, and with little attention to its constitution within a heroic mythology in the dying age of sail.[50] There was a difference between the 'bachelor' culture which gave rise to tales of whoring, drinking sailors in or before the mid-nineteenth century and an equally ebullient, but more aggressive culture of seafarers in the late nineteenth and early twentieth centuries. Dispelling romantic illusions about sail is necessary to probing the other reality, the economic and social marginalization of sailing ship men.[51] Their turn to a rugged masculinity of the workplace may then be explained in ways which respect the more conventional links between capitalist market organization and productive relations and cultural forms sought by labour and working-class historians. Still it is what has been least acknowledged by labour historians – the elements of misogyny and how they feed the mythology of workplace culture – which might, in the end, explain most about the experience of these men.

The men who worked in sail in what is known as sail's 'golden age' were in a very depressed sector of the market. Sailing ship owners made their profits in this declining sector by keeping old, leaky and unsafe vessels in service, deploying them opportunistically in search of cargoes (so that voyages might be very long) and paying wages at approximately half the level prevailing in the steam sector of the industry.[52] With low wages, long voyages and increased hazards due to ageing tonnage and undermanning, sailing ships made far from pleasant berths. The men who took them were of mixed nationalities and, for the most part, were older than their counterparts in steam.[53] The customs and rituals of an 'old-fashioned' seamanship raised their consciousness of what they shared and what distinguished them from landsmen. This was an essential form of bonding in the light of the adversities which they faced at sea, and the less than favourable comparisons with other workers at sea and ashore. If they now burnished their credentials as 'old time' sailors it was in hostility to the appropriation of sailing-ship skills and traditions to a professionalized officer core; it was in resentment at the proliferation of non-sailors as they saw them (mechanics and service workers) with steam; and it was in the absence of an organized trade union to lobby on their behalf.

The more organized and regulated labour market after 1850 was character-ized by regional and sectoral segmentation and this was a factor in the edging out of itinerant seafarers who were progressively displaced to its less lucrative margins as premium jobs went to men settled with their homes and families in their ports of recruitment. After 1860 many vessels were deployed in ways which were less likely to leave their crews out on a limb in foreign or British ports. They were in less need of the services provided by brothel and lodging house keepers or of the crimps. The attractions of the all-male workplace grew by contrast. For some sailing ship seafarers their work was an escape from the imperatives of heterosexual social arrangements on shore while others, forced there by their marginality in the labour market, found consolation in an escapist world of male bonding. In any case these seafarers took to minimizing their emotional, financial and psychological engagement with women by rejecting what was considered feminine in the social world.[54] Since low wages removed most consumer items from their reach, their lionization of sailortown Jack as a privileged spender was a nostalgic thing. In the narrative context of sailortown legends seafaring still furnished these men with permissive constructs of masculinity – virility, prowess, strength and the unencumbered ability to spend. The mythical Jack was rooted in, but not finally dependent on, the continuation of patterns of work and circumstances associated with the sailing vessel.

Images of physical power and scripts of primitive drives were drawn upon by seafaring men as they negotiated between the world of men at sea and the world shared with women on shore. Men who had never been to sea also accessed these meanings and presumed to believe they contained some kind of truth about seafaring which extended to all men. Their appeal increased as proscriptions on drinking, womanizing and hedonist spending were rounded out in the civilizing process of industrial society. The more the home and family became the site of an idealized manhood, the greater were the attractions of the mythology of the unencumbered male; the more that institutions forwarded their message by introducing indigent wives and children into the legend, the more appealing grew the unrepentant Jack.

Discussing the 'whoring, drinking sailor' by reference to these oppositions has been a fruitful way of addressing a historically changing masculinity. The significance of the apparently firm rule that women did not work at sea has yet led to reflection on what that came to mean when assimilated to the politics of gender and class. I have shown how in the shipping industry the circumstances of seafarers' employment influenced adjustments between work and home. These were in turn supported by, or challenged in, institutional and popular visions of what it was to be a worker and a man. I then discussed the sailor-town legend and the popularity it attained at a time when the character of male spending was contested, and I examined the deliberations of political economists which revealed how economic individualism informed policy imperatives which were applied to the working-class family in an attempt to reign in more than the spending of men. The thinking which helped to consolidate capital's command of labour in the gender divisions of the idealized family also made its pitch at putting family savings to work for capital in the capital-hungry economy of late nineteenth-century Britain.

These indications mostly hold with a view of power exercised from the top down. If I have negotiated them in ways which allow there is efficacy remaining in a 'bottom up' approach, I still draw back from naming sailortown Jack a radical working-class hero. The characterization of rough and rowdy sailors has revealed a masculinity organized anti-hegemonically in its contrast with the 'representative' artisan. I have been careful, however, to identify its potential for protesting hegemonic economic and social arrangements with the discourses of respectability and reform which promoted male breadwinning. Working men's rights to resources over and above women were observed in industrial society in ways other than breadwinning forms. The evidence that proprietorial rights were extended to male wage-earners through essentialist notions of masculinity suggests something which reflects importantly on a society in which wage-earning increasingly differentiated men's lives from women's. This awareness should be brought to the analysis of the workplace and male leisure culture. There it should check historians' readiness to assume that the libertarian life was constituted in a more egalitarian order than was made possible by the disposition of resources elsewhere within the capitalist system. The contours of a class society reconfigured by masculinity present more complex arrangements than were entertained when historians first embarked on the project of 'history from below'

Work still remains central in that project. Here, I have varied and modified many of the assumptions which labour historians have conventionally brought to the subject of work. I have given more space to the labour market than to the labour process; to consumer rather than producer issues; to state policy and to the thinking of political economists; and I have been more attentive to the narrative voices of working men than the articulations of formal labour organizations. Most important however are the considerations I have exercised around the mythologizing of work, the workplace and workers. I do not think that historians can explain the characterization of seafarers as 'whoring, drinking sailors' without reference to how the nineteenth century organized its perception of time by linear patterns of modernization and progress. Nor, when so much evidence shows prescriptive discourses went into the creation of the 'whoring, drinking sailor', do I think that historians can understand his 'popular' identification unless it is by appreciating that the hierarchical morphology of nineteenth-century society was a reflection of understandings created from the same attachments to notions of progress and modernization. Finally, my point must be that as labour historians continue to explore the links between the capitalist organization of industrial society and the cultural forms of its workers there should be room for seeing how those links were made in the past discursively and through the gendered imagination. There is no reason why labour and working-class historians should not use perspectives which admit to the representational qualities of the material as they continue in the exploration of empowerment and disempowerment in working men's and women's history.

Notes

1. My thanks are due to Pat Ayers who has been a constant supporter, adviser and friend in the course of this work, to the staff of the Maritime History Archive at Memorial University of Newfoundland who provided valuable assistance, as ever, in retrieving Crew Agreements and to Keith McClelland who assisted my thinking in his comments on an earlier version of this paper.
2. 'Seafarers' is used here as a generic, applying to all sea-going workers, irrespective of the technology of their vessels, either sail or steam. 'Sailors' I reserve to identify seafarers under sail. These distinctions are important for it is the sailor who is the prime subject of seafaring mythology.
3. Gilmore, David (1990), *Manhood in the Making: Cultural Concepts of Masculinity*, Yale University Press, p. 108.
4. Exceptional women who went to sea have provided historians with material for examining the gender dimensions of seafaring: for example, Bonham, Julia C. (1977), 'Feminist and Victorian: The Paradox of the American Seafaring Woman of the Nineteenth Century', *American Neptune*, 37 (3), 203–18; and Dugaw, Dianne (1989), *Warrior Women and Popular Balladry 1650–1850*, Cambridge: Cambridge University Press. I believe, however, that the pre-eminently male composition of seafaring workforces should make masculinity the key reference and the studies which have done so are limited: see Creighton, Margaret S. (1995), *Rites and Passages: The Experience of American Whaling, 1830–1870*, Cambridge: Cambridge University Press; and Creighton, Margaret S. and Norling, Lisa (eds) (1996), *Iron Men, Wooden Women: Gender and Seafaring in the Atlantic World, 1700–1920*, Baltimore: Johns Hopkins University Press.
5. Rediker, Marcus (1987), *Between the Devil and the Deep Blue Sea: Merchant Seamen, Pirates and the Anglo-American Maritime World*, Cambridge: Cambridge University Press; Sager, Eric W. (1989), *Seafaring Labour: The Merchant Marine of Atlantic Canada 1820–1914*, Kingston: McGill Queen's University Press. See also the discussion of Sager's book in (1990), *International Journal of Maritime History*, 2 (1), 227–58 and Sager's reply ibid., 259–74. Laura Tabili's discussion of ethnicity and merchant seafaring uses pluralist perspectives with some subtlety: Tabili, Laura (1994), *We Ask for British Justice: Workers and Racial Difference in Late Imperial Britain*, Ithaca: Cornell University Press.
6. Kessler-Harris, Alice (1989), 'Treating the Male as "Other": Redefining the Parameters of Labor History', *Labor History*, 34, 190–204; Kessler-Harris, Alice (1989), 'A New Agenda for American Labor History: A Gendered Analysis and the Question of Class', in Moody, J. Carroll and Kessler-Harris, Alice (eds), *Perspectives on American Labor History: The Problems of Synthesis*, DeKalb: Northern Illinois University Press, pp. 217–34; Rose, Sonya O. (1993), 'Gender and Labor History: The Nineteenth-century legacy', *International Review of Social History*, 38, 145–62; Baron, Ava (1994), 'On Looking at Men: Masculinity

  and the Making of a Gendered Working-Class History', in Shapiro, Ann-Louise (ed.), *Feminists Revision History*, New Brunswick: Rutgers University Press, pp. 146–71.
7. Boyd, Kelly and McWilliam, Rohan (1995), 'Conference Report: Historical Perspectives on Class and Culture', *Social History*, **20**, 93–100.
8. See, for example, Clark, Anna (1997), *The Struggle for the Breeches: Gender and the Making of the British Working Class*, Berkeley: University of California Press.
9. McClelland, Keith (1991), 'Masculinity and the Representative Artisan in Britain, 1850–80', in Roper, Michael and Tosh, John (eds), *Manful Assertions: Masculinities in Britain since 1800*, London: Routledge, 74–91; Kessler-Harris, Alice (1989), 'A New Agenda', p. 231; Rose, Sonya O. (1993), 'Gender and Labor History', esp. p. 146.
10. Lake, Marilyn (1986), 'The Politics of Respectability: Identifying the Masculinist Context', *Historical Studies*, **22**, 116–31; Rose, Sonya O. (1993), 'Respectable Men: Disorderly Others: The Language of Gender and the Lancashire Weavers' Strike of 1878 in Britain', *Gender and History*, **5** (3), 384–97.
11. McLeod, Hugh (1977), 'White Collar Values and the Role of Religion', in Crossick, Geoffrey (ed.), *The Lower Middle Class in Britain*, London: Croom Helm, p. 76.
12. Glover, John (1863), 'On the Statistics of Tonnage during the First Decade of the Navigation Law of 1849', *Journal of the Statistical Society*, **26**, 1–18.
13. Burton, V.C. (1985), 'Counting Seafarers: the Published Records of the Registrar of Merchant Seamen, 1849–1913', *Mariner's Mirror*, **71**, 305–20.
14. Lindsay, W.S. (1876), *History of Merchant Shipping and Ancient Commerce*, Vol. 4, London: Sampson Low, Marston, Low, and Searle, chs 5–15; Farrer, T.H. (1883), *The State in its Relation to Trade*, London: Macmillan, pp. 120–31.
15. Burton, V.C. (1989), 'Apprenticeship Regulation and Maritime Labour in the Nineteenth Century British Merchant Marine', *International Journal of Maritime History*, **1** (1), 29–49.
16. Burton, Valerie (1990), 'The Making of a Nineteenth-Century Profession: Shipmasters and the British Shipping Industry', *Journal of the Canadian Historical Association*, **1**, 97–118.
17. Fricke, Peter H. (ed.) (1973), *Seafarer and Community: Towards a Social Understanding of Seafaring*, London: Croom Helm.
18. Journal entry, 19 March 1776, in Birkbeck Hill, George (ed.) (1934), *Boswell's Life of Johnson*, Vol. 2, *The Life, 1766–1776*, Oxford: Clarendon Press, p. 438.
19. See my major research project 'Spanning Sea and Shore' which uses the statutory Agreements and Accounts of Crew and vessel reports in the shipping press to track vessel deployment and voyage length in the period 1850 to 1914.
20. Whall, W. B. (1948), *Sea Songs and Shanties* (sixth edition), Glasgow: Brown, and Ferguson.
21. Leonore Davidoff has observed that 'Admiration for physical prowess and sexual adventuring did not simply disappear in the face of middle-class proselytizing': Davidoff, Leonore (1989), '"Adam Spoke First and Named the Orders of the World": Masculine and Feminine Domains in History and Sociology', in Corr, Helen and Jamieson, Lynn (eds), *The Politics of Everyday Life*, London: Hutchinson, p. 247.
22. McClelland (1991), *Representative Artisan*; Seccombe, Wally (1986), 'Patriarchy Stabilized: The Construction of the Male Breadwinner Wage Norm in Nineteenth Century Britain', *Social History* **2** (1), 53–76; Rose, Sonya O. (1986),

'"Gender at Work": Sex Class and Industrial Capitalism', *History Workshop*, **21**, 125.

23. Burton, Valerie (1991), 'The Myth of Bachelor Jack: Masculinity, Patriarchy and Seafaring Labour', in Howell, Colin and Twomey, Richard J., *Jack Tar in History: Essays in the History of Maritime Life and Labour*, Fredericton, New Brunswick: Acadiensis Press, pp. 193–5.

24. In 1850 Mayhew wrote of the 'reckless and improvident character of sailors': Yeo, Eileen and Thompson, E.P. (1972), *The Unknown Mayhew*, New York: Schocken Books, p. 299.

25. Stodder, Jim (1979), 'Confessions of a Candy-Ass Rough Neck', in Schapiro, Evelyn and Schapiro, Barry M (eds), *The Women Say: The Men Say: Issues in Politics, Work, Family, Sexuality and Power*, New York: Dell, p. 68.

26. 'If the sailor were a provident man and husbanded his money carefully, he could remain where he pleased for as many weeks as he had money to spend. When his money was gone he would do as other people do – turn to work again' *Western Mail*, 13 January, 1871.

27. Porter, Roy (1996), 'Enlightenment and Pleasure', in Porter, Roy and Roberts, Marie Mulvey, *Pleasure in the Eighteenth Century*, Basingstoke: Macmillan, p. 7.

28. McClelland, Keith (1989), 'Time to Work, Time to Live: Some Aspects of Work and the Re-formation of Class in Britain, 1850–1880', in Joyce, Patrick (ed.), *The Historical Meanings of Work* (second edition), Cambridge: Cambridge University Press, p. 184.

29. Picchio, Antonella (1992), *Social Reproduction: The Political Economy of the Labour Market*, Cambridge: Cambridge University Press, pp. 24–53.

30. Brassey, Thomas (1879), *Foreign Work and English Wages Considered with Reference to the Depression of Trade*, London: Longmans, Green and Co., pp. 292, 298, 300.

31. Laqueur, Thomas (1993), 'Sex and Desire in the Industrial Revolution', in O'Brien, Patrick K. and Quinault, Roland (eds), *The Industrial Revolution and British Society*, Cambridge: Cambridge University Press, p.101.

32. Reverend Nugent, a Liverpool prison chaplain, suggested that between one-half and three-quarters of seafarers' wages was spent on drink and prostitution: 'Second Report of the Select Committee on Intemperance', Parliamentary Paper (henceforth PP), 1877, XI q. 8216; Royal Commission on the Poor Law (1909), PP, Volume XVI, 1909, XLIII, p. 68.

33. See Burton, 'Myth of Bachelor Jack', pp. 193–5.

34. 'Naturalization' is the term which has been used to identify that process of ascribing socially constructed ideas (of sexuality) to a natural or pre-ordained state so that they gain a 'specific form of validity'. See the pioneering work of Jordanova, Ludmilla (1989), *Sexual Visions: Images of Gender in Science and Medicine between the Eighteenth and Twentieth Century*, Hemel Hempstead: Harvester Press, esp. p. 5.

35. Gray, Thomas (1892), *Under the Red Ensign or Going to Sea* (second edition), London: Simpkin, Hamilton, Kent and Co. Ltd.

36. This was the system which generated the Agreements and Accounts of Crew which are now preserved in their largest part at Memorial University of Newfoundland. What follows derives from my analysis of vessel deployment patterns and crew recruitment on the ships using two very different ports, Southampton and South Shields.

37. Roughly 200 000 workers were employed on British-registered vessels annually

by the second half of the nineteenth century: Burton, 'Counting Seafarers', pp. 308–9.

38. Gray, Thomas (1887), 'Fifty Years of Legislation in Relation to the Shipping, Trade and the Safety of Ships and Seamen', *Shipping Gazette*, 11 March 1887, p. 148.

39. Parkhurst, P.G. (1962), *Ships of Peace: A Record of Some of the Problems which came before the Board of Trade in Connection with the Mercantile Marine*, New Malden: P.G. Parkhurst, pp.140–83; Bromley, J.S. (1974), *The Manning of the Royal Navy: Selected Published Pamphlets, 1693–1873*, esp. p. xxxi.

40. PP, Final Report of the Commissioners Appointed to Inquire into the Alleged Unseaworthiness of British Registered Ships, 1874, XXXIV, q.18136.

41. Marsh, Arthur and Ryan, Victoria (1989), *The Seamen: A History of the National Union of Seamen*, Oxford: Malthouse Press, pp. 17–35.

42. National Amalgamated Seamen's and Firemen's Union, Executive Committee Minute Book, Warwick University Modern Records Centre, Mss. 175/1/1/1, p. 2; *Shipping Gazette*, 19 March 1886, p. 183 and 16 April 1886, p. 245.

43. See Burton, 'Myth of Bachelor Jack', pp. 191–2.

44. See Havelock Wilson's address to the seafarers of Sunderland published in *Shipping Gazette*, 19 February 1886, p. 183; correspondence in *The Morning Post*, 5 January 1899; and his evidence to two parliamentary committees: PP 'Report of the Committee appointed to enquire into the manning of British Merchant Ships', 1896, XL, p. 37; 'Report of the Committee appointed by the Board of Trade on the question of continuous discharge certificates for seamen', 1900, LXXVII, q.1419.

45. Rowe, Richard (1875), *Jack Ashore and Jack Afloat*, London: Smith, Elder, p. 28; Fox Smith, C. (1924), *Sailor Town Days* (second edition), London: Methuen, pp. 28–9.

46. Board of Trade hand-bill, dated 1885, number 25: uncatalogued holding in the Library of the Department of Transport, London.

47. PP, 'Report of the Committee Appointed to Consider the Question of the Extension to Ports Abroad ... of the Arrangements Now in Force in the U.K. for the Transmission of Seamen's Wages, 1893', 1893–4, LXXX, 130.

48. Weibust, Knut (1969), *Deep Sea Sailors: A Study in Maritime Ethnology*, Stockholm: Nordiska Museet; Doerflinger, William Main (1951), *Shantymen and Shantyboys*, New York: Macmillan; Henningsen, Henning (1969), *Crossing the Equator: Sailors' Baptism and other Initiation Rites*, Copenhagen: Munksgaard.

49. Foulke, R.D. (1963), 'Life in the Dying World of Sail', *Journal of British Studies*, 3, 105–36.

50. Greenhill, Basil and Stonham, Denis (1981), *Seafaring Under Sail; the Life of the Merchant Seaman*, Annapolis: Naval Institute Press; Rediker, *Between the Devil*, pp. 153–204.

51. A prime instance of the glorification of the passing technology of sail is in Fox Smith, C. (1924), *The Return of the 'Cutty Sark'*, London: Methuen, p. 12.

52. These observations are based on my extensive study of British shipping and crews in the late nineteenth and early twentieth centuries using, amongst other sources, the shipping press, business records, parliamentary select committee reports and, most valuable of all, the Agreements and Accounts of Crew and Official Logbooks held in the Maritime History Archive at Memorial University of Newfoundland.

53. Burton, 'Counting Seafarers', p. 317.

54. Weibust, *Deep Sea Sailors*, pp. 138, 244.

CHAPTER SIX

Gendering the Stories of Socialism: An Essay in Historical Criticism

June Hannam and Karen Hunt

Why do labour historians seem to find it so difficult to integrate gender into the historiography of British socialism? In studies of Britain's leading socialist organizations before the First World War, feminist historians have shown how socialism was gendered both in its theory and in its practice.[1] Yet these arguments have had relatively little impact on the framework in which historians continue to narrate socialist politics of this period. Why is this? One reason is that most labour historians ignore the ways in which the identities of organizations such as the Independent Labour Party (ILP) and the Social Democratic Federation (SDF) were constructed by contemporaries. Within what has become the 'received view' of British socialism a myth has developed about the affinity between particular versions of socialism and the women's movement. This chapter is concerned with the origins and effects of that myth.

One of the ways in which an organization establishes a sense of its identity is to narrate its past, to construct a sense of its own tradition and culture. Although this process is often contested, dominant narratives or myths usually emerge. Problems can occur when historians mistake such a constructed narrative for the complex history of a particular organization. This is precisely what has happened with regard to both the ILP and the SDF. This chapter explores how these organizations narrated their pasts in relation to women and the 'woman question'. Both parties constructed a version of the 'pioneering days' in which their individual traditions were established and from which the subsequent narrative of British socialism was woven. In this process only certain decontextualized voices were heard: yet it resulted in a version of the past which most historians have taken up uncritically as *the* narrative of British socialism. This in turn has affected the way in which socialism's relationship to women has been understood.

One way of illustrating the concerns of this chapter is to turn to a number of comments made by Carolyn Steedman in her many-layered study of one socialist woman, Margaret McMillan. Steedman recounts how, prompted by a visit from the socialist propagandist Caroline Martyn, a correspondent to the *Liverpool Chronicle* in 1895 wondered, 'when the story of Socialism in

England comes to be written ... what the historian will say about the little band of women who have done so much to infuse the movement with lofty principle'.[2] Steedman comments, 'We now possess an answer to this question, which would appear to be "not much"'![3] Steedman is, of course, right to draw attention to the partial picture of women's participation in British socialism which is to be found in much of the historiography. What is disappointing is that although there is much in Steedman's biography which is challenging and thought-provoking, her representation of socialist organizations is an unreflecting reiteration of the 'master' narrative. As she observes, women continue to be marginal to the story of British socialism but what she fails to make clear is that when women make their brief appearance, they and their political parties are frozen into an unforgiving and inaccurate stereotype. Steedman herself repeats the traditional characterization of the ILP as offering 'a degree of participation to women that the blatantly misogynist SDF denied them'.[4]

This conventional wisdom relates to the ILP's early commitment to sex equality, in particular its support for women's suffrage. In contrast, the SDF is seen as adopting a more rigid Marxist analysis of social change, based on the class struggle and with little room for gender-based issues. Thus as Olive Banks would have it, the ILP was 'feminist from its inception' while the SDF was 'anti-feminist'.[5] For James Hinton women played 'an exceptionally important role in the ILP',[6] although he provides no real evidence for this judgement. Historians who do offer evidence do so selectively. This is particularly clear when reference is made to the SDF's attitude to women and the woman question. For Jill Liddington and Jill Norris the SDF's 'general attitude to feminism was unsympathetic' and to support this view they cite the views of Hyndman and Quelch.[7] Similarly Jeffrey Weeks has discussed Hyndman and the misogynist Belfort Bax's views on women as though they represented the SDF as a whole.[8] However, this tunnel vision is not confined to historians, for contemporaries also generalized from the views of a few idiosyncratic SDFers. Sylvia Pankhurst described the SDF solely in terms of Hyndman and Bax and their opposition to women's enfranchisement.[9]

Reading the politics of a party from the statements of some of its, usually male, leaders is an approach which has not just been applied to the SDF. The problem lies with representing any organization in terms of its leadership. With both the SDF and the ILP there was a high level of autonomy at a local level combined with a healthy scepticism for 'leaders', as Logie Barrow and Ian Bullock have recently demonstrated.[10] Nevertheless the assumption too often remains that the ILP and its particular version of socialism was sympathetic to the women's cause whilst the SDF's was at best indifferent and often hostile.

This stereotype is given a further twist by the way that women's suffrage – the demand for votes for women on the same terms as men, that is on a property-based franchise – is seen as emblematic of a feminist sympathy. Yet this is to misunderstand the nature of the Edwardian suffrage movement. For there were 'feminist' women in the ILP as well as in the SDF who supported the larger demand for adult suffrage, that is the enfranchisement of every man and woman over twenty-one. However, historians do not always acknowledge this possibility. They often take the advocacy of adult suffrage as evidence of 'anti-feminism'.[11] Since adult suffrage was more favourably received within the SDF, later perceptions of the suffrage debate reinforce the received view of the two parties.

This characterization of the ILP and SDF as feminist and anti-feminist respectively is part of a wider stereotype of the two organizations which has been remarkably tenacious: that the ILP and SDF represent a reasonable/unreasonable dichotomy in which the SDF is all that is alien to the British labourist tradition.[12] Although historians such as David Howell have noted that the stereotype is 'tendentious, partial and misleading',[13] few mainstream labour historians are as sympathetic. Their failure to grasp the complexity of the myths of socialist and labour politics has discouraged retrieval of the richness of socialist women's politics in Britain.

The classic view of the SDF is that it was a 'bitter, dogmatic and impractical sect inherently unsuitable to English politics'.[14] Both contemporaries and historians have contributed to this characterization. Contemporaries of the SDF – particularly members of the ILP – made judgements understandably coloured by political rivalry. But it is surprising that these have been used as 'objective' evidence by historians. One of the judgements of the SDF most cited by historians was made by an ILPer, J Bruce Glasier:

> there is no disguising that the ways of the SDF are not our ways. If I may say so, the ways of the SDF are more doctrinaire, more Calvinistic, more aggressively sectarian than the ILP. The SDF has failed to touch the heart of the people. Its strange disregard of the religious, moral and aesthetic sentiments of the people is an overwhelming defect.[15]

The context of this remark is rarely given, yet it is crucial: it was part of an inter-party polemic. It was written by a leading opponent of the SDF who was attempting to persuade his own party's rank and file not to fuse with the SDF to form a united socialist party. His purpose was therefore to emphasize difference.[16]

A stereotype of the SDF as sectarian and alien to British political culture was clearly of value to the SDF's opponents. As a new socialist party founded nearly a decade after the SDF, the ILP had to carve out a distinct political space for itself. It was therefore in the interests of the leadership of both parties to emphasize difference, particularly when challenged by rank and file demands for socialist unity. In contrast, evidence from the rank and file suggests there was considerably less desire to accentuate difference. In the 1890s, in particular, some individuals were members of more than one socialist organization at any one time, or they moved between parties depending on which organized in a particular location. As the ILP became more focused on parliamentary politics the differences between the parties seemed to increase, but at a local level many SDFers and ILPers continued to cooperate over campaigns and joint candidatures.[17] The desire for socialist unity remained, which suggests that for many being socialists was more important than any party label. Yet the received view is that the two groups were polarized with the ILP representing all that was positive and politically palatable including, for those who would regard this as positive, a particular affinity with the women's movement.

Even those historians who recognize the shortcomings of the stereotype of the dichotomous SDF/ILP, do not always escape the use of other stereotypes. David Howell has been criticized for stereotyping socialist women by spotlighting what could be called the 'Famous Four' (Enid Stacy, Caroline Martyn, Margaret McMillan and Katherine St John Conway), all socialist propagandists in the 1890s.[18] He is by no means the only historian of the labour movement to focus on this 'elite'.[19] Although there are some minor differences between historians on the membership of this group, they generally constitute the signifier of the 'feminism' of the ILP. Such a focus diverts attention away from those broader groups of women who contributed to socialist politics and particularly from early working-class and less well-educated female socialists.[20] Furthermore there is little consideration of the differences within this 'elite' group of women.

None of this is to argue that women propagandists,[21] and these women in particular, were unimportant for the development of socialism in Britain. It is simply to point out that the identification of these few individuals obscures the range of women who contributed to the socialist movement, and not just in the ILP. It is more than curious that even though the Famous Four, or its variants, represent 'women' in much of the historiography, this literature contains very little discussion of the particular contributions that women propagandists, as speakers and journalists, made to the socialist project. Although recent biographies of leading socialist women written by feminist historians[22] are cited by labour historians, the latter find no space to consider how representative these women were. All too often labour historians fail to apply to the category 'woman' the standards of historiographical enquiry that they would habitually use of almost any other analytical term.

Within the historiography of British socialism, the image of the charismatic socialist woman propagandist is tied to the ILP's brand of socialism despite the presence of equally effective propagandists such as Eleanor Marx, and later, Dora Montefiore, within the SDF. The Famous Four have come to symbolize the assumed positive relationship between the ILP and women partly because of the way in which they were mythologized by the party as it invented its own version of its 'pioneering days'. The SDF seems to have been less concerned to dwell on its 'heroic past' and never sought to elevate their 'martyr to the Cause', Eleanor Marx (who died in 1898), to the saint-like status that Caroline Martyn (who died in 1896) acquired in ILP and Clarion circles. Martyn's premature death was felt across the movement as a whole and she was represented initially as a socialist rather than as a specifically ILP 'martyr'. Her obituary in *Justice* emphasised this:

> Miss Martyn's catholicity of spirit evinced itself in the fact that it mattered not what organisation was in want of a lecturer, she was equally willing to place her time and her indomitable energy at the disposal of the SDF, the ILP or any other Socialist body. With her Socialism was no mere sectarian movement – it was the cause of suffering humanity ...[23]

Although maybe 'the best-loved of the Socialist women speakers',[24] she, like the rest of the Famous Four in the 1890s, spoke at meetings organized by groups across the socialist and labour movement. They were all more concerned to make socialists rather than ILPers or SDFers. Yet as the ILP sought to differentiate itself from other socialist organizations Martyn was claimed unhesitatingly for the ILP pantheon,[25] an apparent example of the ILP's particular affinity to women and to female emancipation.

In many ways then, historians' attachment to the idea of the Famous Four prevents a much more considered version of British socialism's attitude to women and its understanding of gender. A focus on the Famous Four too often substitutes for a discussion of the more challenging question of the extent to which socialist politics were gendered. This means uncovering the way in which the 'woman question' was constructed by socialists, and how this affected the priority given to women's issues on the socialist agenda. How socialists theorized 'women' and represented them in socialist propaganda, as well as the extent to which the socialist rhetoric of sexual equality was translated into practice, all affected women's participation in socialist political life. The degree to which women were marginal to the socialist project, in theory and in practice, is a measure of the gendering of socialist politics.

If labour history is to recognize a gendered history of British socialism a much more critical reading is needed of the way in which the parties and individuals narrated their own pasts and the ways in which historians have continued to select a particular version of events from the various narratives on offer. This approach to historiography has been pioneered by feminist historians of the women's suffrage movement. They have shown how the histories of the movement written in the interwar years by those who had participated in the campaign, taken with the autobiographies of suffragettes and suffragists, created a very specific view of the movement. This was influenced more by the context of the 1920s and 1930s than by the way in which the campaign was experienced in the prewar years.[26] These historians have suggested that such texts need to be read carefully against material written during the campaign itself and that the former should not be taken at face value. Similar research has not been undertaken in relation to the histories and autobiographies written by socialists in the same period.

Yet there was a considerable outpouring of histories and reminiscences, particularly by ILP members, from 1913 into the 1920s. This activity was prompted by the ILP's 'Coming-of-Age' Conference in 1914 which celebrated twenty-one years of the party and what was seen as the growing success of the movement. The ILP made much of this anniversary, inaugurating in 1913 a specific propaganda campaign across the country which was to culminate in the anniversary conference.[27]

Unsurprisingly, this prompted reflections not only on what the party had achieved but also what the early 'pioneering days' of the 1890s had been like. Members wrote into *Labour Leader* with their memories and the paper produced a special supplement for what was always called the 'Coming-of-Age' Conference. This was well-advertised in advance and included a 'Beautiful Art Supplement suitable for framing, containing the portraits of the Chairmen of the ILP from 1893 to 1914'[28] – not, of course, a woman amongst them. Apparently the rather different images presented by the postcards of the youthful and feminine Famous Four, which had sold so well for the party in the 1890s, had been forgotten despite the nostalgic air of celebration. Instead, the supplement had a rather different gender message. For as a backdrop to the imposing figures of the various party chairmen there was a faint tableau. At its bottom stand two workers who are clearly male while at the top a number of figures gaze towards the bright rays of socialism, which appear to reside somewhere behind Fred Jowett's head! To the left is a man and a male child and to the right stands a woman with a female child – men and women appear to be separate although equal in their distance from the socialist goal. This image, and others like it, have to be set beside the ILP's rhetoric on sexual equality and their claim to be 'the women's party'.

The 'Coming-of-Age' Campaign prompted a range of reminiscences. Some sought to narrate the origins of the party so that the differences between the ILP and competing socialist groups were as distinct as possible. So Alfred Settle in his 'Early Reminiscences' remembered the SDF was 'preaching Marxian economics to crowds who, for the most part, adjudged them to be either amiable idiots or revolutionary scoundrels'.[29] Part of the reason why the party encouraged these memories was to assert the distinctiveness and success of the ILP as opposed to the SDF, which by implication had not learnt the lessons that the ILP had and which was therefore unlikely ever to 'Come-of-Age'. Part of this distinctiveness was the ILP's appeal to women. So in 1919, J Bruce Glasier, so important to the construction and maintenance of the wider stereotype of the ILP and SDF, chose to remember:

> while as yet the question of the women's suffrage was wholly ignored on Liberal and Tory platforms, Hardie, Isabella Ford, Enid Stacey [sic] and others were urging it to the front in ILP meetings ... I am right I think in saying that the ILP was the first political party to promote the candidature for women for election on public bodies. It has the distinction also of being the first political body to elect women on its National Executive.[30]

The latter assertion was made despite the fact that women had been elected to the SDF and Socialist League's Executives before the ILP was even founded, and that the ILP never elected more than two women at any one time to its executive, the National Administrative Council (NAC).[31] The ILP's record in this area was not much more impressive than its rival socialist parties. Yet Glasier's version of the socialist past remains the orthodox view even today.

Some socialist women who had been active in the suffrage cause also made similar retrospective claims for the ILP. The most interesting is perhaps that of Ethel Snowden who, once the vote was won, claimed that the ILP was 'The REAL women's party' since:

> in all those hard years of fierce struggle for women's political freedom, the women of the country had no greater friends than the members of the Independent Labour Party. From the beginning of its existence the ILP has stood for the political equality of women and men. ... Its members of Parliament were amongst the most intrepid and selfless leaders in the suffrage campaign in the House of Commons.[32]

Snowden made much of the fact that the ILP at every level was open to women implying, erroneously, that this was unique in the socialist movement. She also made a case to those who had been involved in women's suffrage organizations to return to the mixed-sex parties of the mainstream, specifically to the 'real women's party', the ILP.

This was a time of competition for the 'women's vote' amongst the political parties, and this pamphlet was part of that battle. In 1920 the ILP needed to persuade itself and potential supporters that it was *the* party for women. Snowden was writing at a time when some ex-suffragettes briefly established a Women's Party and socialists feared that this and other women's organizations, like the Women's Citizens Association, could draw women's support away from labour politics. Yet it was curious that it should be Snowden who voiced these sentiments. For, in her praise for the ILP, Ethel Snowden managed to ignore, or conveniently forget, the fact that in 1909 she had resigned from the ILP because of what she saw as its half-hearted support for women's suffrage –

for failing to be the 'real women's party'. In particular, she protested against the involvement of two members of the NAC in the Adult Suffrage Society. Other women, such as Emmeline and Christabel Pankhurst and Teresa Billington, left the ILP to give their energies entirely to the suffrage cause. It was far more unusual to return to the party as Snowden later did. Despite her own experiences before the First World War, Snowden contributed to a narrative that describes a party which was unequivocal in its support for women's suffrage. The disenchantment of those ILP women who founded the Women's Social and Political Union (WSPU) and were its early activists did not have a place in this story, nor did the kind of choices faced by Snowden herself find an echo in this, the dominant, narrative of British socialism and its relationship to the women's cause.

Margaret McMillan remembered a different version of the ILP of the 1890s. With hindsight she said that the party 'was not formed to champion women. It took the battle in its stride, and might drop it in its ardour. It was born to make war on capitalism and competition'.[33] But in 1895, McMillan, like other socialist women, clearly hoped and believed that there was a complete identity of interests between the women's cause and that of socialism – 'At bottom all their efforts have the same aim: self realisation, a full and conscious life of social and personal activity'.[34] For the ILP's 'Coming-of-Age' Conference Katherine Bruce Glasier, who, with McMillan, was the only other survivor of the Famous Four, also chose to look back to the earliest days of the party. Under the heading 'The Part Women Played in Founding the ILP. Reminiscences Of The Time When It Was Hard For A Woman To Be a Socialist', she recalled:

> When I came up to Yorkshire as a Fabian lecturer in June 1892, there was an atmosphere in the Labour movement there of swift and eager welcome for every woman comrade, and of settled conviction as to the women's equal right of citizenship with the men, that not only won me, for all my life, for the service of the Independent Labour Party, but also completely disarmed what little of the narrower 'feminist' attitude had been left to me from my Newnham training.[35]

According to this account, women were welcome and the party was convinced of the need for women's full citizenship while feminism was too narrow for true socialists.

Yet there is another narrative which has been identified for the SDF *and* for the ILP in which socialist parties of whatever hue were not so welcoming to women and were much more ambivalent when it came to placing any priority on women's claims to citizenship.[36] Other speakers at the ILP's 'Coming-of-Age' Conference raised these issues, as they had before and would have to again. One of these was Hannah Mitchell, who later recalled that 'None who attended this event will ever forget it'. She spoke in the debate on suffrage

109

in order to protest against the indifference of socialists.[37] The voices of women, like Mitchell, who stayed in the ILP despite all their concerns about the gendered nature of socialist practice and the frustrations of being a suffragist in a socialist organization, are silenced by the easy stereotype of the ILP as 'friend to women'. As Marion Coates-Hansen tried to explain to George Lansbury, her experience of the socialist movement (she had been in the SDF and then joined the ILP) had left her with:

> A passionate hopeless feeling that women don't count. ... Imagine an enthusiastic boy – yourself for example ... going into a movement in the hope of becoming of use – and then finding that you did not count – that another sex only had power etc. You've got to *feel* it to know what it means.[38]

Although Coates-Hansen was certainly not alone in these feelings, it does not seem that Katherine Bruce Glasier shared them. If she had done, she would not have been the sole woman invited to contribute to the *Labour Leader*'s 'Coming-of-Age' supplement. She had, after all, been a member of the party's first NAC. As much as anyone she symbolized the 'pioneering days', particularly the feminine version of them. She also formed part of a famous socialist partnership with the principal architect of the stereotype of the SDF/ILP, her husband J Bruce Glasier. Nevertheless, there is more in Katherine Bruce Glasier's 'Coming-of-Age' piece than merely a repetition of the ILP 'as friend to the woman's cause'. In her reminiscences of the early days of the ILP, she recalled SDF women too (although they are not named as such) and made a real effort to be inclusive of women well beyond, and very different from, the Famous Four. She remembered sharing her room one night with Eleanor Marx, who for half the night 'held us spellbound' with her memories of the International and:

> Sternly she bade us renounce, if we were to be worthy of the comradeship of the workers of the world, all the older feminist demand for equal political rights with men, until the franchise should be granted to human beings and not to property. It was the price of the workers' trust in us. Middle-class men had barely used the workers in their battle for freedom. Let middle-class women, at any rate the Socialists among them, strive to make atonement.[39]

Glasier then proceeded to use Eleanor Marx's words as the explanation, and even inspiration, for the way that middle-class women like herself had heeded this call and had thrown in their lot with the workers' movement. She continued, 'There lies the apology, if apology be needed, for the earlier ILP women's attitude so sternly upbraided years afterwards by Mrs Pankhurst and others as "treachery to our sex". Since then, as we know, the position has been reversed.'[40]

By 1914 this jibe at the WSPU would play well with an ILP audience – particularly as the 'Coming-of-Age' Conference was disrupted by WSPU hecklers.[41] Glasier was writing her own experience as though it were that of the movement as a whole, thereby justifying her own position as an ILP woman who in 1906 had denied 'that the question of getting the vote for women transcends all other questions'[42] and for whom the passing years of militancy had only confirmed this judgement. She then brought her comments up to date by claiming that:

> With generous and enlightened zeal, the men of the ILP ... have declared that they have no right to ask such sacrifice of their sisters, and in our ILP today the twain battles for women's equal political freedom, and for economic freedom of the workers go forward side by side, and I think our men have found their reward even as did we, their women comrades long ago.[43]

This, for Katherine Bruce Glasier, was why socialism was the only ideology for women of all classes, including women of a middle-class background like herself. Yet despite the sub-title of her article, she did not make it clear how in twenty-one years it had become easier for a woman to be a socialist. Nevertheless, this is a rare piece as it was part of a self-conscious attempt to construct a history for the ILP in which women had a real rather than merely a rhetorical contribution to make, particularly as propagandists. It is also an account in which women's suffrage is not mentioned once.

Suffrage, as Ethel Snowden's 1920 version of the 'ILP as friend to women' demonstrates, was, and is, a crucial lens through which the competing narratives of British socialism should be read. This is reflected in the reminiscences and autobiographies of ILPers and SDFers and the parties' 'official' histories. Joseph Clayton, looking back in 1926, claimed that 'in the SDF no one woman save Helen Taylor had been in any real sense of importance' whereas '[i]n the ILP women were a great deal more than mere helpers to men; they were quite literally the co-leaders'.[44] Although he saw women's suffrage as the badge of socialist rectitude and the ILP as 'on the whole sympathetic', he also saw that the struggle for 'Votes for Women' did not create socialists and, more worryingly for socialists, that, 'It diverted, for the time, both men and women from the Socialist movement, and the women thus diverted did not for the most part return'.[45] This suggests that women were forced to choose between suffrage and socialism, and that suffrage and socialist activism did not sit as comfortably together as the later reminiscences of some ILPers might suggest. Yet Clayton's account cannot be taken at face-value either. Although entitled *The Rise and Decline of Socialism in Great Britain, 1884–1924* this book was not 'objective' history. It was written by someone who had been the secretary of Leeds ILP in the 1890s and who was an ardent suffragist.[46] For Clayton the ILP had been 'the women's party' in the 1890s but had wavered a little in its commitment when confronted with militant suffragism, and so this was how he narrated the party's history. Who he was contextualizes but does not devalue his account; yet who he was is rarely mentioned by the historians who cite his work and thus misrepresent it.

To histories written by contemporaries in the 1920s must be added the volumes of autobiography and columns of newsprint filled with the reminiscences of ILPers. Most of these are by men who are self-consciously reaching back to a forgotten time. In a *Clarion* series in 1924 entitled 'Ben Turner Looks Back. His Own Story of the Old Days', an important part of that story were the women fighters. After a roll-call of ILP women who went well beyond the Famous Four, Turner concluded that 'The sacrifice of the women ... has been the greatest. ... To the dead ones Praise, to the living ones Honour'.[47] For him the story of the ILP was one where men worked together with particular women, like Isabella Ford whom he venerated but saw as different. This collaboration represented a form of equal membership, in that there were no formal barriers to women's participation, but it was not a politics of empowerment. It was a socialist version of separate spheres. Nevertheless, it is a version of the ILP in which women are not only present but make a crucial contribution.

Although the SDF never held a 'Coming-of-Age' Conference and their official history was not published until 1935, they too have a narrative of their collective past. H.W. Lee and E. Archbold recorded the names of women activists such as Eleanor Marx, Amie and Margaretta Hicks, Dora Montefiore, Mrs Bridges Adams, the Countess of Warwick and Mrs Murray, but the tone was much less eulogistic than the equivalent ILP 'guardians of the flame'. The woman question is only referred to indirectly in terms of the 'discordant note' of women's suffrage, although 'our untiring comrade' Dora Montefiore was commended for her work for adult suffrage. As for the WSPU, 'It was but natural, in the light of their past work, that leading Social Democrats like E. Belfort Bax and H. Quelch should consider these activities as a declaration of war upon the public'. Yet, pulling back slightly from the brink of the stereotype of the party, the authors continue 'Leonard Hall, the incisive ex-ILPer from Birmingham, amongst others, bitterly espoused the cause of the women'.[48] So suffragist SDFers were included in the official history, even if only represented by a man.

This particular narrative can at least partially be explained by considering the author, H.W. Lee, who as the long-time secretary of the SDF, was a self-conscious member of the Old Guard and could not hide where his sympathies, and indeed, loyalties, lay. It is, of course, significant not only who became the historians of the movement but also which socialist women and men chose to write their autobiographies. It may seem that in the language of today, the ILP had more effective 'spin doctors' when it came to official representations of the relationship between their party and the woman question. Yet among the SDF autobiographers are Margaret Bondfield and Dora Montefiore, who in their rather different ways give a voice to a woman-focused socialism and an unapologetic adult suffragism.[49] Nevertheless, the stereotype of the ILP as the only socialist 'friend to women' remains.

Recent studies which focus on women in individual socialist groups question these conventional wisdoms. June Hannam[50] argues that although many women found that local ILP branches were welcoming to their sex, in particular in Yorkshire, the ILP did not make gender-based issues a priority before the First World War. Annual conferences passed resolutions in favour of a limited franchise for women, and individual MPs such as Keir Hardie were consistent in their support for women's suffrage in parliament, yet the ILP as an organization did not work very hard to promote the cause. Some of its leading members were adult suffragists and were wary of an issue which seemed to privilege sex over class. This interpretation has been supported by Laura Ugolini's research into the attitudes of ILP men to women's suffrage.[51] She found that the party concentrated on winning the support of male trade unionists and showed little interest in franchise reform of any kind in its day-to-day politics.

Karen Hunt's work on the SDF,[52] on the other hand, suggests that women were more extensively involved in the organization than is usually conceded. She compared the attendance of women at SDF and ILP conferences and the extent to which they held national or local office and found very little difference between the two organizations. In both cases around ten per cent of conference delegates were women and very few were secretaries or treasurers of local branches. The SDF made it clear that gender issues were of secondary importance to the class struggle but, at the same time, by making them a matter of individual conscience, it enabled a widespread debate to take place on the woman question within the organization. Fundamental to Hunt's argument is the way in which the socialist theorizing of the woman question was itself gendered. This impacted on the practice of socialist women in various ways and framed socialists' attitudes to women. Although focusing on the SDF, much of Hunt's evidence suggests that the party and its male and female members were very like other Second International socialists. It would seem that not only is the traditional dichotomous view of the SDF/ILP unhelpful but that, perhaps, loyalties other than party such as sex, class, local political culture and position on suffrage were more important to individual socialists. Both Hannam and Hunt's biographical work[53] has shown that these nuances, shifts and re-negotiations change over a lifetime.

So why does the received view still persist despite this questioning of socialist history, the overlapping work of revisionist suffrage historians and the important research still largely hidden in doctoral theses? Or, to reframe the question, why have feminists exploring women's complicated relationship with British socialism had such a limited and particular impact on mainstream labour historians? It is much harder now to write a history of a socialist party which fails to acknowledge its female membership, although Martin Crick's *The History of the Social Democratic Federation*[54] comes very near to achieving this. But are a few pages within a larger work sufficient? Keith Laybourn in his recent book, *The Rise of Socialism in Britain*, specifically marketed as an account which is inclusive of women, seems to think so. He quotes Clayton's judgement that in the early ILP women 'were quite literally the co-leaders', continuing that 'it is even suggested that this meant that the ILP was more inclined to support the women's suffrage issue and the "women's question"'. Though he acknowledges that June Hannam's research throws doubt on some of these suggestions, he still concludes that 'the ILP was one of the most obvious sources of support for women'.[55] Aside from this fairly brief consideration, which is not really integrated into the book's overall argument, and the mention of a few female names in his analysis of other socialist organizations, women do not feature. There is simply no space given to the gendering of socialism. The challenge posed by recent feminist history has simply not been absorbed into the story of British socialism. Another approach to writing women and the gendering of socialist politics into labour history can be found in Neville Kirk's *Labour and Society in Britain and the USA*. In his brief treatment of women in relation to socialist and labour politics, the whole literature is so thoroughly telescoped that all that is really left is that ILP women were not 'submissive, doormat material' while in the SDF women were viewed as a problem.[56] Hunt and Hannam are both cited, but the heart of their individual arguments have barely been probed, let alone explored and incorporated. There is no space here for a complex analysis of gender, only for one of class.

These points are not made in order to engage in 'male labour-historian bashing'; rather we are raising the question, why mainstream labour history is sometimes deaf and often very hard of hearing when it comes to the contributions which feminist historians have made to the history of British socialism. It is no longer so easy to leave out 'women', even though only certain versions such as the Famous Four seem palatable. Yet British labour historians remain reluctant to integrate gender into their work. There is little attempt to explore the extent to which the theory and practice of socialist organizations were gendered and the ways in which women and men negotiated over this across time, place and party.

Perhaps British historians should look abroad for inspiration! The historiographies of other countries have been more open to the challenge that feminist history poses. In Australia Marilyn Lake's article 'The Politics of Respectability: Identifying the Masculinist Context'[57] was seen as breaking new ground 'by naming the politics that had constituted "the Lone Hand", the free-wheeling bushman, untrammelled by domestic ties, as the symbol of Australian nationalism'.[58] She termed these politics 'masculinist'. Her article provoked a heated debate in the mainstream historical establishment and the controversy established the term 'masculinism' as a distinct political position, loosely analogous – though diametrically opposed – to the political positions represented by feminism. As much of the evidence for the debate was drawn from the terrain of labour history, the issues could not be ignored by Australian labour historians. In *Labour History*, Bruce Scates and Lake debated her argument that 'The socialist beliefs and commitment of many working men arose from an anxiety about their gender status as well as a consciousness of class'.[59] These arguments over the extent to which socialist politics were also masculinist politics showed how labour history might be revised if viewed through the lens of gender. To some extent the debate on masculinism prepared the ground for the controversial *Creating a Nation*,[60] in which Lake and others attempted to de-centre the dominant narrative of the making of Australia by foregrounding gender and race. It is striking that there is no equivalent text for Britain. If British labour historians are to produce equally gender-sensitive work, do they need to come up with a sexy term like 'masculinism' or are there other ways to make the concept of gender effective?

In our current research[61] we foreground gender in an exploration of the British socialist movement as a whole between the 1880s and the 1920s, in order to offer a new 'angle of vision'. In recognition of the complexity of the politics of socialist women, we explore the competing tugs on the individual of class and sex as well as party, place and 'the private'. This work challenges not only the received view of the British socialist movement but also what socialism meant to women. For many women their criticisms from *within* socialism stretched across all parties as did their desire to make concrete the belief that the socialist and the women's cause was one. It is only by interrogating what it meant to be a 'socialist woman' in relation to contemporary notions of 'feminism' and of socialism that we can come to a more nuanced understanding of the political identity that was 'socialist woman'.

This process is part of the re-narrating of the history of women's politics in this period. It can also contribute to a revised socialist/labour history which has learnt to integrate gender into its conceptual frameworks. For this to happen, the dominant story of the British socialist movement has to be deconstructed and the implications of this deconstruction assimilated by labour historians. As socialists in the past narrated their own political histories, not always self-consciously, so they also participated in the construction of the identities of their political parties. Yet these early versions of the SDF and the ILP were often rhetorical devices in polemical inter-party struggles. If feminist historians can recognize that the 'women's cause' was a complex matter and that socialism was gendered in its theory, its language and its practices, how do we persuade labour historians, with a few honourable exceptions,[62] to remake their projects in recognition of this?

Notes

1. Hannam, J. (1987), '"In the Comradeship of the Sexes Lies the Hope of Progress and Social Regeneration": Women in the West Riding ILP, *c*.1890–1914', in Rendall, J. (ed.), *Equal or Different. Women's Politics, 1800–1914*, Oxford: Blackwell, pp. 214–38; Hannam, J. (1992), 'Women and the ILP, 1890–1914', in James, D., Jowitt, T. and Laybourn, K. (eds), *The Centennial History of the Independent Labour Party*, Halifax: Ryburn, pp. 205–28; Hunt, K. (1996), *Equivocal Feminists. The Social Democratic Federation and the Woman Question, 1884–1911*, Cambridge: Cambridge University Press.
2. *Liverpool Chronicle*, 1 August 1895, quoted in Steedman, C. (1990), *Childhood, Culture and Class in Britain. Margaret McMillan 1860–1931*, London: Virago, p. 131.
3. Ibid., p. 132.
4. Ibid.
5. Banks, O. (1981), *Faces of Feminism*, Oxford: Blackwell, p. 123.
6. Hinton, J. (1983), *Labour and Socialism. A History of the British Labour Movement 1867–1974*, Brighton: Wheatsheaf, p. 78.
7. Liddington, J. and Norris, J. (1978), *One Hand Tied Behind Us*, London: Virago, p. 44.
8. Weeks, J. (1981), *Sex, Politics and Society: The Regulation of Sexuality since 1800*, London: Longman, pp. 169–70.
9. Pankhurst, S. (1931), *The Suffragette Movement* (1977 edn), London: Virago, p. 111.
10. Barrow, L. and Bullock, I. (1996), *Democratic Ideas and the British Labour Movement 1880–1914*, Cambridge: Cambridge University Press, particularly chs 1, 2 and 4.
11. Strachey, R. (1928), *The Cause* (1974 edn), Bath: Cedric Chivers, p. 302; Liddington, J. (1979), 'Women Cotton Workers and the Suffrage Campaign: The Radical Suffragists in Lancashire, 1893–1914', in Burman, S. (ed.), *Fit Work for Women*, London: Croom Helm, p. 107. More recently suffrage historians have given a more nuanced account of the various suffrage positions but have still not given full attention to adult suffrage.
12. Hunt, *Equivocal Feminists*, pp. 7–16.
13. Howell, D. (1983), *British Workers and the Independent Labour Party, 1888–1906*, Manchester: Manchester University Press, p. 389.
14. Thompson, P. (1967), *Socialists, Liberals and Labour: The Struggle for London, 1885–1914*, London: Routledge and Kegan Paul, p. 297. Thompson argues that this stereotype provides a 'misleading picture' of the SDF.
15. *Labour Leader*, 14 April 1898.
16. For the socialist unity debate of 1896–7, particularly the ways in which the ILP leadership 'managed' the debate by emphasizing differences with the SDF, see Howell, *British Workers and the Independent Labour Party*, pp. 314–16, 393–4;

Barrow and Bullock, *Democratic Ideas and the British Labour Movement*, pp. 75–87.

17. Howell, D. (1984), 'Was the Labour Party inevitable?', *Labour's Turning Point in the North West, 1880–1914*, Southport: North West Labour History Society, pp. 1–18; Morris, D. (1982–3), 'The Origins of the British Socialist Party, *North West Labour History Society Bulletin*, **8**, 29–43; Laybourn, K. (1997), *The Rise of Socialism in Britain c.1881–1951*, Stroud: Sutton, pp. 49–60.
18. Hannam, 'In the Comradeship of the Sexes', p. 215.
19. For example, Pelling, H. (1965), *Origins of the Labour Party*, Oxford: Oxford University Press, p. 155; Pierson, S. (1973), *Marxism and the Origins of British Socialism*, Ithaca: Cornell University Press, pp. 161–9.
20. Howell, *British Workers*, p. 335; Hannam, 'In the Comradeship of the Sexes', p. 215.
21. Hannam, J. and Hunt, K. (1999), 'Propagandising as Socialist Women: The Case of the Women's Columns in British Socialist Newspapers, 1884–1914', in Taithe, B. and Thornton, T. (eds), *Propaganda 1300–1990*, Stroud: Sutton.
22. Steedman, *Childhood, Culture and Class*; Hannam, J. (1989), *Isabella Ford*, Oxford: Blackwell.
23. *Justice*, 30 July 1896.
24. Pye, D. (1995), *Fellowship is Life. The National Clarion Cycling Club, 1895–1995*, Bolton: Clarion Publishing, p. 39.
25. See, for example, J.B. Glasier's speech at Stacy's funeral, *Labour Leader*, 19 September 1903.
26. See, for example, Kean, H. (1994), 'Searching for the Past in Present Defeat: The Construction of Historical and Political Identity in British Feminism in the 1920s and 1930s', *Women's History Review*, **3** (1), 57–80; Mayhall, L. (1995), 'Creating the "Suffragette Spirit": British Feminism and the Historical Imagination', *Women's History Review*, **4** (3), 319–44.
27. *Labour Leader* carried reports of the 'Coming-of-Age Campaign', see for example 31 July 1913.
28. *Labour Leader*, 2 April 1914.
29. *Labour Leader*, 5 March 1914.
30. Glasier, J.B. (1919), *Keir Hardie: The Man and His Message*, London: Independent Labour Party, p. 9.
31. See appendix 1 in Hunt, *Equivocal Feminists*, p. 259, for a comparison between women on the executives of the SDF and the ILP.
32. Snowden, Mrs P. (1920), *The Real Women's Party*, Glasgow: Reformers' Bookstall, p. 2.
33. McMillan, M. (1927), *The Life of Rachel McMillan*, London: Dent, p. 85.
34. McMillan, M. (1895), 'Women in Relation to the Labour Movement', *Labour Annual*, pp. 138–9.
35. *Labour Leader*, 9 April 1914.
36. Hunt, *Equivocal Feminists*; Hannam, 'Women and the ILP'.
37. Mitchell, H. (1968), *The Hard Way Up. The Autobiography of Hannah Mitchell, Suffragette and Rebel* (1977 edn), London: Virago, p. 178.
38. M Coates-Hansen to G Lansbury, 30 October 1907, quoted in Collins, C. (1991), 'Women and Labour Politics in Britain 1893–1932', PhD, London School of Economics, p. 86.
39. *Labour Leader*, 9 April 1914.
40. Ibid.
41. Ibid.

42. *Labour Leader*, 17 August 1906.
43. *Labour Leader*, 9 April 1914.
44. Clayton, J. (1926), *The Rise and Decline of Socialism in Great Britain, 1884–1924*, London: Faber & Gwyer, p. 83.
45. Ibid., pp. 83–4, 155–8.
46. Hannam, *Isabella Ford*, p. 111.
47. *Clarion*, 28 March 1924.
48. Lee, H. W. and Archbold, E. (1935), *Social Democracy in Britain. Fifty Years of the Socialist Movement*, London: Social Democratic Federation, pp. 184, 191.
49. Bondfield, M. (1948), *A Life's Work*, London: Hutchinson; Montefiore, D. B. (1927), *From a Victorian to a Modern*, London: Edward Archer.
50. Hannam, 'In the Comradeship of the Sexes'; Hannam, 'Women and the ILP'.
51. Ugolini, L. (1997), 'Independent Labour Party Men and Women's Suffrage in Britain, 1893–1914', PhD, University of Greenwich. See also Ugolini, L. (1997), '"By all means let the ladies have a chance". *The Workman's Times*, independent labour representation and women's suffrage, 1891–1914', in John, A. V. and Eustance, C. (eds), *The Men's Share? Masculinities, Male Support and Women's Suffrage in Britain, 1890–1920*, London: Routledge.
52. Hunt, *Equivocal Feminists*.
53. Hannam, *Isabella Ford*; Hunt, K. (1999), 'Journeying Through Suffrage: The Politics of Dora Montefiore', in Eustance, C., Ryan, J. and Ugolini, L. (eds), *A Suffrage Reader: Themes & Directions in the Study of British Women's Suffrage History*, London: Cassell-Mansell.
54. Crick, M. (1994), *The History of the Social Democratic Federation*, Halifax: Ryburn.
55. Laybourn, *The Rise of Socialism*, p. 35.
56. Kirk, N. (1994), *Labour and Society in Britain and the USA*, vol. 2, Aldershot: Scolar Press, pp. 201–5, 240–1.
57. Lake, M. (1986), 'The Politics of Respectability: Identifying the Masculinist Context', (Australian) *Historical Studies*, **22** (86), 116–31.
58. Magarey, S., Rowley, S. and Sheridan, S. (eds) (1993), *Debutante Nation. Feminism Contests the 1890s*, Sydney: Allen and Unwin, p. xvii.
59. Lake, M. (1986), 'Socialism and Manhood: The Case of William Lane', *Labour History*, **50**, 54. See also Scates, B. (1990), 'Socialism, Feminism and the Case of William Lane: A Reply to Marilyn Lake', *Labour History*, **59**, 45–59; Lake, M. (1991), 'Socialism and Manhood: A Reply to Bruce Scates', *Labour History*, **60**, 114–20.
60. Grimshaw, P., Lake, M., McGrath, A. and Quartly, M. (1994), *Creating a Nation*, South Yarra, Victoria: McPhee Gribble.
61. Hannam, J. and Hunt, K. (1999), *Women and Socialism, 1880–1930*, London: Routledge.
62. See, for example, Savage, M. (1987), *The Dynamics of Working-Class Politics*, Cambridge: Cambridge University Press.

CHAPTER SEVEN

'Giving them Something to Do':
How the Early ILP Appealed to Women[1]

Krista Cowman

From its foundation, the Independent Labour Party (ILP) took self-conscious pride in its ability to attract a female membership. In an article written in 1894 Enid Stacy, herself a prominent woman member, remarked that her party had made good progress in its first year which:

> augurs well for a still more rapid advance in the future as the objects of the ILP are calculated to especially enlist the sympathy and support of women. The party makes no distinction between men and women, all are equally eligible for membership and office; its political programme is far more thoroughly in favour of women's sexual equality than the most advanced of the orthodox political women's bodies.[2]

Stacy's words are representative of a broad consensus amongst both early ILP activists and the first wave of its historians that their party was 'as much a women's movement as men's' and somewhat ahead of its time in its views on the woman question.[3] More recently feminist historians have been keen to emphasize the more woman-friendly aspect of the ILP, especially in comparison with its political counterparts.[4] However, there has been little investigation as to how this 'woman-friendliness' was perceived or experienced by the women who actually joined the ILP. Indeed, even identifying the female membership has proved somewhat problematic. The difficulties that might attach to this were unconsciously predicted as early as 1895, by John Edwards, himself a staunch supporter of women's rights within the ILP. In a short article in the *Liverpool Labour Chronicle* introducing Caroline Martyn who was about to embark on propaganda work in Liverpool, he wrote:

> we who stand in the midst of the fray see less of the struggle than those who stand on the distant hill-top and view the whole battlefield at a glance ... I venture to prophesy, however, that the intense earnestness and holy passion which now animate the disciples of Socialism will be in great part attributed to the three or four women who have become prominent speakers at our meetings during the last few years.[5]

Here, unwittingly, Edwards identified two of the key problems for those future historians to whom his words were explicitly directed. First, there is the question of identity. The prominence of a small group of women has been acknowledged repeatedly. Edwards cites 'three or four' here, whilst Henry Pelling agreed that three were noteworthy, and Stephen Yeo raised the number to eight.[6] However, although public acknowledgement of the importance of women in building the ILP is to be welcomed, such specific identification of individuals can convey the impression that those named were unique rather than representative of a broader layer of women activists. Second, there is the problem of roles conveyed by the areas in which these women are shown to be working. 'Holy passion' may have its adherents, but it looks awkwardly feminine, in a pejorative sense, when placed adjacent to some of the industrial or economic conflicts through which the ILP recruited many of its first generation of parliamentarians. Hence 'women's issues' appear peripheral to the main business of party from the outset.

In this chapter I want to contribute to ongoing debates assessing the true extent of the ILP's woman-friendliness. Although some of my discussion will concern the perceptions and attitudes of male ILPers, my main focus will be on relationships between women, and especially on the ways in which women socialists attempted to recruit other women into the party in its earliest years. It is my intention to demonstrate that much of what has been interpreted as 'feminist' or 'woman-centred' about the ILP was viewed with suspicion by many of its female contemporaries.[7] Yet this interpretation is not intended to dismiss any claims for ILP feminism. Indeed, I will re-evaluate certain other tactics which have been condemned as anti-feminist in an attempt to reclaim some of the radicalism such tactics may have offered in their own time.

Whilst the extent of the ILP's commitment to feminism remains uncertain, there is no question that it did number amongst its most enthusiastic founders a small but significant group of women. The most visible members of this group – Enid Stacy, Caroline Martyn, Isabella Ford, Eleanor Keeling, Katharine St John Conway and Margaret McMillan – had a certain amount in common. They were similarly aged (mainly in their mid twenties in the ILP's formation year) reasonably educated and very articulate, with no fear of the public platform.[8] Yet despite speaking talents which left local branches the length and breadth of the country clamouring to hear more of them, these women could be quite contemptuous of those whom they thought of as 'mere head socialists' who spouted empty theory without relating it to daily life.[9] All of them looked to socialism for much more than enthralling rhetoric or a re-organization of the economic basis upon which society was founded. Through their politics they sought nothing less than a total rearrangement of *all* aspects of society, stretching into the private sphere and the realm of human relationships.[10] Much of their political activity involved working with, or attempting to recruit and organize working-class women.[11] Although like all socialists they were concerned with contemporary poverty and desirous of a more equitable distribution of wealth, they gave equal weight to other issues – marriage, housework, dress reform. These scarcely featured in the writings of their male comrades but were a key feature in meetings of socialist women or in their writings and they often despaired of those who 'would ... crowd to a meeting of ordinary gassy politics' but had 'little interest in ... health, education' and similar questions.[12]

It follows that as public platform women who expressed radical views on a whole number of issues, these prominent women socialists were all 'rather proud than otherwise' of the label 'New Woman' which frequently attached itself to them.[13] This phrase was introduced to Britain in 1894 via the *North American Review*, and passed rapidly into common use as journalists and social commentators alike sought a response to the advances of feminism. The populist portrayal of the New Woman was an amusing caricature, an aggressive bluestocking: manly, harpyish and decidedly non-aspirational.[14] 'This nagging New Woman can never be quiet!' was how *Punch* introduced its readership to the concept.[15] Unsurprisingly, the ILP women took a different view, and defended this personification of feminism. In one of her earliest women's columns for *The Clarion*, Eleanor Keeling, who saw great possibilities within the figure of the New Woman, explained to her female readership that this was an identity to cherish. 'A New Woman is one who has high ideals on what life should be and ... is determined *to think for herself* to use her newly discovered reasoning powers'.[16] Such conceptualizations had important organizational implications for the gendering of the new party. New Women did not need men to speak for them or to represent them in public, but would take on this work themselves. 'The New Woman ... is the true woman, seeking the fullness of life and possibility' agreed Caroline Martyn.[17] Adopting this identity would open up an exciting number of directions for political women.

Yet despite the best efforts of leading women like Keeling and Martyn, the ILP did not offer New Women a safe harbour against the broader prejudices of society, and such public affirmations were as necessary inside the movement as they were elsewhere. Some socialist men attacked the idea of a New Woman in terms which would have been quite at home in *Punch*. Visual representations of the New Woman signified by the presence of trousers or bloomers on images of the female body were the most common caricature. These were also encouraged by socialist men. Eleanor Keeling sought the opinion of James Sexton, a member of her home ILP branch and was enraged by the condescending tone of his reply. 'I quite approve of the New Woman', he responded, 'all but the *trousers*!' Many prominent male socialists held similar views. Dangle (Alec Thompson), one of the all-male team behind *The Clarion*, claimed that he was a staunch supporter of the women in his party but confessed to some worries as to where claims for equality would end. As evidence he pointed to the case of Miss Edith Walker of Bogota, Colombia, who wished to join the police force. 'Make of them policemen ... they will want to become music hall managers, shopwalkers, perhaps even football referees' he wrote in alarmed concern.[18] Local branches also fretted about the threat to gender conventions, trawling equally far afield for examples, In 1896, *The Bradford Labour Echo* informed its readers that 'the New Woman has made her appearance in Kentucky ... working as a bricklayer!'[19] In the face of these attacks, Isabella Ford warned socialists to 'stand against the silly sneering at the New Woman ... as if she were some new or intolerable species'. She believed that such attitudes ought to concern all socialists, as 'surely the New Woman, the intelligent, questioning human being is the one we want in the Labour Movement?'[20] Mocking caricatures were not only misogynist, but would eventually prove detrimental to the spread of socialism by keeping many progressively-minded women away.

Attacks on New Women represent only one aspect of the problems faced by women who joined the ILP. As Karen Hunt has recently demonstrated, the very language of the early socialist movement found it difficult to cope with an active female membership.[21] Despite its grand public claims for equality the ILP continued to make heavy use of the term 'comrade'. This was a supposedly genderless term, but in reality denoted a male socialist as occasional awkward references to 'women comrades' made clear.[22] There simply was no equivalent female term. Socialist women unsuccessfully tried to overcome this by finding their own language. Eleanor Keeling sought an alternative fraternal term and suggested in her *Clarion* column the use of 'sisters as well as brethren', but her phrase never took hold in other *Clarion* articles.[23] Then there was the Mrs/Miss problem faced by women activists which was especially thorny to those who married after becoming recognized figures in the movement. Early on in her career, Enid Stacy complained of 'being taken for a man' when receiving letters addressed 'E. Stacy Esq.' and felt that there was a 'convenience' in the prefixes Mr, Mrs and Miss.[24] After her marriage to Percy Widdrington she retained her maiden name for public work, and in an apparent change of heart over prefixes used her Christian name whenever possible but remained Mrs Widdrington in private.[25] Katharine St John Conway attempted a similar compromise but was soon speaking and writing as Katharine Bruce Glasier.[26] Only Eleanor Keeling succeeded both in retaining her maiden name and convincing others to use it despite her high-profile marriage to Joseph Edwards, editor of the *Labour Annual*. This public independence made her a target for unpleasant criticism, notably by one anonymous correspondent who claimed that, if she were neither a Miss nor a Mrs she must be a man. Stung by this, Eleanor called for a revival of the term Mistress 'as a title for grown women' but to no avail.[27]

The difficulty in finding a name for women socialists gives some indication of the extent of the problems accepting equality posed for many socialist men. Examples abound in the labour press of women as somewhat unusual, or peculiar beings. 'Women are after all, truly engaging creatures' George Samuels wrote in his account of a lecture in Liverpool in 1896, 'and I discovered an immense number of pretty women [at the lecture] ... I might have carried home a specimen or two for observation.'[28] In similar fashion, a member of Bradford ILP reported on a socialist ramble in April 1895 attended by '17 women and ... only 2 men [who] braved the interminable chatter of the feminine tongue with the full determination to do our best with 8 and a half women each.'[29] These examples must question the validity of the ILP's 'reputation for treating women as equals'.[30] They also emphasize the difficulties facing attempts to build up a female membership in the ILP when women drawn to meetings were publicly dismissed in such terms.

Outside the realm of semiotics many women who encountered the socialist movement discovered very real problems of male indifference to their situation which sat unhappily at odds with equality rhetoric. These appeared at their worst in domestic situations. There were complaints about men who espoused socialism in public but did nothing to alter their behaviour towards women. They would happily listen to the national leaders of socialism lay down arguments for equality, but not translate these into their own lives. 'I know of one socialist who I was told stayed out till two o'clock you know, dearie' Eleanor Keeling's sister complained to her. 'I think a man who does those kind of things isn't a socialist at all, at all! He may advocate the nationalization of mines, railways etc, but nevertheless he is no socialist.'[31] Such indifference towards their nearest and dearest by socialist men was also encapsulated in the famous quotation from early ILP activist Hannah Mitchell, immortalized through the work of Jill Liddington and Jill Norris: 'No cause can be won between dinner and tea, and those of us who were married had to work with one hand tied behind us'.[32] Yet whilst the treatment that women socialists received from some men in the movement gave leading women socialists cause for complaint and concern, it did not shake their own commitment to their political cause. Rather, in certain instances, such treatment served to strengthen links between them as they began to increasingly work together possibly as an antidote to frequent attacks on their sex.[33] Space within the socialist press such as women's 'columns', 'pages' or 'letters' also helped provide a female socialist identity where the converted could unite together as both socialists and women.

There was a further problem, however, which was more serious than occasional jibes or instances of male political incorrectness. This problem directly threatened the sense of sisterhood which leading women socialists appeared to rely on to underpin their political lives. As the ILP increased in number, it became increasingly clear that outside its ranks, potential female recruits looked upon its women activists with much more suspicion than they did men. Far from identifying with them on the grounds of gender, the prominence of female propagandists in the ILP provoked a range of feelings in the women who encountered them from jealousy to inferiority. Although such feelings were more common amongst women unfamiliar with the day-to-day life of propagandists, even activists were not immune to the problem. What was worse, some prominent women socialists appeared to openly invite such antipathy. Hannah Mitchell spoke bitterly in her autobiography of the rudeness of a nameless female speaker who stayed at her home. The visitor, Hannah recalled, 'fl[ung] her hat and coat on the sideboard to the imminent danger of my cherished bits of china and silver' and threw herself into animated conversation with Hannah's husband, ignoring her hostess completely. This, claimed Hannah, was not a rare event, as she encountered 'many women who made this fatal mistake of treating their less gifted sister with intellectual contempt.'[34]

If Hannah Mitchell, a noted speaker and rising star of the movement could be treated like this, women who were not active socialists themselves would have found the situation even more difficult. To them, especially if they were married, the New Women of the movement posed a very real threat. Sally Blatchford, wife of *Clarion* editor Robert, confided to Margaret McMillan that she often feared losing her husband to women socialists who were less encumbered by domestic duties than herself and, 'though very willing to talk' to her Robert, 'had nothing to say to her except to ask for another cup of tea'. 'I can sympathize with you' McMillan replied, 'I also have found myself in company with those who would not deign to speak to me. I used to feel it so much I truly suffered.'[35] Marginalization of women, it would appear, was not simply to be laid at the door of socialist men.

It was not only the perceived threat women activists posed to their marriages which led the wives of socialists to suspect or dislike their husband's politics. Many wives also resented playing second fiddle to a movement which took up increasing amounts of their husband's leisure, time which was often sparse to begin with within working-class households. For women socialists who were also feminists, the realization that socialism was actually *worsening* the lives of many working-class women became a painful concern. It cut across much of the work they had attempted to do with such women to draw them into the movement, and directly challenged their personal belief in equality. In an attempt to address the problem, socialist women began to publish a variety of articles in the labour press which explored marital tensions around socialism.[36] In one of the first of these to appear, 'Dorothy Scott' (an acknowledged pseudonym) contended that faced with the persistence of traditional gender roles in many socialist households it was hardly surprising that women were often accused of being unsympathetic towards socialism. 'We may well be ... when a man comes in all aglow ... and then wonders that the wife who has

never had a chance of hearing any of those fine speakers, seems a bit quiet ...'
Scott clearly felt that the threat such situations posed to socialism was best
rectified by a more patient attitude on the part of men ensuring that women had
this chance, although she acknowledged that the attitudes of male 'chums'
could be a stumbling block in the way of more sympathetic men.[37]

The wife in Scott's article is simply marginalized by socialists and it is
assumed that once she gets to a meeting the problems will dissolve. More
seriously, in her essay 'The Labour Movement and the Home', Enid Stacy
presents a picture of a woman whose contacts with the movement leave her torn
with sexual jealousy. She opens with the story of a recent male convert who
complains of his home life since his conversion to socialism. His wife is
'ignorant, foolish and quite unsympathetic ... when she says anything it is only
to upbraid me for neglecting her and the children, for staying away from home'.
She starkly contrasts with the New Women he meets through his politics:

> All women are so, people say, and yet I meet a few in the Labour Movement
> itself, educated women too, with whom it is a relief and a pleasure to talk
> who seem to me to fill a void in which no men comrades can. Yet if I dare to
> make a friend of one of the women, jealous recriminations are added to the
> spiteful words ... which greet me on my return home from a hard evening's
> work.[38]

Although Stacy reserved most of her advice in this particular piece for men, she
also had a word for her 'married sisters' outside of the socialist movement,
acknowledging that this was a complex issue. Changing attitudes would not be
achieved simply by allowing hostile and threatened women to attend a meeting.
To achieve sexual equality within the socialist movement and prove Stacy's
claim that it really was 'as much a women's movement as men's' required effort
on the part of men and women.[39]

Socialist feminists also attempted to encourage practical changes which they
hoped would foster new attitudes. Whilst acknowledging the individual, if
understandable prejudices of working-class wives, they identified the domestic
situation in many working-class households as one of the main factors keeping
women away from socialism. 'One of the great reasons why there was so little
sympathy between husbands and wives' Stacy informed the ILP conference in
1894, 'was that the woman was so much shut up in the home and her interests
were so largely apart from those of her husband'.[40] From this analysis women
within the ILP began to turn their attention to the domestic sphere as a way
of recruiting other women. There was a general unwillingness to challenge
the belief that this was above all else a female arena. However, some serious
attempts were made to proclaim that socialism would remove some of the
domestic burden. The ILP's First Annual Report in 1894 closed with 'an appeal
to women' which acknowledged that any system which demanded that 'a wife

and mother' should 'be called upon to do her housework at night' after a full day at work was 'sufficient to drive one to revolting point'.[41] Julia Dawson, who succeeded Eleanor Keeling as editor of the *Clarion* Woman's Page, went further and explained how socialism would overcome this and alleviate domestic drudgery. It would:

> so organise household work that no one woman will have the burden of a whole house to look after and the cleaning, cooking, mending and general 'doing for' a whole family. Experts will come into our homes to do the cleaning as regularly as we now get our drains flushed by the local authorities ... our meals will be cooked by the very best cooks that can be trained, in one big co-operative kitchen for so many families so that the heaviest and dirtiest part of all housework, namely cooking and washing up, will be entirely done away with in private houses. Likewise the washing ... this burden alone lifted off women's backs is enough to make them cry Hallelujah for Socialism![42]

Such schemes were not without their critics, however, and there was concern even amongst the women who advocated them that they could undermine the already tenuous position of women within their homes, or destroy valuable areas of autonomy in working-class lives. Although Enid Stacy acknowledged that domestic inequality could only be ended through such communal approaches, she warned that 'many will consider the cure worse than the disease – I among the[m]'.[43] Much more practical was the comment of Katharine St John Conway who wrote, apparently without coercion, to the *Labour Woman* to endorse 'the really wonderful advantages of the patent mop and wringer advertised in our paper ... [for] a labour woman who has to do a good deal of rough cleaning work and yet would like to keep her hands as nice as possible'.[44]

Rhetoric of this type makes it clear that many of those socialists who would describe themselves as 'New Women' were happy to retain an acceptance of particular roles for men and women. These roles were further emphasized via many of their public statements on the usefulness of women to socialism. Much was made of the alleged innate sensitivities of feminine nature. Margaret McMillan, speaking on her work on the Bradford School Board, explained that women socialists did this far more effectively than 'stupid men, occupied with their ridiculous "business" [who] don't know how pretty children are – far less how pretty they might be'.[45] Eleanor Keeling felt that the best hope of abolition of the 'shameful' workhouse system lay in 'an army of firm-handed big-hearted women, deft with the use of the broom – to sweep away the whole vile rubbish heap.'[46] This state of affairs, Enid Stacy argued, called for tactics which recognized that, when attempting to recruit women, sentiment was more important than reason. Men are first attracted to socialism via their intellect 'then their feelings and their sympathies are forced'. With women 'a different order prevails. Touch their quick and ready sympathies, then render the feeling ... stronger and lasting by giving them something to do.'[47] Isabella Ford took this argument even further when she tired of 'the continued outcry about the stupidity or tiresomeness or selfishness ... inherent in the female mind' which kept women out of the movement. The remedy, she felt, was obvious. To attract 'the best and strongest part of woman's character ... that exists by reason of her physical nature ... we must give her a religion, not just mere economics'.[48]

It is perhaps this question of what role the ILP allocated to women, or what female recruits were given to do which has caused most problems for feminist historians when dealing with the party. As Christine Collette has remarked, 'the ILP perhaps got off to a bad start in that *women* founders cleaned the hall prior to its inaugural conference, decorating the trestle with a red cloth.'[49] Those seeking to establish a more concrete record of political activism for women within the party in its early years are forced to wade through columns of reports of meetings at which women cleaned, decorated, handed round the songsheets, took the collections and made the tea. Many of the early banners of the party were stitched by women members in socialist sewing circles, although the number of women who sat underneath these same banners on public platforms remained small. And whilst there was often one woman on the ILP Executive, this was by no means automatic in spite of the suggestion made by a Nottinghamshire member, Fred Greasley in 1895 that there ought always to be at least two places reserved for women.[50]

It is easy to interpret such incidents as anti-feminist, or at least as off-putting to potential female supporters. However, as June Hannam has recently pointed out, this can be missing the point.[51] The early socialist movement which surrounded the ILP was as much concerned with lifestyle as economics, and the development of a socialist culture was crucial to establishing the lifestyle members sought. Social activities such as soirees and rambles in which women took a leading part lay at the forefront of socialist cultural developments. This is most definitely the case, but other supposedly secondary or supportive political activities also need to be reinterpreted within their original context. Take, for instance, the task of passing round the hat for a collection at meetings. This appears a tame and unradical job, especially when compared with the more public roles a meeting offered. It sometimes appears to have been assigned to women in a dismissive manner such as when the (male) executive of Liverpool ILP publicly reminded 'women comrades ... that their services will again be required ... as collectors, their only role in a three-day long campaign'.[52] However, surprisingly when Enid Stacy first advocated this as an obvious task for new women recruits, she was initially hesitant about promoting her idea. Her hesitation was not due to a concern that she was offering or reinforcing a secondary role for women. Rather, she claimed, her proposal *challenged* predominant gender assumptions and offered women a job which had previously been restricted to men: 'At open air meetings [women] can take the collection instead of always leaving it to the men. This may seem a startling proposal, but I have known instances where it has been tried and with great success.' In support of her challenge, Stacy further justified her 'startling proposal' by resorting to more pragmatic arguments. 'Women collect more and unscrupulous listeners are less likely to remove money from the plate when it is received from a female hand.'[53] In this she may have been concurring with a somewhat essentialist view of the 'better' female nature, but was nevertheless attempting to alter gendered norms of behaviour and open up more space for women to participate.

Another area where a reassessment of intentions may be made is around the ways in which socialist feminists constructed marriage and motherhood. These themes featured prominently within their discourses on the gendered roles that a future, socialist society would provide. As with the task of collecting donations at a public meeting, the presentation of these ideas often falls short of the expectations of late twentieth-century feminism. None of the activists discussed in this chapter went so far as to call for the total abolition of marriage.[54] However, this does not mean that they were all committed to a Victorian ideal of the institution. Rather, many of them were actively searching for a new construction of marriage which would fit into a future socialist society. Such new marriages would be between 'twin-spirits' in sympathy with each other's highest aims.[55] Together, such couples could 'win the victory of right over might and put to rout the armed forces of materialism'.[56]

For many leading women socialists there was another dimension to their conception of marriage. In the 1890s many of them were making marriages themselves: Eleanor Keeling with Joseph Edwards, Katharine St John Conway with John Bruce Glasier and Enid Stacy with Percy Widdrington. Marriage was a step that each of them agonized over before taking, fearing its effects on their feminism, their independence or their work. Katharine St John Conway and Eleanor Keeling both refused to marry in church, and Eleanor worried about her decision to wear a ring until a fellow socialist assured her that it was 'little more than the blue ribbon of the temperance people'.[57] Enid Stacy was marrying a clergyman which ruled out a civic ceremony, but the bride went to great lengths to ensure that the word 'obey' was not used during the ceremony, substituting it with 'serve'.[58] All three women married men who were active socialists, and in sympathy with their work which must have contributed towards the high public profiles that they were able to retain in the years after their marriages.

Within each of these socialist marriages it appears that part of the decision to enter a partnership was inspired by the usefulness that both partners believed such alliances could bring to the broader movement. Inspired by the belief that couples 'might be more useful together' Enid Stacy published a short playlet intended to demonstrate the advantages socialist marriages might have for local branches. The drama involves two characters, 'A' and 'B', returning from a socialist meeting. Whilst B wishes to go to the pub, A is keen to return home and tell his wife the result of a crucial vote. B is nonplussed. 'Do you mean to say she cares twopence about that? It's more than mine does!' he exclaims, before explaining that his wife only complains that socialism makes him neglect his home. Stacy uses 'A' to outline the domestic bliss which would proceed from an ideal socialist marriage. Socialist papers are read together, childcare shared and the party social a focus for family outings. The rewards are plain, as A explains: a wife who is a 'co-worker' and 'friend' '[who] will have entered into your life because you have entered into hers'. Much of this advice is aimed at changing men, who continue to be presented as the main problem, despite increasing tensions in relationships between women activists and recruits. However, Stacy also encouraged women to look at things slightly differently. Married women especially are urged to 'take your part' and again the rewards spelt out; 'how many magnificent battles will be won ... when women of all countries realise fully that the best way is for all workers to stand together, women equally with men'.[59]

Personal experience also intruded on the way that leading women socialists attempted to conceptualize motherhood. It is true that there was a tendency amongst some socialists to take a 'sentimental view of the mother's role within the family'.[60] Margaret McMillan frequently drew on 'maternalist imagery and arguments' which focused on the beauty of the maternal bond.[61] Jeannie Mole, founder of socialism in Liverpool and a familiar name to readers of both Eleanor Keeling and Julia Dawson's *Clarion* columns went further. Her belief that mothers were 'moulding the destiny of men' and missing 'much of real joy ... through ... not fashioning and stitching her own loved one's garments' would not have looked out of place amongst the prescriptive writings of Hannah More.[62] It is easy (and perhaps tempting in the case of Jeannie Mole) to subject such writings to a critical feminist analysis which, in the latter twentieth century, views them as slightly less than radical. However, as with interpretations of some of the activities which socialists offered to women, they can appear somewhat different within their own time. Often, leading women socialists felt obliged to defend their politics against accusations that they were morally corrupt and intent on destroying the family.[63] In such a climate it is hardly surprising that some women in the ILP felt the need to overemphasize their 'respectability' or to stress repeatedly that theirs was a party which supported marriage. Highlighting motherhood was an obvious way to do this and one which avoided some of the more thorny issues of religious or state involvement in the private sphere raised by 'conventional' marriage. It was also an area in which socialism and feminism could combine into something practical. Such a useful convergence has also been suggested within the field of maternity provision and child welfare. Seth Koven, for example, has demonstrated 'women ... making specific claims about why they ... as a sex, were especially qualified to shape welfare policy and provide care for working-class children'.[64]

Yet as with the rhetoric surrounding marriage there was another motivation for many of the activists' views mentioned here. The equal partnerships which they had envisaged on marriage were soon complemented by the arrival of children. Becoming mothers allowed active socialists a further opportunity to attempt to merge theory with practice in their own lives. Eleanor Keeling was the first nationally recognized speaker to have a child. Prior to this, she had equated motherhood with paid work, and argued for some form of wage or state endowment to recognize its status.[65] After the birth of her daughter in 1897 she attempted to find other ways in which she could combine socialism and motherhood, offering a new conception of both roles. Fay Keeling Edwards was named after the late Edward Fay of *The Clarion*, her surname acknowledging her father and reflecting Eleanor's determination to retain her own name after marriage. She was presented to the movement at a socialist naming service held on a Merseyside beach at which her mother presided and offered 'a few earnest words of dedication to the cause' on behalf of her child.[66] As with her marriage, Keeling viewed motherhood as something personal, but also as something undertaken for the cause. Rearing children was not simply the lot that fell to women after marriage; it was important work for society, and a task to be shared by both parents.

The lives of many prominent women speakers after they became mothers demonstrates the extent to which they were able to put these ideals into practice. Within their households both parents took a part in childcare and in introducing their children to a broader socialist culture. John Bruce Glasier frequently took his daughter Jeannie, on whom he clearly doted, when travelling on business. During these trips he paid as much attention to her reactions as to the socialist work he was engaged in. In October 1902 he visited Liverpool where friction between *Clarion* and ILP supporters was holding back local work. Rather than dwell on the reasons for this in his accounts of the visit, his main memory was of the reactions of Jeanniebell (as she was known) to the dogs owned by the socialist couple with whom they stayed.[67] Fay Keeling Edwards became an equally familiar figure within the movement who 'fraternised with [adults] in true socialist manner'.[68] Percy Widdrington managed to combine his pastoral work with almost sole care of his young son Gerard when Enid Stacy undertook a lecture tour to the USA the year after Gerard's birth.[69] However, even this much support did not compensate Stacy for the absence of her child and she resolved not to undertake similar work in the future until Gerard was older. Furthermore, these examples offered little in the way of practical aid to women with a passing interest in socialism who lacked a committed spouse.

What these seemingly unradical tactics do demonstrate is that early women socialists were attempting to resolve the very serious problem of women's hostility towards their party through offering alternative visions of how marriage and the home could look under socialism, and to put some of their theories to the test in their own lives. In so doing, they were tackling much more than the simple problem of a numerical lack of women. Their efforts can be interpreted as a real attempt to achieve a form of sexual equality within the party to underpin the new order of society for which its members strove. Undeniably, many of their actions and beliefs rested on an acceptance of separate roles for men and women, although these were not defined as indivisible. Furthermore, many divisions which were accepted were done so from a position which affirmed power for women within the party but also celebrated the contribution that women and men could make together for a socialist future. As Enid Stacy put it in an article in 1893, 'we [women] have so many calls on our time ... we are ... practical busy people with a desire for new dreams ... we want to be doing something'.[70] The choices of the new women of the 1890s may no longer mirror those which we would make a century later, but this ought not to be allowed to diminish their importance in their own time.

Notes

1. Stacy, Enid (1893), 'What Women Can Do', *The Labour Prophet*, August.
2. Stacy, Enid (1895), 'Women's Work and the ILP', *The Labour Annual*.
3. Letter from Fred Greasley to Eleanor Keeling, 7 April 1895; Joseph Edwards Papers, Liverpool Record Office. (Hereafter cited JEP, LRO). Similar opinions can be found in Clayton, Joseph (1926), *The Rise and Decline of Socialism in Great Britain, 1884–1924*, London: Faber & Gwyer.
4. See, for example, Hannam, June (1995), 'Women and politics', in Purvis, June (ed.), *Women's History in Britain 1850–1945*, London: UCL Press, p. 231; Gordon, Eleanor (1991), *Women and the Labour Movement in Scotland*, Oxford: Clarendon Press, p. 265.
5. Edwards, John (1895), 'Caroline E. D. Martyn', *Liverpool Labour Chronicle*, August.
6. Pelling, Henry (1965), *The Origins of the Labour Party*, Oxford: Oxford University Press, p. 155; Yeo, Stephan (1977), 'A New Life: The Religion of Socialism in Britain', *History Workshop Journal*, 4, Autumn, 5–55.
7. The word 'feminist', although not in common usage during the 1890s, will be used throughout the chapter rather than the more cumbersome 'woman-friendly' or 'woman-centred'.
8. For individual biographies see, for example, Tuckett, Angela (1980–81), 'Enid Stacy', *North West Labour History Society Bulletin*, 7, 41–8; Thompson, Laurence (1971), *The Enthusiasts: A Biography of John and Katharine Bruce Glasier*, London: Gollancz; Fidler, Geoffrey (1979), 'The Work of Joseph

Edwards and Eleanor Keeling, Two Liverpool Enthusiasts', *International Review of Social History* **XXIV**, 293–379; Steedman, Carolyn (1990), *Childhood, Culture and Class in Britain: Margaret McMillan, 1860–1931*, London: Virago. Their similarities and differences are further discussed in Cowman, Krista, 'Good Woman Socialists in Late Victorian and Edwardian England', in Cubitt, Geoff and Warren, Allen (eds), *Exemplary Lives*, Manchester: Manchester University Press (forthcoming).

9. Letter to Eleanor Keeling from 'your sister Annie', n.d., JEP, LRO.
10. Hannam, June (1992), 'Women and the ILP', in James, D., Jowitt, T. and Laybourn, K. (eds), *The Centennial History of the Independent Labour Party*, Halifax: Ryburn Publishing p. 207, contains an excellent discussion of this point.
11. Eleanor Keeling, for example, took on one of her earliest public roles as secretary of Liverpool Women's Industrial Council. See also Hannam, June (1989), *Isabella Ford*, Oxford: Blackwell; and Steedman, Carolyn, *Childhood, Culture and Class*, for similar concerns in the early public works of two other prominent socialist women.
12. Enid Stacy to Percy Widdrington, 13 November 1895. Angela Tuckett Papers, Working Class Movement Library, Salford. (Hereafter cited ATP, WCML.)
13. Anon. (1895), biography of Enid Stacy, *The Labour Annual*.
14. For discussions of the New Woman, see Rubinstein, David (1986), *Before the Suffragettes: Women's Emancipation in the 1890s*, London: Harvester, pp. 3–12; Bland, Lucy (1995), *Banishing the Beast: English Feminism and Sexual Morality, 1885–1914*, London: Penguin, pp. 143–9
15. *Punch*, 26 May 1894, cited by Rubinstein, p. 17.
16. *The Clarion*, 23 March 1895.
17. *Labour Prophet*, July 1895.
18. *The Clarion*, 19 January 1895.
19. *Bradford Labour Echo*, 26 September 1896.
20. *Labour Prophet*, December 1894.
21. Hunt, Karen (1997), 'Fractured Universality: The Language of British Socialism Before the First World War', in Belchem, John and Kirk, Neville (eds), *Languages of Labour*, Aldershot: Ashgate, pp. 65–80.
22. The use of this phrase is discussed in Cowman, Krista (1994) 'Engendering Citizenship: The Political Activity of Women on Merseyside, 1890–1920', University of York, unpublished DPhil thesis.
23. *The Clarion*, 9 February 1895.
24. Stacy, Enid (1892), entry in 'Our Fabian Circle' mss notebook 5 April. Bruce Glasier Papers, Liverpool University.
25. *Bradford Labour Echo*, 14 September 1895. During her speaking tours abroad letters from her husband and family are addressed to 'Mrs Widdrington' although she speaks as 'Miss Stacy' which continues to prefix her business correspondence. ATP, WCML.
26. Thompson, *The Enthusiasts*, p. 83.
27. *The Clarion*, 13 April 1895.
28. *Labour Leader*, 25 January 1895.
29. *Bradford Labour Echo*, 27 April 1895.
30. Liddington, Jill and Norris, Jill (1978), *One Hand Tied Behind Us*, London: Virago, p. 45.
31. Letter to Eleanor Keeling from 'your sister Annie', n.d., JEP, LRO.
32. Liddington and Norris, *One Hand Tied Behind Us*.
33. Some branches began to form women's sections, although this was a matter of

heated debate within the national party, or to provide occasional women's meetings.

34. Mitchell, Hannah (1977), *The Hard Way Up*, London: Virago, p. 119.
35. Thompson, L. (1951), *Robert Blatchford: Portrait of an Englishman*, London: Gollancz, p. 141.
36. See for example 'Scott, Dorothy' (pseud.) (1892), 'The Wife's Sunday Out', *The Labour Prophet*, February; Anon. (1892), 'The Workman's Wife by One of Them', *The Labour Prophet*, March; Stacy, Enid (1893), 'The Labour Movement and the Home', *The Labour Prophet*, March.
37. Scott, 'The Wife's Sunday Out.'
38. Stacy, 'The Labour Movement and the Home'.
39. Stacy, 'Women's Work and the ILP'.
40. Stacy, Enid (1894), Independent Labour Party *Annual Report*.
41. Anon (1894), Independent Labour Party *Annual Report*, my italics.
42. Dawson, Julia (1904), *Why Women Want Socialism*, ILP pamphlet.
43. Tuckett, Angela (n.d.), unpublished mss biography of Enid Stacy, ATP, WCML.
44. *Labour Woman*, May 1913. Writing as 'Iona' in the *Labour Leader*, Katherine St John Conway made frequent reference to the importance of women as home-makers. See Hannam, 'Women and the ILP', p. 211.
45. *Labour Prophet*, November 1895.
46. *The Clarion*, 9 February 1895.
47. *Labour Prophet*, August 1893.
48. *Labour Prophet*, December 1894.
49. Collette, Christine (1989), *For Labour or for Women: The Women's Labour League 1906–1918*, Manchester: Manchester University Press, p. 18.
50. Letter from Fred Greasley to Eleanor Keeling, 7 April 1895. JEP, LRO.
51. Hannam, 'Women in the ILP', p. 206.
52. *Liverpool Labour Chronicle*, May 1895.
53. *Labour Prophet*, August 1893.
54. One possible exception is Caroline Martyn who, June Hannam has argued, was 'sympathetic' to the alternative unions to marriage, believing they would lead to a 'higher' union between men and women. See Hannam, 'Women and the ILP', p. 210.
55. Moira Addison, letter to Joseph Edwards in response to his comments on his union with Eleanor Keeling, 15 February 1894. JEP, LRO.
56. *Labour Prophet*, July 1895.
57. Thompson, *The Enthusiasts*, p. 83. For Eleanor Keeling see letter from Annie, 31 October 1894, JEP, LRO.
58. Tuckett, ms biography of Enid Stacy, ATP, WCML.
59. Stacy, Enid (1893), 'The Labour Movement and the Home', *The Labour Prophet*, March.
60. Hannam, June (1987), 'In the Comradeship of the Sexes Lies the Hope of Progress and Social Regeneration' in Rendall, Jane (ed.), *Equal or Different: Women's Politics, 1800–1914*, Oxford: Blackwell, pp. 214–38.
61. Koven, Seth (1993), 'Borderlands: Women, Voluntary Action and Child Welfare in Britain 1840–1914', in Koven, Seth and Michel, Sonya (eds), *Mothers of a New World: Maternalist Politics and the Origins of Welfare States*, London: Routledge, pp. 94–135. See also Steedman, *Childhood, Culture and Class*, pp. 119–20.
62. Mole, Jeannie (1895), 'Housewives and Queens', *Liverpool Labour Chronicle*, December. For Hannah More see Davidoff, Leonore and Hall, Catherine (1987),

Family Fortunes: Men and Women of the English Middle Class 1780–1850, London: Hutchinson, pp. 167–72.

63. For a discussion of this, see the description of the case of Edith Lanchester, and the SDF's reaction to it, in Hunt, Karen (1996), *Equivocal Feminists: The Social Democratic Federation and the Woman Question 1884–1911*, Cambridge: Cambridge University Press, chapter 4, especially pp. 94–104.
64. Koven (1993), p. 125.
65. *Shafts*, July 1895.
66. *The Labour Leader*, 29 May 1897.
67. John Bruce Glasier diary, 4 October 1902, Liverpool University.
68. *Bradford Labour Echo*, 7 October 1899. For further descriptions of socialist home life, see Pankhurst, E. Sylvia (1911), *The Suffragette*, London: Sturgis and Walton, pp. 5–6; Thompson, *The Enthusiasts*, pp. 112–13.
69. He did have some domestic help in the form of a Swedish girl who was lodging in the household learning English in return for light duties. See Mrs Widdrington to Enid, 27 November 1902, STP, WCML.
70. *Labour Prophet*, August 1893.

CHAPTER EIGHT

From the Periphery to the Centre: Changing Perspectives on American Farm Women

Margaret Walsh

Introduction

> Most men lived in the households of their parents until they married, because until they married most men could not muster the labor necessary to begin farms of their own. ... The work of children was important, but it was the work of farm wives that made the difference between the success or failure of productive strategies.[1]

> Women contributed twice as much to the value of farm output in the Northeast and on the Frontier as they did in the Old Northwest. In the Northeast their contribution approximated the wage of a hired hand for seven to eight months, which represents the standard contract length for hired hands at that time ... [but these estimates] ... omit the value of domestic production or housework. In fact, if one imputes the wages of a full-time domestic to a woman, then the market value of the total contribution to the household by a woman exceeds that by a man in every region.[2]

Such a fair representation of the female contribution to agrarian livelihood is a recent phenomenon in historical writing about American farming. For most of its past, agriculture has been depicted as a triumph or a tragedy of productivity, dependent on male physical labour aided and abetted by machine technology, mercantile intermediaries, the idiosyncrasies of the weather and natural hazards.[3] Not for nothing did Carolyn Sachs entitle her 1983 study of American farm women, *The Invisible Farmers*.[4] Yet she, like the many other recent writers who have contributed to recovering a female presence on the farm, aimed to do more than discuss women's reproductive work. They also wanted to challenge the gendered division of labour which assigned women to a supportive role in what has been a major sector in the national economy.

Thanks to the energies and resourcefulness of this generation of academics, women's multiple functions in American agriculture can no longer be ignored. These female activities have most frequently been recounted and assessed in terms of running the farmhouse and managing the barn and yard enterprises.

Here women worked in domestic space and fulfilled their traditional roles in both a pre-capitalist and a commercialized economy.[5] They also, however, successfully undertook 'male' or outside tasks, working in the fields and selling crops in the marketplace. Furthermore, women's social skills in family and community relations and their consumer skills in managing modern farm households are no longer dismissed as irrelevant to material success.

Yet despite the mounting evidence of female contributions, farming is still seen as a masculine occupation. Domestic responsibilities have not been ac-credited with valuable status because they contributed mainly to reproduction and self-sufficiency and generated little income. Even when technology shifted the emphasis of female inside work from domesticity towards managerial operations, these office functions have been deemed of only secondary importance. Furthermore, any crossing of gender confines whereby women moved into the male space of outside work or remoulded shared workspace has made little impact on rebalancing traditional interpretations. Patriarchal notions of gender difference have remained.[6] Another generation of gender-conscious scholarship will be needed to redefine the boundaries of womanhood and manhood in agricultural life. Then perhaps women's accomplishments in serving the family enterprise will be more fully appreciated.

The triple work load

Most discussion of women's work on the family farm has focused on domestic functions which include both the running of the home and the management of the kitchen garden and the farmyard. Until the post-Second World War years most American agriculture was organized around the small family farm. Whether viewed in terms of the Jeffersonian ideology of an independent self-sufficient yeomanry or measured statistically at 140 acres in the mid-nineteenth century and 433 acres in 1982,[7] this small farm was impractical without a female partner to run the home. Here the farm woman's main function as wife and mother included food preparation, cleaning, washing, making and mending clothes, bearing and raising children. Testimonies ranging from pioneers on the Oregon frontier in the 1840s to settled farmers in Florida in the 1980s agree that such home tasks were fundamental to the success of farm enterprise.[8] Industrial technology in the shape of mass produced food and clothing and household equipment has enabled farm women to consume rather than produce many goods and services, but the time and labour thereby saved have frequently been directed to new household tasks which can include the secretarial and administrative servicing of the farm.

On frontier farms in the eighteenth and nineteenth centuries domestic tasks were both arduous and time-consuming. In one-room homes which lacked basic amenities women spent a large proportion of the day cooking simple meals over an open fire or a primitive stove and keeping the house and clothes clean. Carrying water alone was a chore which took hours every week while washing clothes and bed linen was a dreaded weekly task. When much of the family's food had to be raised and processed as well as cooked, housework became more daunting. Grain required pounding into meal, animals needed slaughtering and curing and fruit and vegetables picking, preserving and storing. Prior to the advent of ready-made clothing – for men after the Civil War and for women towards the beginning of the twentieth century – clothes frequently had to be made as well as mended. Add to this list women's 'natural' role as mother then domestic tasks became endless. Pregnancies were frequent and childbirth was dangerous. Nurturing children and nursing them through illnesses was exhausting.[9] Household tasks were a full-time occupation whose only relief was provided by some assistance from older children and occasionally from a husband.

Yet women managed *and* took on extra work in the vicinity of the home. The kitchen garden, the yard and the barn were frequently considered the female domain. Their operation became a form of rural outwork which was sometimes recorded in the Census of Agriculture in the form of home manufactures.[10] Official documentation, however, marginalized such female efforts to keep the family farm solvent, by registering their financial contributions in their husbands' names. Detailed evidence of female outwork has only emerged in private sources like diaries and letters which frequently discuss the 'butter and egg' money. Chickens, eggs, butter, cheese, milk, fruit and vegetables were both consumed on the farm and sold locally. These cash sales could support a farm during difficult times, or in more prosperous years, were considered as female 'perks' available to purchase store goods. Baked products, sewing, spinning, weaving, taking in laundry or a lodger offered women other means of making cash. In exchanging the products of their labour for money, women entered the 'male' productive sphere and the commercial market.[11] Their enterprise, whether classified as home produce for self sufficiency or as gainful employment, was essential to the welfare of the farm.

Women also entered the 'male' sphere and contributed to farm output when doing outdoor work. In the pioneer West and proto-capitalist communities labour was frequently in short supply during the planting or harvesting of crops. At such busy times women helped in the fields. They also herded cattle and drove the teams for hauling. When their husbands were ill or were away from home earning money, women often ran the farm and undertook all the farm tasks.[12] Farm women were genuine working partners in this family enterprise, although they frequently deferred to their husbands' decisions and usually preferred to undertake domestic work. Conditioned by cultural norms of femininity they took second place. Such deference has been judged by

137

feminists as exploitation by a patriarchal system. Yet contemporaries regarded women's part-time field work as a pragmatic response to labour shortage. Increasingly, historians now view 'crossovers' into male space as genuine possibilities for altering gender boundaries.[13]

Diversity in women's triple work load

Variations in the triple work patterns of farm women stemming from income, geography, technology, ethnicity and race, have offered academics more opportunities to point out flexible responses to the division of labour and to assess the economic value of female and male members of the family, while still retaining the basic proposition that women's contributions were essential to running American family farms. Independent female farmers are a case in point. Traditionally women have not been associated with landholding, but the fact that they were in a minority should not detract from their existence. Whether they were 12 per cent of the homesteaders in Wyoming in the late nineteenth and early twentieth centuries or 21 per cent of single owners and operators in the USA in 1982, their presence clearly showed that women could operate farms.[14] These proprietors were more likely to be single women or widows than wives, and their farms were generally smaller than those operated by men because of the financial and legal problems of female ownership. In running their farms, women faced considerable difficulties acquiring credit, and they encountered managerial problems in hiring male help. Yet the concerns arising from combining female and male roles were daunting rather than debilitating.[15] Possibly under a different ideology and with less restrictive property and inheritance legislation American women would have been as capable as their male counterparts of running a farm enterprise.

Regional and ethno-cultural differences further illustrate American farm women's work flexibility. In the South and southwestern parts of the USA in the nineteenth century, the production of cotton and tobacco as commercial crops were often more important than cereal and livestock raising. Then in the twentieth century the development of truck farming (market gardening) on a large scale depended on seasonal and migratory farm labour. Both systems of farming exploited the unskilled farm labour of minority groups.

Before the Civil War slave labour was essential to large-scale or plantation farming. The 'peculiar institution' altered both white and black women's contribution to farming. Planters' wives had a dual role. They were both mistresses of households directing domestic work done by slave women and, in the absence of their husbands, overseers of slaves and any hired labour involved in crop production. As such they could demonstrate managerial capacities more associated with twentieth-century small business enterprises.[16]

African-American farm women in slavery faced dire circumstances. They either worked in the plantation home as domestic help or in the fields alongside male slaves. Here they usually assumed the same workloads as males other than when pregnancy temporarily altered assignments. They were also responsible for whatever limited yard crops could be raised to supplement their families' diet. Furthermore, as victims of white male sexuality as well as white control of their physical labour they were forced to demonstrate their reproductive capacity. As chattel, African-American women demonstrated a capacity to undertake both 'male' and 'female' work.[17] Any ideological constraints on the proper female farm role were conveniently abandoned.

The legacy of slavery shaped the contributions of African-American farm women after emancipation. Freed into poverty and illiteracy, lacking access to land and capital many African-American families became share-croppers or tenant farmers raising cotton as a cash crop.[18] Some wives withdrew their field labour as a recognition of their free status, but many, together with their children, worked beside their husbands in the fields and replaced them when men took temporary jobs to supplement family income. African-American women were much more involved in field work than were their Euro-American counterparts. Yet they and their children worked in the kitchen garden, raising chickens and eggs for sale in local markets and vegetables for their own consumption. They also undertook other forms of outwork, most notably taking in laundry, in an effort to meet economic needs and, like all women, they did housework.[19] Trapped in indebtedness and ground down further by racial discrimination African-American farm women in the postbellum South remained an essential part of their families' economic team fighting for survival.

African-American women were not the only female farm workers in the southern parts of the USA who were exploited as a result of their race. In California, Florida and Texas in the twentieth century, Mexican migrants and Mexican-Americans (Chicanas) were part of an unskilled family endeavour when they followed the fruit and vegetable crops which required harvesting by hand.[20] Those migratory farm wives and daughters who worked alongside their menfolk in the fields faced long hours and low pay in difficult and dangerous conditions and they endured poor living accommodation. Both male and female workers suffered discrimination on the grounds of race, but women fared less well than men as temporary employees of large farm operators because they were hired on piece rates rather than hourly rates and were frequently hired only for casual work.[21] Nevertheless, minority women's paid work was essential both to individual family survival and to truck farming production. Their contributions again demonstrated that women's work in a rural environment was remunerative.

For Euro-American farm owners and tenants, crop mixes and productivity levels did not remain static. Access to urban markets and machine technology changed the forms and balance of women's farm contributions. Even in the pre-Civil War years the growth of East coast cities offered farmers in nearby areas opportunities to sell dairy products, vegetables and fruit at higher prices than they would receive for cereal crops. This market incentive, together with competition from grain farms in the newly settling western regions, expanded throughout the nineteenth century and altered the economic value of women's work in the Northeast. The most noticeable changes developed in the 'middle ground' of the barnyard and kitchen garden. As the value of dairy and market garden products increased, men and boys often helped out with the milking, churning, preserving and tending of the garden, thereby increasing the tendency to make these jobs either joint activities or 'men's work'.[22] Then depending on family dynamics and preferences, women spent more of their time in domestic pursuits and in extending their community ties, thereby cementing the social bonding which was so essential to rural well-being.

Machine technology has altered patterns of American farming in perhaps more significant ways, reducing labour inputs, increasing productivity, providing easier access to markets and generally improving the quality of life. Whether in the form of reapers, combine harvesters, railroads, fertilizers, electricity, the internal combustion engine or the computer, technology has shifted the shape of women's farm contributions rather than their substance. The threefold division of work – domestic, yard and field – still remains, but the contents have been modernized or externalized.[23] The balance assigned to each part remains a family or individual response, partly influenced by the economic pressures for well-being and partly by a greater awareness of cultural concepts of womanhood.

Farm women's roles in the late-twentieth century illustrate this new balance which emerged directly and indirectly from technological advances. Domestic work still involves child care and housework, but as much, if not more, time is spent in consuming goods and services as in producing them. Food is both bought in the supermarket and processed at home, and children require frequent chauffeuring to peer-group activities as well as home supervision. Domestic appliances have eased the laborious parts of cleaning and cooking, but higher standards have required that the time allotted to these tasks was not necessarily different from that required at the start of the century.[24]

The 'butter and egg' style contributions of farm women's outwork have also been remoulded. In the 1980s wives' 'On Farm Activities' included roadside stalls for the sale of fresh and processed fruit, vegetables and poultry as well as stalls in the local market. Other activities sometimes involved running farm restaurants or craft shops for the sale of such commodities as macramé, knitted goods or quilts or even managing a mail order business for speciality fruits or pecan nuts. Such activities – estimated in 1980 to take two hours labour a day –

complemented men's work on small farms. On larger, specialized and more heavily mechanized units, technology made women's on-farm income-earning capacity less important and even obsolete.[25]

On both small and large farms, however, wives remained employed, though they have not often been recognized as 'gainfully' employed. They 'filled in' on outside work when and as necessary, whether this called for milking, driving farm machinery, 'gofering' (running errands) for their husbands or standing in for hired labour. As general educational levels increased and farming became more bureaucratized women assumed inside farm tasks which required management skills in bookkeeping and accounting, keeping abreast of marketing and technical information and operating the computer. Furthermore, they contributed financially to the family enterprise by taking off-farm jobs. As professionals, some women taught and nursed, either on a part-time or a full-time basis, while others found less skilled employment in clerical, retailing and factory work. Home dealerships and home computers enabled women to earn money while remaining on the farm. Though none of this work is well-paid because the rural neighbourhood labour market is frequently saturated, it has enabled many farm women to improve their families' material well-being in new ways.[26]

The social processes of farming

Women's economic contributions to American farming have been significant and varied. These efforts have increasingly been recognized and absorbed into historical knowledge thanks to a greater awareness of both the value of household work and homework and of the shared nature of family enterprises, irrespective of patrilineal ownership. Yet the worth of the female contribution to the social processes of farming activities remains only partially appreciated. As central agents in cultivating reciprocal relationships both on the farm and within the rural community, farm women brokered both survival and success with a form of moral capital and a process of neighbouring. They thus became custodians of a rural culture which seemed antithetical to mercantile and industrial capitalism and as such was unAmerican. Yet farm women accepted life within a market-driven society. What they wanted from this society was not a return to rural self-sufficiency, but a lifestyle which prioritized kin relationships over individualism and a system which allowed women participation and recognition.[27]

Women's primary contributions to the social processes of farming lay in securing the intergenerational transfer of the farm and the stability of the family in the rural community. Though most farm women were formally marginalized by a patriarchal culture and a male inheritance pattern, they, as well as their menfolk, were concerned about the security of the family farm. Not only did they look after their own positions when their husbands died; they wanted to ensure that each child, female as well as male, could make a living. As a family concern, the farm unit should meet the needs of all family members and not just the father and the inheriting son.[28]

Historically, American farm women have obeyed their husbands or their sons. Though some independent women owned land and some widows ran farms while their children were still minors, most women had to bargain with their husbands for a share in family decision-making. Occasionally they used their domestic and housekeeping assets to secure influence. More often their particular economic value – whether in textile processing in the Philadelphia hinterland in the eighteenth century, in selling butter and eggs in the newly settled prairies in the mid-nineteenth century or in raising chickens and vegetables in Florida in the 1970s – provided leverage to persuade men to adopt specific paths. Yet even when buttressed by financial contributions, women frequently preferred to use their womanhood, either as wife or as mother, to negotiate social relations within the family. Much brokering focused on intergenerational transfer and revolved around husbands who were reluctant to share power even though their success was dependent on family contributions. Faced with sons anxious to participate in the running of farms, mothers frequently intervened. They either persuaded them to accept a lengthy apprenticeship to paternal authority, coaxed fathers to grant them more autonomy or gave up their own partnership role to make a place for their children. Accustomed to patriarchy, mothers preferred to be displaced as managers than to see children leaving the community.[29]

This familial brokerage could take different forms. The family farm might provide a living for the family and subsequently for one or two sons, but it was too small to be divided between all the children.[30] Women thus sought to endow their other children with a bequest which would give them an equal or better start than that which they themselves possessed on their marriage. Such a bequest could take the form of nearby land if available. Alternatively, it could be a dowry or training for gainful employment. Throughout much of the nineteenth century, cash in hand for native-born sons eased acquisition of a farm if they moved west where land was more abundant and cheaper. For daughters, a dowry or training in farm skills could facilitate marriage into a neighbouring farming family. The provision of education rather than a dowry enabled some farm daughters to become teachers. On marriage they might return to the farming community or move to a nearby town from where they could maintain contact with the family.[31]

Farm women, whether native-born or immigrant, could only be successful in building connections within rural communities if they belonged to the land-owning minority. Then they lived and worked together for many years inter-marrying and passing on their improved lands to their children. More women, however, were likely to be part of the land-hungry majority who were geographically mobile. As wives of propertyless sons or farmers who failed, they migrated to new lands in the west. There they hoped to acquire rather than to rent farms, or to build larger farms which would better provide for their families. If they succeeded they would remain in the newer settling west. If they failed they could move further west again in search of land or they could move into cities in search of alternative employment. Many mobile farm wives struggled alongside their would-be-owner or tenant-husbands to eke a living from the land, and their social functions lay more in surviving than in providing for their children's future.[32]

In the mid-twentieth century the family farm both increased in size and competed with agribusiness. In this more impersonal and less labour-intensive arena women strove for more flexible arrangements to enable their children to make a living in the rural community. Initially, daughters left the farm sooner than sons because cultural values still favoured male inheritance and males were better able to attain the specialized skills which were necessary to modern farm management. More recently, with equal rights, daughters have claimed a share in the family farm. In this situation, families adopted ways of co-ordinating the on and off-farm activities of several members. Kin ties and working relationships with neighbours also enabled farming interests to be merged in a variety of small, but profitable ways.[33]

In the wider social arena of the rural community, farm households often depended on 'exchanges' for both their livelihood and their way of life. Here women used their negotiating skills to barter for or to transact an exchange of resources, including labour, and to build or retain a rural culture. Neighbouring or developing reciprocal relationships were significant ways of making farming viable and ones which have become more visible since the advent of oral history.[34]

In the formal economy men reciprocated with neighbours on commercial terms. Sharing a reaper or working together to slaughter farm animals or raise barns could be assigned a specific value at current prices. Yet such an exchange still required the cooperation of women both in being available as extra labour for specific periods of time and in being willing to feed and support a larger temporary work force. The exchange of auxiliary work and hospitality created a community in which men and women contributed in different, but integrated ways to the running of the farm.[35]

In the informal community the social interactions of female visiting and mutual aid was important in sustaining many farms both during the early years of development and in maturity. Indeed women provided a 'moral capital' in their womanly nurturing. For example, in the Nanticoke Valley of western New York in the nineteenth century and in the Midwest of the early twentieth century women exchanged help with female kin and neighbours in tasks ranging from gardening, through canning and dressmaking to child and sick-care. This work-sharing was important not only because it enabled women to accomplish tasks efficiently and to keep farm running costs low, but also because it broke the monotony of daily routine and moderated the isolation of household work. Indeed in hard times neighbouring became a type of social security system for families on small farms. They felt that they could barter informally for assistance and make repayments and could thus avoid going into financial debt.[36]

This swapping of help was consolidated into a rural culture by visiting neighbours socially and by celebrating family or national occasions. Participation in life transitions like birth and death strengthened economic assistance by building emotional ties. Help during pregnancy and at childbirth was a specifically female-centred neighbouring, but death and sickness could often involve men in 'lending a hand'. Extended visits during periods of ill-health or economic crises showed further rural solidarity. Celebrations, like birthday parties, weddings, school graduations or Christmases, which often involved giving gifts, provided other opportunities for women to maintain ties through rituals. Such reciprocity, bonded not only adults of both sexes, but also socialized children into community awareness.[37] Women's skills in creating links within and across gender lines and between families and generations were significant contributions to enhancing the quality of rural life, especially before the spread of mass communications and rural electrification.[38]

Informal neighbouring was often institutionalized in schools and churches or in farm organizations. Though originating out of a need to provide children with education and to have some spiritual and moral fellowship, schools and churches often served as centres for social and cultural activities. From these institutions women organized events like Sunday school picnics or Christmas programmes which often linked entire communities. On a broader level, farm groups like the Grange in the 1870s, the Farmers' Alliances in the 1880s, the Populists in the 1890s or the Farmer's Union in the early twentieth century depended on the energies of both sexes. Women's contributions focused on community-building functions like providing food and entertainment for meetings. Besides sustaining occasions where agrarian politics could be fully discussed, women, as members and potential office-holders also became involved in the largely male world of politics.[39] Farm women may not have had formal power in rural society prior to female suffrage or have wielded much thereafter, but they had long developed a variety of social bases from which they could exercise influence.

Not all rural women were involved in neighbouring, nor was neighbouring all inclusive. Length of residence, economic or tenure status, ethnicity, religion and race often created barriers to the formation of communities. Those who did not belong to rural networks, like the native-born Americans in ethnic enclaves or those who had few resources, like share-croppers, encountered more difficulties in exchanging goods and services and in remaining on the land. Then, as agriculture became more complex and impersonal and farm communities were drawn more into consumerism, in the mid-twentieth century, farm women modified some of their gendered work patterns. A higher commitment to gainful employment, whether on or off the farm, lessened the time available for filling in as auxiliary farm labour, for rural outwork and for voluntary and non-cash activities. The balance of the triple work load and of the social activities of neighbouring changed, but women's farm contributions remained essential.

Conclusion

Much research and writing remain to be tackled in the revision of the female rural past in the USA. Regional variations have worked against the creation of any major theoretical frameworks. The multicultural dimensions of the non-Euro-American presence remains hidden, while the differential impact of technology and financial arrangements are barely uncovered. Many more case studies are needed to explore the diversity of women's farming experiences. Yet a quarter century of women's and gendered research has already brought American women from the periphery to the centre of agricultural history.

Notes

1. Faragher, John M. (1986), *Sugar Creek. Life on the Illinois Prairie*, New Haven: Yale University Press, pp. 99, 101.
2. Craig, Lee A. (1993), *To Sow One Acre More. Childbearing and Farm Productivity in the Antebellum North*, Baltimore: Johns Hopkins University Press, pp. 79, 81.
3. Gates, Paul W. (1960), *The Farmer's Age: Agriculture, 1815–1860*, New York: Holt, Rinehart and Winston; Shannon, Fred A. (1961), *The Farmer's Last Frontier: Agriculture, 1860–1897*, New York: Holt, Rinehart and Winston; and Cochrane, Willard W. (1979), *The Development of American Agriculture. A Historical Analysis*, Minneapolis: University of Minnesota Press.
4. Sachs, Carolyn E. (1983), *The Invisible Farmers. Women in Agricultural Production*, Totowa, NJ: Rowman & Allanhead.
5. More recent surveys of American agriculture acknowledge women's presence by adding in paragraphs or sections on the home and home products. See, for example, Hurt, R. Douglas (1994), *American Agriculture. A Brief History*, Ames: Iowa State University Press; and Danbom, David B. (1995), *Born in the Country. A History of Rural America*, Baltimore: Johns Hopkins University Press.
6. For insights into gender roles in farming see Garceau, Dee (1997), *The Important*

Things of Life: Women, Work and Family in Sweetwater County, Wyoming, 1880–1929, Lincoln: University of Nebraska Press; McMurray, Sally (1995), *Transforming Rural Life. Dairying Families and Agricultural Change, 1820–1885*, Baltimore: Johns Hopkins University Press; Neth, Mary (1995), *Preserving the Family Farm. Women, Community, and the Foundations of Agribusiness in the Midwest, 1900–1940*, Baltimore: Johns Hopkins University Press; Osterud, Nancy G. (1991), *Bonds of Community. The Lives of Farm Women in Nineteenth Century New York*, Ithaca: Cornell University Press; and Osterud, Nancy G. (1993), 'Gender and the Transition to Capitalism in Rural America', *Agricultural History*, **67** (2), 14–29.

7. Craig, *To Sow One Acre More*, p. 52; Rosenfeld, Rachel A. (1985), *Farm Women. Work, Farm and Family in the United States*, Chapel Hill: University of North Carolina Press, p. 12; Hurt, *American Agriculture*, p. 395.

8. Jeffrey, Julie R. (1979), *Frontier Women. The Trans-Mississippi West, 1840–1880*, New York: Hill and Wang, p. 54; Gladwin, Christina H. (1985), 'Values and Goals of Florida Farm Women: Do They Help the Family Farm Survive?', *Agriculture and Human Values*, **II** (1), 40–7.

9. Historians of the American West have drawn on numerous diaries and letters to document women's domestic work on pioneer farms. See, for example, Jeffrey, *Frontier Women*, pp. 51–78; Myres, Sandra L. (1982), *Westering Women and the Frontier Experience, 1800–1915*, Albuquerque: University of New Mexico Press, pp. 141–66; Riley, Glenda (1988), *The Female Frontier. A Comparative View of Women on the Prairie and the Plains*, Lawrence: University Press of Kansas, pp. 42–101; Stratton, Joanna L. (1981), *Voices from the Kansas Frontier*, New York: Simon and Schuster, pp. 57–76; Webb, Anne (1986), 'Forgotten Persephones: Women Farmers on the Frontier', *Minnesota History*, **50** (Winter), 134–58; and Schweider, Dorothy (1980), 'Labor and Economic Roles of Iowa Farm wives, 1840–80', in Peterson, Trudy H. (ed.), *Farmers, Bureaucrats and Middlemen. Historical Perspectives on American Agriculture*, Washington, DC, Howard University Press, pp. 155–9. Social and rural historians have placed women's household work in a pre-capitalist framework for earlier years and other parts of the country. See, for example, Faragher, *Sugar Creek*, pp. 77–118; Clark, Christopher (1990), *The Roots of Rural Capitalism. Western Massachusetts, 1780–1860*, Ithaca: Cornell University Press, pp. 121–55; and Jensen, Joan M. (1986), *Loosening the Bonds. Mid-Atlantic Farm Women, 1750–1850*, New Haven: Yale University Press.

10. For a discussion on under-enumeration of women's outwork and part-time work in the US Census see Goldin, Claudia (1990), *Understanding the Gender Gap. An Economic History of American Women*, New York: Oxford University Press, pp. 219–27.

11. Jensen, *Loosening the Bonds*, pp. 79–112; Clark, *Roots of Rural Capitalism*, pp. 139–55; Faragher, *Sugar Creek*, pp. 104–5; Myres, *Westering Women*, pp. 159–60; Riley, *The Female Frontier*, pp. 118–19, 146; Schweider, 'Land and Economic Roles', pp. 161–4; Craig, *To Sow One Acre More*, pp. 37–42; Jensen, Joan (1980), 'Cloth, Butter and Boarders: Women's Household Production for the Market', *The Review of Radical Political Economics*, **12** (2), 14–24.

12. Craig, *To Sow One Acre More*, pp. 53–92; Jensen, *Loosening the Bonds*, pp. 36–56; Myres, *Westering Women*, pp. 162–4; Riley, *The Female Frontier*, pp. 117–18, 132; Faragher, *Sugar Creek*, p. 101.

13. Osterud, *Bonds of Community*, pp. 139–58; Garceau, *The Important Things of Life*, pp. 89–111.

146

14. Bauman, Paula M. (1986), 'Single Women Homesteaders In Wyoming, 1880–1930', *Annals of Wyoming*, **58** (Spring), 48; Effland, Anne B., Rogers, Denise M. and Grim, Valerie (1993), 'Women as Agricultural Landowners: What Do We Know About them?', *Agricultural History*, **67** (2), 260. In northeastern Colorado, Katherine Harris found that before 1900 between 10 and 13 per cent of homestead entries were made by women; after 1900 the proportion rose to 18 per cent. Harris, Katherine (1993), *Long Vistas: Women and Families on Colorado Homesteads*, Niwot: University Press of Colorado, p. 158.

15. Webb, Anne, (1989), 'Minnesota Women Homesteaders: 1863–1889', *Journal of Social History*, **23** (1), 115–36; Bauman, 'Single Women Homesteaders', pp. 39–49; Harris, *Long Vistas*; Peterson-Black, Sheryll (1976), 'Women Homesteaders on the Great Plains Frontier', *Frontiers*, **1** (Spring), 67–88; Effland, Rogers, and Grim, 'Women as Agricultural Landowners', pp. 235–61; Sachs, *The Invisible Farmers*, pp. 77–117. See also George, Susan K. (ed.) (1992), *The Adventures of the Woman Homesteader. The Life and Letters of Elinore Pruitt Stewart*, Lincoln: University of Nebraska Press.

16. Cashin, Joan E. (1991), *A Family Venture. Men and Women on the Southern Frontier*, New York: Oxford University Press; Fox-Genovese, Elizabeth (1988), *Within the Plantation Household: Black and White Women of the Old South*, Chapel Hill: University of North Carolina Press.

17. hooks, bell (1982), *Ain't I A Woman! Black Women and Feminism* (1992 edn), London: Pluto Press, pp. 15–49; White, Deborah G. (1985), *Ar'n't I a Woman? Female Slaves in the Plantation South*, New York: Norton, pp. 91–118; Jones, Jacqueline (1985), *Labor of Love, Labor of Sorrow. Black Women, Work and the Family From Slavery to the Present*, New York: Basic Books, pp. 11–43; Stirling, Dorothy (ed.) (1984), *We are Your Sisters. Black Women in the Nineteenth Century*, pp. 13–17; White, Deborah G. (1983), 'Female Slaves: Sex Roles and Status in the Antebellum South', reprinted in DuBois Carol E. and Ruiz, Vicki L. (eds) (1990), *Unequal Sisters. A Multicultural Reader in U.S. Women's History*, New York: Routledge, pp. 22–33.

18. For discussions of the crop-lien system in the postbellum South see Ransom, Roger L. and Sutch, Richard (1977), *One Kind of Freedom: The Economic Consequences of Emancipation*, Cambridge: Cambridge University Press; Fite, Gilbert (1984), *Cotton Fields No More. Southern Agriculture 1865–1980*, Lexington: University Press of Kentucky, pp. 1–29.

19. Jones, *Labor of Love*, pp. 79–109; Janiewski, Delores, E. (1985), *Sisterhood Denied. Race, Gender and Class in a New South Community*, Philadelphia: Temple University Press, pp. 27–54; Fite, *Cotton Fields*, pp. 45–6.

20. Not all wives and daughters accompanied their husbands and fathers to the fields because Mexican and Mexican American women were more employable as domestics or in factories than were their male kin. See Gonzalez, Rosalinda M. (1983), 'Chicanas and Mexican Immigrant Families 1920–1940: Women's Subordination and Family Exploitation', in Scharf, Lois and Jensen, Joan M. (eds), *Decades of Discontent. The Women's Movement 1920–1940*, Westport: Greenwood Press, pp. 66–8; Blackwelder, Julia K. (1997), *Now Hiring. The Feminization of Work in the United States*, College Station: Texas A&M University Press, pp. 71–2.

21. Gonzalez, 'Chicanas and Mexican Immigrant', pp. 61–6; Jasso, Sonia and Mazorra, Maria (1984), 'Following the Harvest: The Health Hazards of Migrant and Seasonal Farmworking Women', in Chavkin, Wendy (ed.), *Double Exposure. Women's Health Hazards on the Job*, New York: Monthly Press,

pp. 86–90; Weber, Devra A. (1989), 'Raiz Fuerte: Oral History and Mexicana, Farmworkers', reprinted in Ruiz and DuBois (1994), *Unequal Sisters* (second edition), pp. 395–404. See also Daniels, Cletus E. (1981), *Bitter Harvest. A History of California Farmworkers, 1870–1941*, Berkeley: University of California Press; and McWilliams, Carey (1942), *Ill Fares the Land. Migrants and Migratory Labor in the United States* (1976 reprint), New York: Arno Reprints.

22. Craig, *To Sow One Acre More*, pp. 67–73; Osterud, *Bonds of Community*, pp. 139–86, 202–27; Osterud, Nancy G. (1988), 'The Valuation of Women's Work: Gender and the Market in a Dairy Farming Community during the Late Nineteenth Century', *Frontiers*, **10** (2), 18–24; McMurray, *Transforming Rural Life*. Christine Kleinegger suggests that the barn and yard site might be called an androgynous zone. She also considers that a male 'take-over' might be called masculinization. Kleinegger, Christine (1987), 'Out of the Barns and into the Kitchens: Transformations of Farm Women's Work in the First Half of the Twentieth Century', in Wright, Barbara D. et al. (eds), *Women, Work and Technology, Transformations*, Ann Arbor: University of Michigan Press, pp. 163, 169.

23. Craig, *To Sow One Acre More*, pp. 101–3 uses externalization in preference to modernization to capture the process of social change whereby farming families turned outwards beyond the family and local community to interact with a widening network of social and economic institutions.

24. Bush, Corlann G. (1986), 'The Barn is His, The House is Mine. Agricultural Technology and Sex Roles', in Daniels, George H. and Rose, Mark H. (eds), *Energy and Transport. Historical Perspectives on Policy Issues*, Beverley Hills: Sage Publications, pp. 235–59; Jellison, Katherine (1993), *Entitled to Power. Farm Women and Technology, 1919–1969*, Chapel Hill: University of North Carolina Press; Jellison, Katherine (1988), 'Women And Technology on the Great Plains, 1910–40', *Great Plains Quarterly*, **8** (Summer), 145–57; Colman, Gould and Elbert, Sarah (1984), 'Farming Families: The Farm Needs Everyone', *Research in Rural Sociology and Development*, **1**, 61–78 and Sachs, Caroline F. (1988), 'The Participation of Women and Girls In Market and Non-Market Activities on Pennsylvania Farms', in Haney and Knowles (eds), *Women and Farming*, pp. 123–34. Most discussions about the hours spent in housework have focused on urban women. See, for example, Vanek, Joanne (1979), 'Time Spent in Housework', in Cott, Nancy F. and Pleck, Elizabeth H. (eds), *A Heritage of Her Own. Towards A New Social History of American Women*, New York: Simon and Schuster, pp. 499–50 and Cowan, Ruth S. (1983), *More Work For Mother. The Ironies of Household Technology from the Open Hearth to the Microwave*, New York: Pantheon Books.

25. Boulding, Elise (1980), 'The Labor of U.S. Farm Women. A Knowledge Gap', *Sociology of Work and Occupations*, **8** (3), 278–81; Fink, Deborah (1986), *Open Country, Iowa. Rural Women, Tradition and Change*, Albany: SUNY Press, pp. 161–97; Gladwin, 'Values and Goals', p. 41.

26. Fink, *Open Country*, pp. 161–97; Gladwin, 'Values and Goals', pp. 42–3; Boulding, 'The Labor of U.S. Women', pp. 278–81; Rosenfeld, Rachel A. (1985), *Farm Women. Work, Farm and Family in the United States*, Chapel Hill: University of North Carolina Press, pp. 52–97, 141–85; Elbert, Sarah (1987), 'The Farmer Takes a Wife: Women in America's Farming Families', in Beneria, Lourdes and Stimpson, Catherine R. (eds), *Women, Households and the Economy*, New Brunswick, NJ: Rutgers University Press, pp. 187–91; Kohl,

Seena B. (1977), 'Women's Participation in the North American Family Farm', *Women's Studies International Quarterly*, **1**, 48–50; Salamon, Sonya (1992), *Prairie Patrimony. Family, Farming and Community in the Midwest*, Chapel Hill: University of North Carolina Press, pp. 131–6.

27. Fink, Deborah (1988), 'Sidelines and Moral Capital: Women on Nebraska Farms in the 1930s', in Haney, Wava and Knowles, Jane (eds), *Women and Farming. Changing Roles, Changing Structures*, Boulder: Westview Press, pp. 55–70; Neth, Mary (1980), 'Building the Base: Farm Women, The Rural Community and Farm Organizations in the Midwest, 1900–1940', in Haney and Knowles, *Women and Farming*, pp. 339–55; Barron, Hal. S. (1985), 'Staying Down on the Farm. Social Processes of Settled Rural Life in the Nineteenth Century North', in Hahn, Steven and Prude Jonathan (eds), *The Countryside in the Age of Capitalist Transformation. Essays in the Social History of Rural America*, Chapel Hill: University of North Carolina Press, pp. 327–43. See also Barron, Hal. S. (1997), *Mixed Harvest. The Second Great Transformation in the Rural North, 1870–1930*, Chapel Hill: University of North Carolina Press, for a fuller discussion of how northern country people adapted to and rejected some of the national corporate culture.

28. Colman and Elbert, 'Farming Families', pp. 65–6. Mark Friedberger discusses the problems of documenting inheritance practices in rural America in Friedberger, Mark (1983), 'The Family Farm and the Inheritance Process: Evidence from the Corn-Belt, 1870–1950', *Agricultural History*, **57** (1), 1–13.

29. Colman and Elbert, 'Farming Families', p. 69; Jensen, *Loosening the Bonds*, pp. 49–50, Myres, *Westering Women*, pp. 158–60; Riley, *The Female Frontier*, pp. 118–19, 146; Gladwin, 'Values and Goals', p. 41.

30. Women's brokerage was connected to family size, sex of children and cultural values. Historians have more often estimated fertility rates and migration patterns than they have examined persistence in rural communities and the transmission of inheritance patterns from settled parts of the USA or from Europe. For discussions of fertility issues see Craig, *To Sow One Acre More*, pp. 1–26, 93–105; Easterlin, Richard A. (1976), 'Factors in the Decline of Farm Fertility in the United States: Some Preliminary Results', *Journal of American History*, **63** (3), 600–14; Leet, Don R. (1975), 'Human Fertility and Agricultural Opportunities in Ohio Counties: From Frontier to Maturity, 1810–1860', in Kingaman, David C. and Vedder, Richard K. (eds), *Essays in Nineteenth Century Economic History: The Old Northwest*, Athens: Ohio University Press, pp. 138–58; and Atack, Jeremy and Bateman, Fred (1987), *To Their Own Soil. Agriculture in the Antebellum North*, Ames: Iowa State University Press, pp. 49–70. For persistence see Barron, Hal. S. (1984), *Those Who Stayed Behind. Rural Society in Nineteenth Century New England*, New York: Cambridge University Press, pp. 78–111; Jensen, *Loosening the Bonds*, pp. 18–35; and Clark, *Roots of Rural Capitalism*, pp. 121–55. For ethnic differences see Conzen, Kathleen N. (1985), 'Peasant Pioneers. Generational Change Among German Farmers in Frontier Minnesota', in Hahn and Prude (eds), *The Countryside in the Age*, pp. 259–92.

31. Salamon, *Prairie Patrimony*, pp. 138–79; Clark, *Roots of Rural Capitalism*, p. 91: quoting Ditz, Toby L. (1986), *Property and Kinship: Inheritance in Early Connecticut, 1759–1820*, Princeton: Princeton University Press, 1986, pp. 158–60; McMurray, *Transforming Rural Life*, pp. 100–22; Osterud, *Bonds of Community*, pp. 53–85.

32. Craig, *To Sow One Acre More*; Faragher, *Sugar Creek*, p. 145.

33. Colman and Elbert, 'Farming Families'.

34. Neth, 'Building the Base', and Neth, *Preserving the Family Farm*, use the term 'neighbouring' to describe supportive systems of repeated exchanges and social interactions. Women were the primary organizers of this informal social world.
35. Neth, *Preserving the Family Farm*, pp. 40–70; Bush, Corlann G. (1987), 'He Ain't So Cranky as He Used to Be', in Groneman, Carol and Norton, Mary Beth (eds), *'To Toil the Livelong Day'. America's Women At Work, 1780–1890*, Ithaca: Cornell University Press, pp. 217–22; Danbom, *Born in the Country*, pp. 90–1; Faragher, *Sugar Creek*, pp. 130–6; Osterud, *Bonds of Community*, pp. 244–8.
36. Fink, 'Sidelines and Moral Capital', p. 55; Osterud, *Bonds of Community*, pp. 187–201; Neth, *Preserving the Family Farm*, pp. 40–70.
37. The social neighbourhood system is discussed in Neth, *Preserving the Family Farm* and in Osterud, *Bonds of Community*.
38. There is some debate about the breakdown of neighbouring and its community value system when automobiles, the radio and then the spread of rural electrification enabled rural Americans to more fully participate in consumerism. The full impact of these technologies was not felt in the countryside until after the Second World War. There is also some discussion about the impact of government policies and the Home Economics movement on promoting a rural gender division which conformed more to the ideology of separate spheres. See Barron, *Mixed Harvest*, pp. 193–241; Neth, *Preserving the Family Farm*, pp. 187–266; Elbert, Sarah (1988), 'Women and Farming: Changing Structures, Changing Roles', in Haney and Knowles, *Women and Farming*, pp. 245–64.
39. Neth, *Preserving the Family Farm*, pp. 68–70, 122–46; Osterud, *Bonds of Community*, pp. 249–74; Marti, Donald B. (1984), 'Sisters of the Grange: Rural Feminism in the Late Nineteenth Century', *Agricultural History*, **58** (3), pp. 247–61; Watkins, Marilyn P. (1993), 'Political Activism and Community-Building Among Alliance and Grange Women in Western Washington, 1892–1925', *Agricultural History*, **67** (2), 197–213; and Pratt, William C. (1993), 'Women and the Farm Revolt of the 1930s', *Agricultural History*, **67** (2), 214–23.

CHAPTER NINE

Gender and Technology: Inverting Established Patterns. The Lancashire Cotton Weaving Industry at the Start of the Twentieth Century

Jutta Schwarzkopf

In the interplay of gender and technology in the labour process, machinery has emerged as one, if not the most, important way of anchoring the allocation of tasks along gender lines. The particular usefulness of technical artefacts as markers of gender lies in the seemingly objective quality they bestow on what is in fact a social construction. Gendering of technology as a way of buttressing, or legitimizing a reversal of, the established allocation of jobs along gender lines occurred, for example, in cotton-spinning in the wake of mechanization,[1] in typesetting prior to computerization[2] or in office work following the introduction of the typewriter.[3] These few examples suffice to demonstrate that the relationship between technology and the gender-typing of jobs is by no means clear-cut, with machinery being able to be used as an argument for upgrading a given job and thereby claiming it as a male domain, as was the case in cotton spinning, or conversely for downgrading and relinquishing it to women, as happened in the transition from the male office clerk to the female typist.

The relation to specific technical items in which male and female workers are placed at particular historical junctures thus throws into relief the volatility of gender. The same technical features that allegedly show an affinity to femininity may in some other instance be linked to masculinity.[4] The fluidity of gender, as it is constructed and contested, reinforced and inverted, becomes particularly obvious when the established relationship between technology and gender in a given labour process is modified.

Such reconstruction of gender lies at the centre of this case study, which investigates the relationship between gender and technology in Lancashire cotton weaving in the decade prior to the First World War. Particular attention is paid both to the way in which employers tried to defuse trade union opposition to the introduction of new technology by proposing a special deal for their male workers and to the reasons why collusion between manufacturers and unions ultimately foundered. Established patterns of the relationship between gender and technology were inverted at three stages in the process: first, in Lancashire cotton weaving, machinery initially bore no gender connotation; second, the change-over to a new type of loom appeared to afford the opportunity for introducing a gender division of labour into this industry through collusion between employers and male weavers at the expense of women workers; finally, male collusion failed to materialize, because class-based notions of masculinity clashed with each other, and the desire to maximize profit overrode solidarity along gender lines.

To begin with the first stage: in Lancashire cotton weaving, men and women worked side by side on the same kind of machines, producing the same types of cloth and, most significantly, receiving the same rates of pay.[5] This marked degree of gender equality in the labour process was particularly characteristic of, but not necessarily confined to, the weaving districts in the north-east of the county. As a result, women weavers counted among the most highly paid groups of female workers,[6] while men were effectively paid a woman's wage. Hence, in order to make ends meet, weaving families were dependent on the joint earnings of husband and wife,[7] at least until older children had reached the age at which they could start work at the mill. Conditions in the industry thus militated against male authority both in the workplace and the home.[8] Relations of power in weaving families were largely shaped by the absence of a male breadwinner wage and wives' continued factory employment.

These conditions stemmed from women's consistent predominance in the industry since the onset of mechanization. The newly erected weaving sheds had been staffed mainly by female and infant workers, who were joined by men on any significant scale only when handloom weavers' resistance to the factory system had finally crumbled. To gain any foothold at all and subsequently to retain their jobs, men had had to insist on being paid the same as women.

Apart from receiving better wages than the majority of their peers, female cotton weavers were also unionized to a higher degree, their union membership reflecting their preponderance in the industry.[9] Yet despite women's numerical strength among the rank and file, officials were exclusively male, and they smarted under the inability of their membership to maintain their families without recourse to the earnings of kin, usually their own wives. Enmeshed as they were in the world of labour organizations with its strict code of respectability, to which highly segregated gender roles were central, union officials saw the large number of women weavers as a blemish on their trade. Thus in 1893 the editor of the *Cotton Factory Times*, the trade-union-friendly weekly targeted at the cotton workforce, asserted that:

> Weaving is not a branch of the cotton industry suitable for men to follow, simply because the wages to be earned are not sufficient to enable men to keep a home and bring up children as modern society requires. On an average, the earnings of a man weaver come under a pound a week, and any

152

one with experience in domestic life will admit that such a sum is quite
inadequate to meet the charges coming against a household.[10]

D.J. Shackleton, the President of the Northern Counties Amalgamated
Association of Weavers, deployed a similar argument when campaigning for
membership. In 1909, at a meeting at Shaw, near Oldham, he reputedly said he
would be pleased to see their own trade in Lancashire

> being carried on without work in the mill being a mother's choice or a
> mother's necessity. The men ought to take their proper places, and their
> women folk ought to demand their right to be kept out of the mill.[11]

Amalgamation officials, who operated at a regional and even national level,
were clearly dissatisfied with the failure of their male rank and file to fulfil their
role as breadwinners. By contrast local officials appear to have been primarily
concerned with safeguarding the family economy of their union members.[12]
Their acknowledgement of the vital role played by the earnings of wives for the
well-being of weaving families may well reflect the attitude of the male rank
and file. Yet this primary concern with living standards did not involve any
endorsement in principle of wives' right to work.

By the beginning of the twentieth century, an opportunity to invert the
established pattern of the weaving family's dependence on the combined
earnings of husband and wife appeared to present itself in the shape of the
so-called automatic, or Northrop, loom. This machine had been developed in
the USA by James Northrop, a machine designer with the company of George
Draper & Sons, and was commercially viable by 1894.[13] Its central feature, a
mechanism replacing empty with full bobbins in the shuttle without stopping
the loom, relieved weavers of the need to change shuttles manually, their main
and most time-consuming task, thereby significantly increasing their output.
After more than a century of working with the original powerloom design, the
Northrop represented a true innovation.

If employers were fully to exploit the labour-saving and hence cost-cutting
potential of the automatic loom, the labour process had to be fundamentally
re-organized.[14] This involved expanding the machine assignment per worker
beyond the four to six looms customary in Lancashire[15] and confining the job of
the loom operative to weaving proper, with all operations incidental to weaving
delegated to ancillary labour. It also necessitated adjusting the piece rates
downwards, because weavers could operate more machines and increase their
weekly earnings. In Lancashire, piece rates were laid down in agreed price lists,
which specified in minute detail the prices to be paid for each type of cloth. Such
price or wage lists had been pioneered in cotton weaving[16] and were, by the
closing decades of the nineteenth century, generally respected by employers, a
state of affairs which weaving unions then were strong enough to enforce.

153

Given the economic need for both the intensification of labour and alterations to the long-established price lists, manufacturers warily anticipated fierce trade union opposition to any attempt at introducing the new machines. As the *Textile Recorder*, a manufacturers' journal urging the need for technological innovation, opined in 1902:

> ... it is certain that, failing the willingness of the operatives, not only to acquiesce in, but also to aid in effecting a change in the present system of working a weaving shed, the adoption of looms of this type will be slow and halting.[17]

Those manufacturers intent on innovation were therefore at pains to dispel any fears that union officials and the rank and file might harbour about the new loom. Thus the *Textile Mercury*, a trade journal of cotton spinners and manufacturers, stressed that increasing global demand for cotton goods would enable the industry in Lancashire, now more competitive thanks to the Northrop loom, to absorb any weavers made redundant. Failing that, unemployment would be averted by a re-formation of the weaving workforce, where employment on the automatic looms was reserved for male weavers, who would receive a family wage.[18]

Put into place, this proposed de-feminization of the workforce, the second stage in the inversion of established patterns, would have amounted to a revolution in weaving. To enhance its acceptability, the scheme was discussed in the context of mounting national anxiety about population decline. It was presented as both an individual and a national advantage in that the relegation of married women weavers to the home would significantly reduce infant mortality.[19] Appealing to male anxieties arising from the large-scale employment of women, including wives, in cotton weaving, the *Textile Mercury* depicted the prospect of increased male authority in the following terms: 'By men becoming weavers and earning more money at the work than is possible at present, they will be able to take their proper place as the breadwinners of the family and keep their wives at home, which is their proper sphere.'[20] By focusing on their desire to relieve wives and mothers from the need to earn money, manufacturers glossed over the fact that male exclusivity on Northrop looms would eventually put all women weavers, regardless of marital status, out of work.

Employers could be certain that the prospect of a breadwinner wage would strike the right chord among union officials, if not their rank and file. The Northern Counties Amalgamation of Weavers had for a long time been concerned about the fragility of male weavers' headship of the family, which stemmed from the negligible differential between male and female earnings in the weaving industry. Pleas for a breadwinner wage can be traced back at least to 1878 when 100 000 North Lancashire operatives stayed out for two

154

months in an abortive attempt to ward off a reduction in pay.[21] In 1892 the absence of a family wage was cited as one of the deplorable conditions in the industry by Amalgamation representatives appearing as witnesses before the Royal Commission on Labour. Then, David Wilkinson, speaking on the organization's behalf, asserted:

> I think the husband, the head of the family, ought to be able to keep his wife at home to look after her household duties, and that he ought to earn as much as would keep the family in a satisfactory condition.[22]

The attraction of making automatic weaving a male preserve, the improvements in men's status and the buttressing of male authority in both the workplace and the home proved wellnigh irresistible. In contrast to powerloom weaving, which was considered semi-skilled mainly because of its large constituency among women, the new loom opened up the long-term possibility of claiming that weaving was skilled work. Intricately bound up with masculinity as it was, such skilled work would rightfully be the domain of men, and their masculinity would be further enhanced by their ability to earn a family wage without any recourse to a secondary female income. While male handloom weavers had responded to mechanization by holding out as long as possible against submission to factory discipline, male powerloom operatives appeared to be determined to use machines at this stage of technological development to their advantage. The Northrop loom would be given a masculine connotation, and automatic weaving would become a male preserve. Moreover such a gender division of labour according to the type of machine operated would enable male weavers on automatics to shroud their work in 'craft mystery', in very much the same way as did members of skilled trades. Such a status was denied them in powerloom weaving, because men and women performed identical work.

If male weavers could see a double advantage to accepting the automatic loom, employers incurred a considerable risk. By promising to tie the introduction of the new loom to payment of a family wage, they provided workers with the yardstick by which conditions for the use of the Northrop would be measured. Unions would insist on the size of the machine assignment and the corresponding cuts in prices staying within limits that they deemed reasonable.[23] These conditions were thrashed out in the protracted struggle with the firm which pioneered the automatic loom in Lancashire.

The concern of Ashton Brothers at Hyde, east of Manchester, differed from the average cotton weaving enterprise in several ways, which made it particularly suited to technological innovation on a large scale. Non-membership of the employers' association[24] removed any restriction upon the firm's wish to experiment with new technology and new ways of organizing the labour process. Moreover, the firm specialized in the production of plain goods – drills for China and shirting and sheeting for the domestic market. Not only were the early Northrop looms particularly suited for the making of this class of cloth,[25] but competition from cotton cloth produced on automatic looms in the USA was also keenest in the lower qualities of goods exported to China.[26] Furthermore, since the early nineteenth century, and quite exceptional by Lancashire standards, the firm had been vertically integrated, making textile goods from spinning through to finishing and marketing these goods. Finally Ashton Brothers prided themselves on having consistently been in the vanguard of technological innovation.[27]

Thus in May 1902 Ashton Brothers installed 500 Northrops in their Throstle Bank Mill, with the first of these going into operation on 24 September of that year.[28] Previously the firm had sought assurance from Amalgamation representatives that the organization would do nothing to impede the adoption of the new looms. It had, however, at the same time been warned that acquiescence was conditional upon the weavers concerned being satisfied with conditions and wages.[29] Both issues were to remain contentious for some time.

Contrary to their original intention and despite their professed belief in the primacy of women's domestic role, Ashton Brothers had not refused employment on the new loom to women. In this they claimed to act out of loyalty to their existing workforce.[30] The 500 Northrops were allocated to 50 female weavers at the rate of 10 wide and 12 narrow ones per operative.[31] They used weft that had been spun on mules into packages which had to be skewered through with a metal prong[32] for use in the shuttles of the Northrop loom. Furthermore, weavers filled their own batteries, from which shuttles were replenished, and wove coarse cloth.[33]

These conditions of labour and the attendant pay rates failed to satisfy the female weavers set to work on the new looms. Rather than negotiate terms of employment with the Amalgamation, the firm preferred dealing with their workforce directly. In this way they avoided any undue interference by outsiders.[34] Union recognition was thus added to the list of grievances that was slowly building up. Even so Ashton Brothers procrastinated for two years, and only the threat of strike action by the female Northrop operatives pressured the firm finally to agree to meet personally with the Amalgamation representatives – all previous exchange having been by letter. The compromise worked out by both parties was unanimously accepted by the weavers as a temporary settlement for 12 months.[35] Under the terms of the compromise, the firm slightly increased the rates of pay. More importantly this increase was a time wage rather than a piece rate, which, though it relieved Northrop weavers of some of the strain imposed by the machine assignment, left that assignment the same. However strain was further reduced by the supply of better material, which was less likely to break and require mending, and by the employment of one spare worker per 100 looms to help mend faulty places in the cloth and fill the batteries. Furthermore, a boy was taken on to keep the looms supplied with weft.[36]

Yet when the twelve-month trial period was up, the firm reverted from the standing wage to piece rates, which the weavers only accepted 'under protest', feeling that their working conditions had not improved.[37] They still had to operate more looms than they felt able to cope with and make do with inferior qualities of yarn, while their earnings failed to reflect the arduous nature of their job. Moreover, the aspect of Ashton Brothers' Throstle Bank Mill in October 1904 drove home the impact of the new technology on the industry's workforce. Where previously 300 weavers had tended 700 ordinary looms, now 77 weavers tended 800 Northrops. Given the size of the firm and its determination to make the new loom a success, the workers made redundant had been found employment either at the firm's other mills or as ancillary labour about the Northrops.[38] Nevertheless, many issues remained unresolved in the initial use of the new loom.

Exasperated by the firm's refusal to improve conditions substantially, in October 1904 the female weavers together with the operatives in the preparatory departments at Throstle Bank Mill walked out, causing the workers in the mill's other departments to be locked out.[39] Women recognized the need to take a stand on the introduction of new technology as expressed by Ada Nield Chew from the Women's Trade Union League when addressing the audience at a popular concert in support of the Northrop weavers' strike. After lauding the women weavers for their high degree of unionization, she pointed to the significance of the strike as setting a precedent for the entire industry. She thus called on the women to resist tyranny and injustice and pledged their union's support.[40] The exhortative slant of her speech did less than justice to the fact that women as England's pioneer workers on the automatic loom had shown a great deal of courage and determination in their consistent refusal to be browbeaten by their employer. Throughout they had displayed a marked degree of awareness of their role as forerunners in shaping the conditions under which the Northrop was to be operated in England. Unfortunately Ada Nield Chew's promise of trade union support proved to be in vain.

Given the local importance of the firm as one of Hyde's major employers – roughly one-half of the district's cotton operatives worked for Ashton Brothers[41] – the mayor felt that the strike was sufficiently serious to act as a mediator between both parties. He managed to bring about a compromise within three days.[42] The speedy ending of the strike was helped by the fact that the dispute occurred during a boom period for cotton cloth.[43] The wages offered by the firm were deemed entirely satisfactory, but the number of looms per operative remained a contentious issue.[44] Weavers were allowed to exchange a set of 12 for one of 10 looms if they wanted,[45] but they did so to the detriment of their weekly earnings.

Undeterred by the opposition they had encountered from their female weavers on automatic looms, Ashton Brothers pressed ahead, replacing ordinary looms with Northrop looms and putting into place their original scheme of confining work on these machines in future to men. The type of automatics allocated to male weavers were able to use weft as it had been spun onto wooden bobbins on ring-spinning machines. Thus there was no need to rewind yarn for use in the shuttle, as was the case on ordinary looms. Moreover, bobbin weft was more resistant to breakage than mule-spun yarn and required no skewering.[46] Each male weaver was allocated 20 looms,[47] wove cloth of medium fineness and had helpers to fill their batteries as part of the firm's quest to maximize output from the new machines. Henceforth the firm focused its efforts on increasing productivity on the bobbin looms, tentatively expanding the machine assignment to 24 machines per weaver. But when the trial period had expired, the male weavers unanimously decided to revert to 20.[48]

As interviews with workers who switched to Northrops in the interwar period have shown, weavers strongly resented the intensification of labour and the feeling of competitiveness among the workforce consequent on the introduction of the automatic.[49] Additionally, they considered that the new technology undermined their knowledge and skill. The size of the machine assignment rendered it impossible for workers to be familiar with each loom. Furthermore, the automatic did not allow any of the manual adjustments required on the ordinary looms. Thus weavers were frustrated because of their lack of control over the quality of the cloth they produced, which was consequently poor.[50] The strain and resentment experienced by the weavers in the interwar years were probably similar to those suffered by their predecessors early in the century. Moreover, the deeply engrained habit of watching for broken threads, although obviated by the warp-stop motion attached to the Northrop, died hard.[51] Such change of custom noticeably increased the mental strain under which weavers on the automatic were labouring.

By contrast, the firm considered that the introduction of the Northrops had been a resounding success. By October 1907 Ashton Brothers claimed that 790 of these looms were running satisfactorily,[52] not least because of their ability to use bobbin weft as it came from the firm's own spinning department.[53] In a self-congratulatory lecture on the Northrop's introduction, A.M. Fletcher, the company's managing director, told the Lancashire section of the British Association of Managers of Textile Works that after initial difficulties the workpeople had become proud of being Northrop weavers. He smugly asserted that the firm had effected a revolution in the weaving trade with a stoppage of only two and a half days and proceeded to extol the advantages of the new looms. In the first place the Northrops had enabled the firm to dispense with some of their married women workers, because the men employed on the new looms, who earned 25 per cent more than before, were able to maintain their

158

wives at home. This was a development to be warmly welcomed, because married women's factory work caused a high rate of infant mortality. Secondly the Northrop rendered Britain more competitive in the cotton trade.[54]

As Fletcher knew well, this favourable view was strongly contested by the Northrop weavers back at Hyde, who remained dissatisfied with conditions of work and pay. Their stubborn refusal to submit to the conditions imposed by management appeared to him as an indication of the machine-breaking attitude harboured by operatives and trade union officials. He alleged that

> when the workpeople and others who were prejudiced against any invention that was intended to do away with the old order of things heard that the looms were on the way to Hyde, they declared that they would never reach England, and that if they did they would be broken up and thrown in the cut.

By contrast the *Cotton Factory Times*, speaking for trade union officials, refuted this allegation and reiterated that

> [t]he underlying principles actuating their policy, as representatives and guardians of the workpeople's interest, have been a desire to bring about the transition as amicably as possible, consistent with the indisputable right of their clients to have a voice in saying what was a reasonable number of looms a weaver should run, and what should be considered a reasonable rate of remuneration.[55]

Fletcher may therefore have vented management's frustration with workers' obstinacy. The directors of the firm took what can be described as an enlightened paternalist attitude towards their employees.[56] Such paternalism was premised on the assumption that management knew best what was most conducive to workers' benefit.

At Hyde, meanwhile, dissatisfaction among weavers lingered on. The size of the machine assignment, the level of wages and the speed at which looms were running remained contentious issues.[57] In the union's view the conditions imposed by Ashton Brothers nullified the firm's intention to pay their male weavers a family wage. Yet the firm refused to budge, consistently arguing that any agreement would be premature until the potential of the new loom and its workers had been fully tested.[58]

Exasperated, the union, in 1908, finally balloted its members at all of Ashton Brothers' mills about strike action. Despite the small number of weavers immediately affected – 47 men altogether – the ballot was overwhelmingly in favour of a stoppage.[59] Thus Hyde lived up to its reputation of being among the most highly unionized districts of the Amalgamation of Weavers.[60] The solid support for strike action was based on weavers' concern about family income. To earn a breadwinner's wage on the rates paid by Ashton Brothers required a level of exertion which the operatives found unacceptable. Furthermore, the lack of alternative female employment locally increased the threat to weaving families' standard of living.

In what was presumably a last attempt to avert industrial action just prior to the strike being called, the firm printed a circular which was addressed to all its weavers. It here claimed to have introduced vastly superior conditions of work on automatic as compared to conventional looms and 'hoped to accomplish what [they] had in view, namely that a married man could on 25 Northrop looms, keep his wife at home'.[61] This position was reiterated in an interview which a representative of the firm gave to a local newspaper. He painted a picture of the Northrop as enabling 'a man to keep his wife at home, and ... secur[ing] that comfort which is impossible where both husband and wife go to the shed'. He further repeated that the firm had never dismissed any 'man' in consequence of introducing the new looms, obviously implying that only women would be laid off, and, given the potentially high wages to be earned, there was nothing to fear from the innovation.[62]

The Amalgamation's bid for a breadwinner wage for male weavers provoked an ambivalent response from the local community. The union initially faced considerable hostility, and this even extended to the Trades Council.[63] To many outsiders, the difference between the rates paid by the firm and those demanded by the union appeared to be negligible. They were certainly not enough to warrant a strike, which hit the local economy hard at a time when there was already a good deal of slack even at working mills.[64] Shopkeepers were thus among the most vociferous opponents of the strike. Moreover Ashton Brothers enjoyed a reputation of being particularly good employers who had consistently treated their workforce reasonably. The last strike of comparable scale, which had occurred 27 years previously, had collapsed within three weeks.[65] Yet the firm's alleged failure to fulfil its promise to pay a family wage[66] helped the union win support in some quarters. At an annual dinner of the Hyde Philanthropic Burial Society, Councillor Fildes said:

> we cannot stand by and watch this great struggle going on without admiring the determination of the bread-winner struggling to establish what the firm itself say is to be a living wage for its workers on the Northrop looms.[67]

This quest for a family wage could also be used to legitimize the struggle in trade union circles by presenting the weavers as fighting for gains which other trades had already made. At one strike meeting, William Pope, the secretary of the Hyde Weavers' Association, accordingly took to task those members of the public who had criticized his union for bringing the workers out. These included trade unionists who were members of skilled trades, such as boilermakers, felt hatters, mechanics, fitters and turners. They had claimed that nobody who had not served an apprenticeship like themselves deserved to be paid as much as the male weavers on Northrops. Pope replied to this claim that it cost as much to maintain the family of a weaver as that of a boilermaker.[68] Such a line of argument suggested that the dispute was aimed at bringing male weavers into the ranks of the skilled trades. Yet their claim to status was made not on the basis of any criterion related to work – the completion of an apprenticeship – but rather on the basis of gender – men's duty to maintain their families.

The dispute enjoyed considerable support among weavers elsewhere. Though the strike occurred at a convenient moment for the firm, whose stocks were piled up high at a time of oncoming depression,[69] the local union was backed by the Weavers' Amalgamation, whose coffers were sufficiently full to guarantee strike pay for the duration of even a protracted struggle. Furthermore, regular collections at other mills were made to boost the weekly amount paid out to strikers. Workers' responses showed that they clearly understood the significance of the struggle being waged regardless of whether or not Northrops had already been introduced into their own districts.[70]

Weavers were left in no doubt about both the nature and the relevance of what was at stake. At a public meeting, D.J. Shackleton, the Amalgamation's president, after praising the unity and firmness of the strikers, pressed home the significance of the basic issue when he asserted that

> the general introduction of the Northrop loom into the cotton industry would displace from one-third to one-sixth of the weavers affected, and that was a very serious business. They had to face it completely; and to see to it that it was possible for the man to earn such a wage as would enable him to keep his wife at home. – (Loud applause.) It was something more than a Hyde question; it was a county question. They must not expect a man to keep his wife at home on 24s. or 25s. per week.[71]

Clearly Shackleton had not arrived at this assessment on the basis of sophisticated calculations. The amount of money considered to be a 'family wage' was culturally determined in ways similar to a 'fair price' or a 'fair wage'.

The wages of male breadwinners were the crucial issue. This is why the Amalgamation's representatives did not make an issue of the phasing out of female weavers and the wages and working conditions of women Northrop operatives at Throstle Bank Mill, much to the surprise of the company management.[72] The management recognized that women had their workload increased by the need to skewer through the kind of weft they were made to use. Nevertheless their weekly wages were lower than those of their male counterparts, who were spared this extra operation, but worked a larger number of looms and produced finer cloth, which fetched higher rates.[73] Yet women's concerns were not trade union concerns.

Strikers stood firm for 13 weeks. A compromise negotiated through the efforts of two local clergymen ended the dispute. They had persevered when even the intervention by the Board of Trade had failed to resolve the conflict. Although unable to set a limit on the number of looms per weaver and having to make concessions on the pay rates, union officials accepted the terms offered and urged their rank and file to endorse their decision.[74] The Amalgamation's acceptance of the compromise appears to have derived in large part from some degree of union recognition on the part of Ashton Brothers during the protracted negotiations.

The dispute points to differing notions of gender. Ashton Brothers presented their preference for the employment of male weavers on the Northrop loom to the public as the firm's contribution to the national effort to lower infant mortality. This preference simultaneously appealed to male workers to collude with their employer over the introduction of new technology because it boosted their masculinity. The firm's offer to make work on Northrops a male preserve appears to have been based on the reckoning that men's presumed physical ability to operate more machines than women, would also imply that men only could efficiently operate mechanically complex looms. As it turned out, the men concerned were not prepared to prioritize their masculinity over working conditions which they deemed reasonable. The employers' assumptions about working-class masculinity, geared as they were to their economic designs, involved extra-exploitation based on superior physical strength. In the male weavers' idea of masculinity, by contrast, the effective ability to resist such super-exploitation formed an equally important ingredient. Though willing to work more machines than women, they were not prepared to be stretched out indefinitely. In the dispute, class-based notions of masculinity were at loggerheads and it proved impossible to obtain a cross-class male collusion over the Northrop loom.

This position was shared by both the local weavers' union and the Northern Counties Amalgamation. It was precisely their eagerness to grasp the opportunity to make weaving a skilled trade which required that they take a firm stand on wages and working conditions. Good levels of both were hallmarks of skilled labour. However closure of this particular 'skilled' employment to women appears at times to have taken precedence over wages and conditions and to have lain behind the conciliatory stand that the Amalgamation assumed towards the firm throughout. Their attitude testifies both to the attraction of the ultimate aim – a family wage – and to their reluctance to jeopardize any gains with regard to the de-feminization of the weaving workforce. Any concessions made to Ashton Brothers had to be weighed up against this ultimate goal. In the dispute class-based notions of masculinity clashed with each other as well as with class-based interest in maximizing profit, and it was the latter which held sway, allowing Ashton

162

Brothers to carry on with technical innovation on a large scale, unimpeded by trade union intervention. By 1913 the firm was operating some 3000 Northrops in their sheds.[75] Yet this firm's example was not followed elsewhere. By the late 1930s only a tiny proportion of Lancashire cloth was produced on Northrops,[76] on which men and women were employed in roughly equal numbers.[77] Trade union attempts to reconstruct gender relations in weaving thus had manifestly failed. This failure stemmed from reasons that mark the third stage at which established patterns were inverted.

This attempt to use technology to reconstruct gender relations in the workplace failed not for any lack of determination on the part of the weavers' unions. It was due to the specific conditions of Lancashire cotton weaving, which limited the scope of action available to both employers and trade unions. Cost-cutting through the use of inferior qualities of yarn and running looms at higher speeds, in conjunction with lower wage levels and greater reliance on workers' skill in the adjustment of looms as compared to the USA,[78] militated against the economic viability of a machine that had retained the birthmarks of its origin in that country. A high degree of unionization among the weaving workforce and elaborate procedures in place to defuse conflicts between capital and labour further added to Lancashire manufacturers' reluctance to invest in this costly new machine. Rather than run an incalculable risk they banked on continued trade union support in their pursuit of cost-cutting methods that relied heavily on the cooperation of their competent workforce. The significant degree of feminization of both the workforce and trade union rank and file, which had played an important role in shaping the conditions in the weaving industry, acted to prevent any gains in male authority being achieved at female weavers' expense, because any attempt at reconstructing gender relations in the industry was restrained by ultimate trade union concern to safeguard jobs. Consequently, weaving unions emerged from the dispute over automatic looms as having acted in the interest of their female members by default.

Persistence was not confined to machinery which had been readily scrapped by Lancashire's competitors, but extended to gender relations as well. These continued to be at odds with the contemporary working-class ideal. In Lancashire cotton weaving, masculinity did not revolve around the performance of work deemed skilled and the attendant ability to earn a family wage. Conversely, femininity was not characterized by domesticity. Rather it centred on paid work carried out away from home even after marriage and on a degree of competence in weaving that enabled women to bring home a pay packet matching that of a male weaver. It was the specific way in which conditions in the industry were predicated upon gender that made for the resilience of these versions of working class masculinity and femininity. This resilience emerged clearly when the attempt was made to use new technology to topple relations of gender that were characterized by an unusual lack of inequality. As it turned out, no inversion of this gender equality in Lancashire cotton weaving could be had without a simultaneous erosion of the conditions of work and pay.

Notes

1. Hall, Catherine (1982), 'The Home Turned Upside Down? The Working-Class Family in Cotton Textiles, 1780–1850', in Whitelegg, Elizabeth (ed.), *The Changing Experience of Women*, Oxford: Martin Robertson, pp. 17–29.
2. Cockburn, Cynthia (1983), *Brothers: Male Dominance and Technological Change*, London: Pluto Press.
3. Anderson, Gregory (ed.) (1988), *The White-Blouse Revolution: Female Office Workers since 1870*, Manchester: Manchester University Press.
4. For such variation in the gender division of labour along geographical lines see, for example, Lewis, Jane (1984), *Women in England, 1870–1950*, Brighton: Wheatsheaf Books, p. 162.
5. Rose, Sonya O. (1992), *Limited Livelihoods*, London; New York: Routledge, p. 157.
6. Jewkes, John and Gray, Edward M. (1935), *Wages and Labour in the Lancashire Cotton Spinning Industry*, Manchester: Victoria University, Department of Economics and Commerce, p. 157.
7. Gibson, Roland (1948), *Cotton Textile Wages in the United States and Great Britain*, New York: King's Crown Press, p. 65.
8. Gittins, Diana (1982), *Fair Sex: Family Size and Structure, 1900–39*, London: Hutchinson, pp. 155–6.
9. Liddington, Jill (1977), 'Working-Class Women in the North West: II', *Oral History* 5 (2), 31–45, esp. p. 37.
10. *Cotton Factory Times* (henceforth *CFT*), 7 April 1893, p. 1.
11. *CFT*, 12 March 1909, p. 7.
12. See, for example, the different light in which married women's employment was placed by local union officials as opposed to Amalgamation representatives appearing before the Royal Commission on Labour: Royal Commission on Labour. Minutes of Evidence (Group C Volume I). Parliamentary Papers (henceforth PP), 1892, XXXV, pp. 168, 179–80.
13. Townsend, Irving U. (1902), 'The Northrop Loom', *Scientific American* 4 (supplement) (1393), 22, 324–5.
14. Mass, William N. (1984), 'Technological Change and Industrial Relations: The Diffusion of Automatic Weaving in the United States and Britain', PhD thesis, Boston College, p. 173.
15. Ellison, Thomas (1968), *The Cotton Trade of Great Britain*, New York: Kelley, pp. 36–7.
16. Chapman, Sydney J. (1904), *The Lancashire Cotton Industry: A Study in Economic Development*, Manchester: Publications of the University of Manchester, Economic Series, no. 1, pp. 265–6.
17. *Textile Recorder* (henceforth *TR*), 15 August 1902, p. 97.
18. *Textile Mercury* (henceforth *TM*), 13 September 1902, p. 197.
19. Ibid.
20. *TM*, 27 September 1902, p. 237.
21. Rose, *Limited Livelihoods*, pp. 173ff.
22. PP, 1892, XXXV, p. 190.

23. *CFT*, 15 May 1903, p. 5.
24. *TM*, 27 September 1902, p. 236.
25. Mass, *Technological Change*, p. 235.
26. *TR*, 15 July 1901, p. 65.
27. *Making for a New Age at Ashtons* (1961), Hyde: Ashton Brothers, p. 16.
28. Fletcher, Abraham M. (n.d.), *An Account of the Introduction of the Northrop Loom into the Mills of Ashton Brothers & Co. Ltd. of Hyde, Cheshire, 1902*, Hyde, Cheshire, p. 20.
29. *CFT*, 15 May 1903, p. 5.
30. Ibid.
31. *CFT*, 6 March 1903, p. 5.
32. Mass, *Technological Change*, p. 237.
33. *Hyde Reporter* (henceforth *HR*), 28 March 1908, p. 4.
34. *CFT*, 6 March 1903, p. 5; Fowler, A. (1979/80), 'Trade Unions and Technical Change: The Automatic Loom Strike, 1908', *North West Labour History Society Bulletin* **6**, 43–55.
35. *CFT*, 15 May 1903, p. 5.
36. *CFT*, 22 May 1903, p. 5.
37. *CFT*, 17 June 1904, p. 4.
38. *HR*, 29 October 1904, p. 7.
39. *North Cheshire Herald* (henceforth *NCH*), 22 October 1904, p. 5.
40. *NCH*, 29 October 1904, p. 6.
41. *HR*, 21 March 1908, p. 7.
42. *HR*, 5 November 1904, p. 4.
43. *HR*, 29 October 1904, p. 7.
44. *NCH*, 5 November 1904, p. 7.
45. *CFT*, 4 November 1904, p. 5.
46. Toms, J.S. (1996), 'Integration, Innovation and the Progress of a Family Cotton Enterprise: Fielden Bros. Ltd., 1889–1914', *Textile History* **27** (1), 77–100, esp. p. 81.
47. *HR*, 21 March 1908, p. 7.
48. *HR*, 28 March 1908, p. 4.
49. Bolton Oral History Project, tape no. 5, pp. 7–8, Bolton Central Library, *BO 25.178B/PRO*; collection of taped interviews with Lancashire cotton workers, tape no. 5, North West Sound Archive, Clitheroe.
50. Ross, Priscilla (1991), 'A Town Like Nelson: The Social Implications of Technical Change in a Lancashire Mill Town', DPhil thesis, University of Sussex, pp. 66ff.; Lancashire Textile Project: Technology, Work and Leisure in a Factory Community, AF1, pp. 14–15, Lancaster University Library.
51. Townsend, *Northrop Loom*, pp. 22, 324.
52. *CFT*, 11 October 1907, p. 7.
53. *CFT*, 10 April 1903, p. 4.
54. *CFT*, 11 October 1907, p. 7.
55. *CFT*, 11 October 1907, p. 1.
56. *TM*, 15 May 1907, p. 173.
57. *CFT*, 1 November 1907, p. 1.
58. *CFT*, 13 March 1908, p. 5; *NCH*, 4 April 1908, p. 6; *TR*, 15 May 1903, p. 1.
59. *HR*, 4 April 1908, p. 6. At Ashton Brothers weavers and allied trades were unionized to the extent of 94 per cent: *NCH*, 4 April 1908, p. 6.
60. *NCH*, 4 July 1908, p. 4.
61. *HR*, 21 March 1908, p. 7.

62. *HR*, 4 April 1908, p. 6.
63. *HR*, 11 April 1908, p. 4.
64. *CFT*, 8 May 1908, p. 4.
65. *HR*, 4 April 1908, p. 6; 30 May 1908, p. 4; *NCH*, 11 April 1908, p. 5.
66. *HR*, 11 April 1908, p. 6.
67. *HR*, 18 April 1908, p. 6.
68. *NCH*, 23 May 1908, p. 6.
69. *HR*, 11 April 1908, p. 4.
70. *CFT*, 1 May 1908, p. 5; 8 May 1908, p. 4; *NCH*, 23 May 1908, p. 5; 18 July 1908, p. 5.
71. *HR*, 20 June 1908, p. 7.
72. Report of a Conference between the Directors of Ashton Bros. & Co. Ltd. and Operative Weavers' Officials, held at Bagley Field Mill, March 23, 1908, on the question of wages on the Northrop Loom, p. 22, Tameside Local Studies Library, *DD 236*.
73. *HR*, 4 April 1908, p. 6.
74. *NCH*, 4 July 1908, p. 4; *CFT*, 10 July 1908, p. 5.
75. *CFT*, 1 August 1913, p. 6.
76. Frankel, Marvin (1955), 'Obsolescence and Technological Change in a Maturing Economy', *American Economic Review*, **95** (3), 269–319, esp. p. 313; Lazonick, William (1981), 'Competition, Specialization and Industrial Decline', *Journal of Economic History*, **41** (1), 31–109, esp. p. 32.
77. Gray, Edward M. (1937), *The Weaver's Wage: Earnings and Collective Bargaining in the Lancashire Cotton Weaving Industry*, Manchester: Victoria University, Department of Economics and Commerce, pp. 35, 38.
78. Mass, 'Technological Change', pp. 218ff.

CHAPTER TEN

Equal Pay for Equal Work?: A New Look at Gender and Wages in the Lancashire Cotton Industry, 1790–1855

Janet Greenlees

The historiography of the gender-wage debate

Historians have sought to clarify gender roles during industrialization by examining relationships between gender and work, the family economy and trade unions. They emphasize the significant male–female wage gap, particularly in the textile industries and relate this partly to the gender division of tasks.[1] However, textile historians have relied on the Parliamentary Papers and contemporary observers, including Ure, Baines, Wood and Bowley for statistics. Of the textile industries, cotton manufacturing provides an ideal case study for examining gender-wage ratios because it was the fastest growing industry between 1770 and 1831 and relied on a majority female and child-labour force for this growth.[2] It was also the first major factory manufacturing employer of women. First, this chapter will discuss how historians have viewed the gender wage debate. Then it will analyse gender-wage relationships during industrial development by examining business records from cotton firms between 1790 and 1855, during the transition from predominantly domestic manufacturing to the factory system of manufactures. This study reveals very diversified gender-earnings ratios in the cotton industry. It therefore questions both the validity of the factory returns and the reliability of the contemporary observers.

The neoclassical theory regarding the wage differentials of workers is the one most commonly cited by both economists and historians. This theory maintains that wage rates between groups of workers vary as a result of their different productive capacities or output. Variations in wages are evidence of this differential, but there may also be irregularities in supply preferences. In these situations, some workers can command a lower or higher paid job as a preference, thus allowing for market imperfections or monopoly elements that prevent the equalization of wages.[3] Some historians have declared the neoclassical theory inadequate for explaining wage differentials during the

Industrial Revolution because it neglects the importance of custom. Instead, these historians argue that women received one-third to one-half the wage of men due to traditional gender-based wage differentials and dependency. Maxine Berg supports this customary gender-wage differential when she states that 'it is generally assumed that women by custom received one third to one half the wage of men'.[4] In her classic monograph about women workers during the Industrial Revolution, Ivy Pinchbeck argued that during the period just prior to the mechanization of cotton spinning, manufacturers based spinners' wages on the assumption that female spinners were supported by their husbands.[5] This idea is also supported by Jane Humphries who claims that a 'cult of domesticity' emerged for women as a result of traditional gender differentials and the activity of trade unions.[6] Sarah Horrell and Jane Humphries use household budgets to take this theory further and to argue that women increasingly dropped out of the paid labour force during the nineteenth century and became financially dependent on a male breadwinner.[7] Deborah Valenze supports the family wage ideology with a dependency theory for women where employers did not want to antagonize the male heads-of-households.[8]

Although these historians ignore market influences on the determinations of wage rates, their customary wage theory can be supported by contemporaries. In 1833, Dr James Mitchell reported that the mere nature of women meant '[T]he low price of female labour makes it the most profitable as well as the most agreeable occupation for a female to superintend her own domestic establishment, and her low wages do not tempt her to abandon the care of her own children. Nature therefore thereby provided that her design shall not be disappointed.'[9] Employers adhered to the gender-wage imbalance, because 'indeed, it appears to be a custom in every trade to pay women at a lower rate than men for the same article'.[10] Because women were considered part of a male-headed household, '[T]he earnings of the two sexes, though different in amount, bear a due proportion to their respective expenses'.[11] Working women would neglect their household duties, 'the non performance of which scarcely any amount of earnings can compensate'.[12]

Although these arguments support a male-breadwinner household, they all assume women were not the primary household earner because their gender meant domestic concerns were their priority. Both manufacturing and agriculture offered few opportunities for adult males in Lancashire to earn what might be considered a 'family wage'. As a result, the household income which had characterized the domestic industry remained intact in both spinning and weaving communities. For most working-class families, the household could rarely be a woman's sole concern. Clare Evans has demonstrated that female textile workers were the major earners in just over one-quarter of households in north-east Lancashire prior to the mid-nineteenth century.[13] Females over the age of thirteen constituted an average of 54.4 per cent of cotton workers between 1834 and 1878.[14] A large proportion of married women remained in the workforce in north-east Lancashire and women's marriage age was later in this area than the rest of England.[15] Many Lancashire families had become dependent on the cotton factories because they provided plentiful and relatively well-paid work, thus allowing all family members to contribute to the family income.[16]

Factory wages in Lancashire quickly rose above those offered for agricultural labour. In 1834, Dr James Mitchell reported that '[T]he wages in the cotton factories of Lancashire are the best in England; and in that county the poor's rate is lower than in any other manufacturing district'.[17] However, these women were not always continuously employed. Rather, they worked when the family economy required. The available employment opportunities for women increased alongside the mechanization of spinning, with the throstle machine, and weaving, with the automatic loom. These machines depended on mental concentration for operation, rather than physical force. Thus the strength argument for certain tasks to remain a male preserve was decreased. Women became preferable workers for these tasks, particularly high-speed throstle spinning, because of their perceived quickness and dexterity.[18] Yet women were not preferred for all mechanical tasks. The introduction of the automatic mule did not result in the mostly male hand mule-spinners being replaced by females. Mule-spinning remained a predominantly male task. However, debate remains regarding whether the self-acting mule required physical strength,[19] supervisory abilities or skill;[20] or a combination of these;[21] or whether these were perceived attributes attained and preserved by males through trade unions and from which women were excluded.[22]

If indeed the labour market had been completely segregated by gender, then the wage of one sex would not have affected the employment of the other. Yet none of these afore-mentioned tasks became completely gender segregated. There were many female mule-spinners on both the hand and the automatic mules, but women usually worked shorter and/or fewer hand-mules than their male counterparts. In 1841, factory inspector Leonard Horner reported that mule-spinners 'are generally men from 25 years and upwards; frequently women when mules are small' and the self-acting minder 'is a young person of either sex from 18 and upwards'.[23] A Manchester mill manager stated that '[O]ur mules are all short, and the spinners, who are women, make at present 9s. a week, and they require no piecers, due to the shortness of the pull'.[24] Piece rate wages allowed female mule-spinners to earn as much or more than males.[25] In 1829, male mule-spinners agreed in principle to comparable wages for similar work, but their union refused to support the issue. The men also would not allow women to join their union, and suggested that female mule-spinners form their own.[26] Thus, women's skills were financially valued by family, fellow workers and employers, but male co-workers were sceptical about allowing

169

full gender equality amongst mule-spinners. Gender task discrimination often resulted in more men than women in highly paid positions, including mule-spinning. This gender task discrimination was often instigated or preserved by male unions to exclude female competition. However, tradition did contribute to some gender divisions, with men holding most supervisory and mechanical positions. Yet custom can only dictate wages when a particular task is protected from competition. Although gender segregation of labour and gendered wage discrimination existed, it was not as widespread as previously believed by historians. In many cases women's wage rates were comparable to men's for performing similar tasks.

Several recent studies on gender-wage discrimination during industrialization indicate that job discrimination and productive output were major influences on wage determination. Joyce Burnette has explored the gender productivity ratios for a broad range of British industries, explaining the male/female wage gap during the Industrial Revolution through differences in hours worked, productivity per unit of time worked, payments in kind and the mis-reporting of tasks performed at home. If her measurement of error is correct, then there were no obvious inconsistencies between wages and productivity. Burnette acknowledges the existence of occupational segregation, with the highly paid jobs predominantly reserved for men, thus discrediting the notion of a competitive labour market. During industrialization women suffered more from a declining demand for their labour than from wage discrimination.[27] Similarly, Donald Cox and John Nye have cast doubt on pay discrimination against females in the mid-nineteenth century French cotton industry by estimating gender-production functions. They do not, however, rule out other forms of discrimination, including occupational segregation.[28]

Piece-rate wages had been customary in textile manufacturing since the onset of domestic production and 'four-fifths of workers in factories [were] paid by piece'.[29] Piece rates offered 'a fair day's pay for a fair day's work' and did not discriminate by gender, which would make productivity differentials visible. Michael Huberman maintains that piece rates remained the preferred method of payment in factories because they consolidated elements of fairness and encouraged cooperation between workers and employers.[30] Unfortunately, irregular working hours and a lack of both detailed piece-rate information and gendered output data make a Lancashire study similar to Cox and Nye's unviable. Yet the rates paid and amounts received in the Lancashire wage records confirm that many women were paid comparable wage rates to men and that gender-wage discrimination was not an industrial norm. In most cases, differences in hours worked or productivity could explain the differences in the amounts men and women received. This claim does not imply the lack of gender discrimination within the cotton industry. Rather, it suggests the need to consider factors other than gender and custom, including occupational

170

Table 10.1 Average number of employees by gender from the sample of cotton industry business records used in this study*

Year	Firm & location	Males	Females	Unknown	Total	Comments
1790	S. Greg Styal, Cheshire	54	94	33	181	records damaged
1793	S. Oldknow & Co. Mellor, Lancashire	30	83	8	121	records damaged
1795	M'Connel & Kennedy Manchester, Lancashire	27	41	9	77	
1800	Wm. Gray & Son Darcy Lever, Lancashire	29	36		65	
1801	W. G. and J. Strutt, Ltd. Belper, Derbyshire	236	329		565	approximately half the employees
1821	Owen Owens & Sons Manchester, Lancashire	2	10	6	18	
1822	Owen Owens & Sons Manchester, Lancashire	1	9	2	12	
1826	Owen Owens & Sons Manchester, Lancashire	1	5	3	9	
1828	W. G. and J. Strutt, Ltd. Belper, Derbyshire	172	342		514	approximately half the employees (Feb. only)
1835	Grimshaws & Bracewell Barrowford, Lancashire	17	27		44	(Oct. only)
1836	Grimshaws & Bracewell Barrowford, Lancashire	25	45	6	76	(Oct. only)
1837	Grimshaws & Bracewell Barrowford, Lancashire	28	50	6	84	
1837	A. & A. Crompton Crompton, Lancashire	6	9		15	(Oct. only)
1838	Grimshaws & Bracewell Barrowford, Lancashire	30	47	8	85	
1838	A. & A. Crompton Crompton, Lancashire	32	42	2	76	
1848	R. Greg Styal, Cheshire	125	160		285	at least half the rooms for each task were used
1850	Gardner and Bazley Barrow Bridge, Lancashire	79	19	2	100	
1855	R. Greg Styal, Cheshire	155	143		298	the same rooms were used for each month as for the 1848 records
1876	M'Connel and Co. Ltd. Manchester, Lancashire	46	56		102	

* Where only one or two months were analysed, the other month or months were damaged or not available. Numbers are the average for the months available in a given year.

Table 10.2 Wage rates and amounts received by gender from cotton industry business records between 1790 and 1876

Company	Year	Job	Average rate (f)		Average rate (m)		wgf/wgm rate	Av. amount rec'd (f)		Av. amount rec'd (m)		wgf/wgm amount received
			s.	d.	s.	d.		s.	d.	s.	d.	
S. Greg	1790	carding room	3	4	4	5	0.77	3	4	3	11	0.85
		over-time	0	7	0	11	0.60	3	9	5	6	0.68
		water frame spinning	4	0	5	10	0.69	6	3	8	0	0.78
		over-time	1	3	0	9	1.62			11	0	
S. Oldknow & Co.	1793	carders						3	9	6	6	0.58
		warpers/winders						4	0	28	1	0.14
	1795	spinners						5	4	8	5	0.64
M'Connel & Kennedy	1795	reeling*						6	2	16	6	0.37
		roving	6	4				0	9	1	1	0.80
Wm. Gray & Son	1800	unknown						0	11	1	1	0.85
W. G. and J. Strutt Ltd.	1801	spinners						0	5	0	4	1.25
		reelers						0	8	0	10	0.80
		winders						5	6	6	1	0.90
		carders						0	4	6	0	0.06
	1828	unknown**										
		over-time										
Owen Owens & Son	1821	unknown						5	10	7	6	0.77
	1822	unknown						6	2	4	1	1.53
	1826	unknown						3	1	4	0	0.73
Grimshaws & Bracewell	1835	unknown						11	10	14	6	0.81
	1836	unknown	1	0	1	1	0.92	17	7	18	4	0.96
	1837	unknown	1	1	1	1	1.00	19	9	23	0	0.86
	1838	unknown	1	1	1	5	0.76	19	0	25	0	0.76
A. A. Crompton & Co. Ltd.	1837	unknown	7	0	7	6	0.92	13	8	12	4	1.10
	1838	unknown	8	0	7	6	1.05	13	8	15	0	0.90
	1839	unknown	7	11	8	9	0.91	12	7	17	2	0.73
	1840	unknown	8	2	7	7	1.08	16	2	16	0	1.01

Table 10.2   concluded

Company	Year	Job	Average rate (f) s. d.	Average rate (m) s. d.	wgf/wgm rate	Av. amount rec'd (f) s. d.	Av. amount rec'd (m) s. d.	wgf/wgm amount received
R. Greg & Co. Ltd.	1848	reeling/winding	3 1			2 9		
		weaving	6 10	9 0	0.76	6 6	9 8	0.69
		spinning room***	6 1	7 2	0.83	5 5	5 0	1.08
		mule spinning	4 4	3 1	1.47	4 3	2 6	1.80
		card room	5 0	4 1	1.25	5 0	3 8	1.39
	1855	winders	3 0			3 0		
		weavers	8 1	11 7	0.68	7 10	11 2	0.69
		spinning room	5 10	4 4	1.30	5 10	4 4	1.30
		mule spinning	5 0	4 10	1.04	5 0	4 10	1.06
		card room	6 4	5 6	1.19	5 7	5 7	1.00
Gardner and Bazley	1850	unknown				16 0	35 3	0.45
M'Connel and Co. Ltd.	1876	unknown				10 1.5		

wgf = female wage; wgm = male wage

* The male amount received is that for supervisors of each department or room. They were the only males listed.

** Approximately half the employees were included in this study. The same number were used each month.

*** The same 2 out of 4 spinning rooms and both 3 out of 5 mule rooms and weaving rooms were used for both 1848 and 1855. The wages listed are the averages of the months of February, June and October, whereas the text considers the three months individually. (See Table 1.1 for records which do not include all three months.)

In cases where the supervisor was not noted, it was assumed the person or people with consistent, significantly higher earnings held the supervisory positions. If the gender of workers could not be determined from illegible writing or only a first initial, those people were classified 'unknown' and the earnings for these groups calculated separately.

Table 10.3 Gender and wage ratios in the British cotton industry according to contemporary sources

Year	Job	Male or female task	Amount s.	d.	wgf/wgm	wgf/wgm task	Location	Source
1795	unknown	female	8	0			Manchester and District	8
1797	winders	female	4	6			Manchester and District	4
1803	throstle/ring spinning	female	10	1.5	0.31	throstle/ring/mule	Manchester and District	1, 2, 3, 4, 8
1804/06	mule spinner	male	32	6			Manchester and District	1, 2, 3, 4
1804	mule spinner	male	24	2	0.42	throstle/ring/mule	Manchester and District	1, 2, 3
1804	piecer	male	27	6	0.37	throstle/ring/piecer	Manchester and District	4
1828	spinner	male	27	4			Manchester and District	4
1828	throstle/ring spinners	female	9	1	0.33	ring/mule	Manchester and District	4
1836	little piecer	female	5	6	0.61	little/big piecer	Manchester and District	5, 6
1836	big piecer	male	9	3	1.15	throstle/big piecer	Manchester and District	5, 6
1836	throstle spinners	female	10	6	0.44	throstle/mule	Manchester and District	6
1836	tenters & reelers	female	9	6			Preston	4
1836	spinners	female	10	6	0.39	throstle/mule	Ashton-under-Lyne	4
1836	mule spinner	male	23	11			Manchester and District	5, 6
1836	weavers	male/female	9	6			Manchester and District	4
1837	tenters	female	7	0			Bolton & District	4
1837	self actor minders	male	22	0			Skipton	4
1837	mule spinners	male	24	6			Bolton & District	4
1837	weavers	male/female	10	6			Ashton-under-Lyne & District	4
1838	fine hand mule spinners	male	44	2			Manchester and District	4
1838	throstle spinners	female	7	0	0.16	throstle/fine mule	Glasgow	4
1838	spinners	male	28	10	0.24	throstle/mule	Glasgow	4
1838	piecer	male	29	6	0.27	throstle/piecer	Manchester and District	4
1848	weavers	female	10	0			Manchester and District	5, 6
1848	weavers	female	9	0			Manchester and District	4
1848	tenters	female	7	9			Manchester and District	4
1848	mule spinners	male	28	4	0.27	throstle/mule	Manchester and District	5, 6
1848	card room	male	7	9			Manchester and District	4
			to 12	0				

Table 10.3 concluded

Year	Job	Male or female task	Amount s.	d.	wgf/wgm	wgf/wgm task	Location	Source
1855	mule spinners	male	15	3	0.57	throstle/mule	Preston, Blackburn, Darwen & area	4
1855	mule spinners	male	30	3	0.28	throstle/mule	Bolton & District	4
1855	throstle spinners	female	8	6			Preston, Blackburn, Darwen & area	4
1855	piecers	male	8	6			Bolton & District	4
1855	big piecers	male	10	0	0.86	throstle/big piecer	Preston, Blackburn, Darwen & area	4
1855	weavers av.	female	10	6			Preston, Blackburn, Darwen & area	4
1855	weavers av.	male	8	3	1.29	f/m weavers	Glasgow	8
			to 10	9	0.98	f/m weavers	Manchester and District	9, 4
1855	weavers av.	male	8	6	1.23	f/m weavers	Glasgow	4
			to 11	0	0.96	f/m weavers	Glasgow	4

1 Baines, E. 1835. *History of the Cotton Manufacture in Great Britain*. London: H. Fisher, R. Fisher and P. Jackson.
2 Ure, A, 1835. *The Philosophy of Manufactures*. London: Knight.
3 Factory Inspector's Returns of Wages, *Parliamentary Papers*.
4 Wood, G. H. 1910. *The History of Wages in the Cotton Trade During the Past Hundred Years*. London: Sherratt and Hughes.
5 Bowley, A. L. 1900. *Wages in the United Kingdom in the Nineteenth Century*. Cambridge: Cambridge University Press.
6 Horner (Factory Inspector, in the *Parliamentary Papers*).
7 Chadwick, D. 1860. 'Wages in Manchester and Salford'. *Statistical Society Journal*, cited in Bowley.
8 Wood, G. H. (1903), 'The Course of Women's Wages During the Nineteenth Century', in Hutchins, B. L. and Harrison, A. *A History of Factory Legislation*. London: P. S. King and Son.
9 Baker – Factory Inspector, cited in Bowley.

constraints and the local labour market. The interrelationships between these various factors would enhance the study of the different gender experiences of employment. Thus, this study helps bridge the gap between customary and market-based theories of gender and wages in the textile industries.

Mill records and the role of gender in earnings

This data sample includes comparative evidence of the wage rates and earnings of male and female cotton factory workers drawn from the business records of nine cotton firms between 1790 and 1855. It comprises an industrial cross-section, but the surviving records result in a bias towards larger cotton employers, including M'Connel and Kennedy of Manchester, the Gregs of Quarry Bank Mill in Cheshire and the Strutts of Belper in Derbyshire (Table 10.1).[31] However, this bias becomes less significant as the median size of the cotton labour force increases.[32] Although unable to completely account for the variations in gendered employment, this study considers the different natures of the local labour markets. Labour availability significantly affected both worker recruitment and the wages offered. This will be considered within the context of male–female wage differentials for individual manufactures. The results from this analysis will then be compared with the sources other historians have relied upon for gender-based wage differentials, including Parliamentary Papers and the accounts of contemporaries. Conclusions will then be made regarding the implications of the differing results. Although only a few data sets are discussed in this chapter, the conclusions are based on a larger data sample (Table 10.2). The problems with the data sets will be acknowledged, including the lack of a representative industrial sample, the difficulties of differentiating between adults and children and distinguishing between different types of piece rates and daily rates, and of ascertaining the male and female tasks performed. However, these issues do not detract from the overall hypothesis that cotton manufacturers had many considerations when determining the gender divisions of tasks and different wage rates.

Quarry Bank Mill in Cheshire was founded by Samuel Greg and his 1790 factory records provide the earliest substantial remaining accounts from the cotton industry. The rapid population growth in Britain between 1781 and 1851 meant that there was an abundant labour force, but not necessarily a reliable one.[33] The area around Styal was sparsely populated and isolated from Manchester. Local people were used to combining agricultural activities with domestic manufacture. They were not familiar with factories or with cotton mills. Therefore Samuel Greg had to import workers. Although it is unclear where the hard core of Greg's initial adult workforce originated, approximately half of his early labour force were child, parish apprentices who were housed on the premises.[34] Greg may have tried to lure experienced spinners to his mill from Derbyshire, the early centre of factory-based cotton spinning. As a result, Greg may have offered competitive rates to both men and women to attract their labour. Greg's wages were not so high as in an urban mill since the local agricultural wages were low. However, wages higher than the local average were still unlikely to have been a major incentive for workers. In the eighteenth century people had little reason to try and increase earnings because there was little on which to spend wages and only the wealthy had regular savings.[35]

Although wages were not a major incentive for workers, Samuel Greg paid piece rate wages, as did many early factory masters, in an attempt to try and guarantee productivity. Piece rate wages were also a continuation of traditional payment methods from domestic manufacturing. Both male and female wages were considerably lower at Styal than the 8s. per week women earned in Manchester in 1795, the date of the earliest government wage statistics (Table 10.3). An explanation for this could be that Greg provided housing on company premises; whereas urban manufacturers did not need to provide accommodation. The accommodation and living conditions at Styal were favourable and some workers claimed that they compensated for the lower earnings, while other workers left for higher wages in urban areas.

Throughout 1790, both the rates paid and amounts received at Quarry Bank Mill fluctuated for all groups of employees, including those for overtime. The frequency of workers receiving less than their rate in the wage books suggests that neither males nor females consistently worked full-time and/or that they rarely met the productive quotas on which wages were based. However, female carders either worked more hours or produced more than their male counterparts because the female margins between amounts received and rates paid were lower than those for males (Table 10.4). Female spinners earned more for overtime than males, with a differential of 163 per cent, whereas the female to male differential for the standard work week was only 68 per cent. This suggests that the females may have needed an incentive to work overtime;

Table 10.4   A comparison of amounts received and rates paid for male and female carders and spinners at Quarry Bank Mill in 1790

	carders (%)	spinners (%)
female amount received/rate	100	94
male amount received/rate	89	94

Source: MCL C5/1/15/1 Wage Book 1790

177

females were more highly skilled; or that for the months considered, females were equally or more reliable workers than males. Comparisons of the wages at Styal with those for Manchester reveal vast differences. For Manchester, the years 1803 and 1804 were examined because they provide the earliest available government set of male and female spinning wages. During these years in Manchester, female spinners earned only 31 per cent the amount of males. Whereas at Greg's mill, female carders received 85 per cent and female spinners 68 per cent that of their male counterparts.[36] Possible explanations for these gender-wage differences include that the women were more productive than their counterparts in Manchester; that women at Styal worked more hours than those in Manchester; or that Samuel Greg enticed experienced women to Quarry Bank Mill by offering higher wages. He may have believed in more comparable gender-wage rates than the industrial average for women, so as to improve living standards.

By 1848 Quarry Bank Mill employed 421 workers and Robert Hyde Greg had replaced his father in running the mill. Greg had managed to increase both the spinning and weaving productivity so that output was greater than the national average.[37] Then, the closest gender-pay margins were in the spinning rooms where females earned on average 5d. more than males. In mule rooms, females were equally or more highly paid than males, earning an average rate of 1s. 3d. more than males. However, male employees in the mule rooms significantly outnumbered females and some workers listed were probably piecers. With piece rate wages this would indicate that female spinners were more productive than their male counterparts and/or they worked longer hours.

In the cotton industry, power-loom weaving was the one job where women could earn as much as, or more than, men. Yet Greg's records for both 1848 and 1855 challenge this perception. When comparing the gendered weaving ratios for these years, females rates and amounts received were consistently less than for males (Table 10.5).[38] These earnings fluctuations could partially be explained by the hours worked. The Gregs were firm opponents of

Table 10.5   Female-to-male wage rates for weavers at Quarry Bank Mill in 1848 and 1855

	1848	1855
wgf/wgm rate*	0.76	0.68
wgf/wgm amount received	0.69	0.69

* wgf is the female wage and wgm is the male wage

Sources: MCL C5/1/15/5 Wage Book, 1848 and MCL C5/1/15/7 Wage Book, 1855

Parliamentary regulation of working hours and particularly a reduction from a twelve-hour work day. In spite of this, a letter dated June 1846 suggests hours were partially determined by employees. A worker told the Parliamentary short-time delegates that: 'hands might work ten hours whenever they liked to do so for ten hours wages'.[39] This may suggest a flexibility in working hours and that the firm paid both hourly and piece rates. The wage books do not indicate which tasks received hourly rates. However, these tasks were unlikely to include mule spinning or weaving since piece rates had been standard practice for these tasks since their onset and continued practice throughout the nineteenth century. Thus, an alternative explanation for the gender-wage differential is needed. Productivity or hours worked are the most plausible explanations. In both the eighteenth and nineteenth centuries, women worked on average fewer hours per day than men. In 1843, women worked between eight and twelve hours, with an average of 9.66 hours, whereas most men worked twelve-hour days.[40] Thus women would need to be more productive than men to earn the same amount per week. Yet this does not explain the lower female-to-male wage rate. This lower rate could indicate wage discrimination or it could be a result of women having worked less time at weaving. Then, women weavers would be less skilled than the men and not deserving of the higher rate of the more skilled weavers.

Another source of early information regarding women's wages and working hours are the records of James M'Connel and John Kennedy. They formed a partnership in Manchester in 1795 that went on to become one of the largest and most successful cotton manufacturers in the industry. The 1795 M'Connel and Kennedy (hereafter M&K) data are haphazard in nature and include only information for picking, reeling and roving, which were predominantly female tasks. Picking would probably have occurred in a building near the mill rather than in the mill itself, possibly because women pickers were 'a very irregular set of hands, [and] time is not noted'.[41] The words 'returned unpicked' were entered several times in the wage book, meaning that women may also have been able to take work home. The sporadic nature of the work could also explain why the women's wages of between 4s. and 6s. per week were significantly lower than the 8s. that Wood listed for Manchester. Pickers were paid by piece rate and many pickers at M&K had money subtracted from their wages for being 'short'. Thus, either these women were not very productive, did not meet a required weekly quota, or did not work a full week.[42] The most probable explanation is that women undertook picking when the family required supplementary income. This demonstrates that the women were valued as earners by their families and as employees by M&K. It also shows that M&K allowed flexible employment.

Casual labour patterns could also have been a legacy from domestic manufacturing when there was an assumed standard workday and effort and

179

hours were flexible to allow for other responsibilities.[43] Shorter hours were also common during economic downturns, to preserve fair wages for workers and for business survival.[44] Yet in 1795, M'Connel and Kennedy were one of the largest cotton manufacturers and their steady flow of business[45] diminishes the argument that M&K might have preferred casual labour. Manchester did not have a labour shortage in the late eighteenth century, especially for cotton workers since the industry paid comparatively high wages to both males and females. As a result, M&K did not need to import workers or to employ parish apprentices. The two definite conclusions which can be made from M&K's 1795 wage book are: that few female workers were solely dependent on their own income and that the company accepted casual labour.

M'Connel and Kennedy became M'Connel and Co. in 1831. They continued employing casual labour after the cotton industry was well-established and trade unions were influencing labour issues. This is evident from their only other surviving wage records for the years 1876 to 1879. Although these years are outside the scope of this study and are incomplete, they include the days and hours worked. These records suggest that all the employees listed were females who maintained irregular work patterns. Most women worked different hours with few completing a full week.[46] Without further details, it is impossible to determine the reasons behind these sporadic working hours. Yet the fact that women, and perhaps also men, were not working full weeks is significant when examining output and wages.[47] It indicates that casual employment must have been beneficial to all concerned, since both manufacturers and unions allowed, if not supported, its continuation. Comparisons of male and female earnings must take this into account.

Another large firm which remained in business for many years, alongside the Gregs and M'Connel and Co., is that of the Strutts. The Strutts were another paternalistic firm, similar in some respects to the Gregs. However, unlike the Gregs, the Strutts employed families in the early period. This is evident in the 1801 wage book where frequent entries are found of the same surname, indicating that several family members worked in the mill. Ages are not listed, so it is not possible to distinguish between adult and child labour.[48] In 1801, there was a considerable degree of job mobility within the mill, demonstrated by both male and female workers holding more than one position, with both sexes in all positions. Many names occur in subsequent wage books, probably indicating that some employees stayed with the Strutts for several years. Therefore some workers could progress from a low paying position to a more highly paid one. Workers may also have changed tasks upon request or production demands. However, the latter case is unlikely in such a large company because they maintained a greater division of labour than the smaller mills with less available resources.

Similar to many early cotton manufacturers, the Strutts paid piece rate wages

180

for most positions. Females never earned less than 80 per cent the amount of males (see Table 10.2). However, neither the rates paid nor the hours worked are listed. Therefore, although determining gender-wage ratios is possible, the results cannot be related to worker's ages, output or the hours worked.[49] A comparison with the government wage statistics for 1797 and 1803, the nearest years of available data, reveals the Strutts' weekly wage averages were significantly lower than those in Manchester (see Table 10.3). It cannot be assumed that casual labour was common at Belper or that workers' output was low because rural mills had a reputation for paying less than urban mills due to lower living costs. Another possible explanation for the earnings discrepancies is related to the Strutts' paternalism. The Strutts provided housing for their workers, similar to the Gregs, and often food and clothing, the costs of which were deducted from wages, but which possibly were not listed in the wage payment books. Furthermore, from 1812 onwards, the Strutts, along with other industrialists, combined tokens with cash to pay wages due to the scarcity of specie. The tokens were redeemable either at a later date or at the company store.[50] Unfortunately, the surviving Strutt records are inadequate to determine the relationship between deductions and wage payments.

Another consideration when examining wage rates is length of service with the company. The Strutts' records between 1805 and 1812 are one of the few sets which include information concerning workers who gave notice and their reasons for leaving. High worker turnover would have been an incentive for an employer to pay workers less than their marginal product in the early years of employment. Wages would have increased not only in relation to skills acquired, but also for length of service, since repeatedly training new workers would have been costly in terms of output lost. As a result, workers who left or were dismissed lost the wage premium benefit that came in later years. Of the workers who gave their reasons for leaving the Strutts' employ, 88 per cent of males and only 29 per cent of females stated another occupation as the motivation. Insufficient earnings, dissatisfaction with their work, or health reasons, including pregnancy prompted 60 per cent of the females listed to leave, but only seven per cent of the males.[51] Citing insufficient earnings or dissatisfaction with work would have been risky, should workers later wish to return to employment with the company. It is possible that more women than men thought that they might not need to return to factory work or that the costs of domestic responsibilities outweighed their factory earnings. Because men spent more years than females in the workforce, they may not have wanted to diminish their chances of returning to a large employer. Nevertheless, total employee turnover for the Strutts was only about 16 per cent between 1805 and 1812,[52] possibly because of the Strutts' paternalism. It is difficult to put these figures into perspective without further details surrounding individual cases and without knowing the exact gender percentages in employment. In the cotton industry, female turnover was consistently higher than males, partly because women exited the labour market for child-rearing. Female cotton workers remained in employment for an average of twenty-three years in 1833, compared to thirty-five years for a male.[53] There is little reason to believe there were significant differences in these figures in the first quarter of the nineteenth century, since the main reason women left employment, either temporarily or permanently, was related to pregnancy, child-care and a higher rate of sickness than men.[54] Therefore, should men and women have equal access to skills education, women would not have the same time in employment during which to acquire skills which would result in higher wages. Women would also not have had as many opportunities to receive higher wages for long and faithful service. This sixty-six per cent female to male length of employment differential in the cotton mills contributes significantly to explaining the female to male earnings differential.

So far the analysis has centered around some of the cotton industries giants, the Gregs, M'Connel and Kennedy and the Strutts during the early years of factory manufacture. Yet some of the same issues surrounding male-to-female earnings differentials and employment patterns in these companies remained into the 1830s and can also be found in smaller mills. These include similar female to male wage rates and high female-to-male earnings ratios, with men either working longer hours than women or men having a higher productivity rate. Little information remains for smaller manufacturers during the nineteenth century. The best evidence concerning the wages of cotton workers in medium-sized concerns comes from two Lancashire firms in the 1830s, Grimshaws and Bracewell (hereafter G&B) of Barrowford and A. and A. Crompton and Co., Ltd. of Crompton. G&B's wage book appears to be for the weavers and warpers, but Crompton's records do not distinguish the tasks workers performed. The number of employees listed fluctuated considerably between 15 and 119 at Crompton's mill between 1835 and 1840 and from 76 down to 27 between 1836 and 1846 at G&B's mill. Such employee fluctuations were probably more typical of small and medium-sized cotton firms, who were greatly affected by business cycles. Larger mills had greater capital reserves to be able to endure economic recessions. Yet the variations in gender-wage ratios at both G&B and Cromptons are similar to those for the earlier period.[55] Both record sets reveal that although in many cases females were paid proportionately less than males, the female-to-male earnings ratio was never so low as the 16 to 44 per cent listed in the national statistics for the same years. Rather, the minimum that females earned in relation to males was 76 per cent the rate at G&B in 1838 and 73 per cent the amount at Cromptons in 1839.

The two companies paid different rates, with G&B paying between 1s. and 1s. 5d. and Crompton paying between 7s. and 8s. 9d. (Table 10.6). The ratio between rates paid and amounts received indicates that G&B paid mostly daily

Table 10.6 Gendered earnings for Grimshaws & Bracewell, Crompton and Britain, 1837–1838

	1837				1838			
	rate (f)	rate (m)	amount rec'd (f)	amount rec'd (m)	rate (f)	rate (m)	amount rec'd (f)	amount rec'd (m)
G&B[a]	1s.1d.	1s.1d.	19s.9d.	23s.	1s.1d.	1s.5d.	19s.0d.	25s.0d.
Crompton[b]	7s.	7s.6d.	13s.8d.	12s.4d.	8s.	7s.6d.	13s.8d.	15s.
National statistics[c]			10s.6d.	10s.6d.–24s.6d.			7s.	28s.10d.–44s.2d.

Sources: [a] MCL L/1/16/3/7 Wage book for Grimshaws and Bracewell, 1836–38; [b] LRO DDCp Wage books for A. & A. Crompton and Co, 1837–40; [c] Wood, G. H. (1910), *The History of Wages in the Cotton Trade During the Past Hundred Years*, London: Sherratt and Hughes.

rates, whereas piece rates were standard practice for weaving. Daily wages would indicate that on average, the males at G&B worked more hours than the female weavers and that by 1838 males and females were weaving different widths or types of cloth with varying daily rates; or that gender wage discrimination was introduced in 1838. Crompton either paid a weekly rate, with most employees working overtime or paid a piece rate based on a large quota or a task other than weaving and warping. Both companies paid employees every two weeks, with workers at G&B earning more money than at Crompton's mill.

The female/male wage differentials indicate that both companies valued all their employees because of the similar gender wage rates. The considerable variations in amounts received between individual workers most probably correlates with the hours worked and/or individual output. This counteracts the well-recorded belief that women were cheaper labour than men and preferred for that reason. Therefore there must have been another explanation for the gender-wage differential. Possible explanations include that both men and women were skilled workers, but men were more productive due to a greater number of hours worked, higher quality training or longer time in employment, or that wage discrimination existed. As mentioned earlier, on average women did not work so many hours as did men and many women did not wish to work full time. For smaller mills heavily dependent on the business cycle, it could have been beneficial to have a reserve of skilled workers not seeking full-time employment. However, smaller gender-wage differentials do not eliminate the fact that there were situations when women earned less than men, either as a result of occupational segregation or gender discrimination by some employers and by trade unions.

Conclusion

With the exception of William Gray and Sons of Darcy Lever, Lancashire, the other records considered in this chapter confirm a much smaller, or in some instances reversed gender-wage gap than shown in previous studies.[56] Few definite conclusions can be made because of the various problems inherent in these mill records, including the lack of consistent consecutive records. These include the prevalence of records from paternalistic companies, the paucity of time-keeping records, minimal information regarding hours worked, output, age and in some cases gender, differences between rural and urban mill records with diversified manufacturing priorities and the variety of labour sources. Nevertheless, micro-analysis of several record sets suggests that prevailing evidence regarding male and female wages for the cotton industry needs to be reconsidered.

There are four possible conclusions. First, although wages do not appear to have fluctuated with the cotton markets, gender divisions of labour may have fluctuated. 1838 was a relatively good year for the cotton trade, yet wage rates and amounts paid by G&B and Crompton either remained the same or increased only slightly from 1837. This was also the case for males in the national statistics between 1836 and 1838, whereas the amount females received decreased (see Table 10.6). 1855 was a relatively poor year for the industry, yet at Styal mill, the wages were not significantly lower than in earlier years. However, the Gregs employed a significantly lower percentage of females in the mule rooms, where mule-spinning was traditionally classified as 'skilled' male work, than in 1848 (Table 10.7).[57] This data suggests that during good economic years, females were allowed greater access to more skilled tasks, but during business downturns the better paid jobs remained a male preserve. Another possibility is that social perceptions of male–female appropriate tasks were changing. Both explanations, whether alone or combined, support the cultural hypothesis of the man as the primary family breadwinner. However, such a cultural explanation neglects circumstances

Table 10.7   Males and females in the mule room at Quarry Bank Mill in 1848 and 1855 by percentage

	1848 (%)	1855 (%)
females in mule room	19	8
males in mule room	81	92

Source: MCL C5/1/15/5 Wage book, 1848 and MCL C5/1/15/7 Wage book, 1855

where females received higher rates or amounts than males. Traditionally, males had greater educational opportunities than females to acquire the skills required for higher paying jobs. During periods of economic hardship, it was unlikely that families could afford to allow daughters to train for skilled work. Therefore, either these females who earned greater wages than males were exceptions in acquiring the skills or for being more productive than men – more females than previously believed received skills training – or, access to skilled, higher waged jobs came through varying routes.

Second, working hours were flexible, especially in the early years of the industry and particularly for women. This may have allowed women to contribute to the family income while maintaining their domestic responsibilities. Employment flexibility is congruent with the neoclassical hypothesis where output is the basis of workers' pay. It also incorporates traditional work patterns from domestic manufacturing, where females were able to combine household responsibilities with paid work. If indeed flexible hours were common practice, then this pattern could contribute to the explanation of gender earnings differentials.

Third, gender-wage ratios in the cotton industry did not follow consistent patterns. Individual mill owners set pay rates in relation to competitors and to local labour markets and wages. In cases where females were paid a lower rate than males, this ratio was not as large as the one-third to one-half differential indicated by other sources. Situations where females received the same rate or more than males, including Crompton's mill in 1837 and Quarry Bank Mill carders and spinners in 1848 and 1855, could indicate a labour shortage in the area, where employers had to pay higher rates for females to attract workers. However, a more plausible explanation is that workers were paid a rate based on their skills and output, not gender. In this instance, gender would be the silent inter-connector between the other variables.

The gender-wage ratios in the business records leads to the fourth conclusion: that it is necessary to question the validity of traditional wage sources. Many nineteenth and early twentieth-century historians cited each other and the Parliamentary Papers. G. H. Wood made use of Bowley's work, and he, in turn cites Baines, Ure and the Parliamentary Papers.[58] With the exception of Baines, these authors assumed both the correctness and completeness of the reports given to the factory inspectors. Edward Baines was given a preview of the cotton industry statistics by the factory inspectors before they were finished and he states that they were inconclusive.[59] When the factory inspectors began collecting their data, there was no uniform system for counting factories. This lack of a definite methodology remained to the 1850s. The inspectors themselves stated that the 1835 reports were incomplete and that their returns for 1836 may not have been accurate.[60] This means that although the inspectors' reports were thorough for the manufactories counted, it is not possible to rely on their data as being an accurate cross-section of the British cotton industry.

There is also the possibility that both the mill records and the contemporary sources are correct, thus indicating great diversity within the cotton industry. The inspectors used a different, and certainly larger, mill sample than was used in this study, due to the few remaining mill records. Industrial diversity may thus be the most credible explanation for the varying gender-wage differentials, both interregional and between rural and urban manufactures. There were no defined methods for starting and expanding a business and labour regulation was only in the formative stages by the 1830s. Expansion occurred at the manufacturers' discretion and not always in conjunction with economic and local forces. Work patterns were usually local. Manufacturers had to take into consideration traditions regarding working hours and gender divisions of tasks with associated wage rates during the change from domestic to factory production. Manufacturers based decisions regarding labour and wages on their financial resources, the markets for both raw materials and goods produced, and local traditions regarding gender and work practices.

The incomplete manufacturing records and factory returns leave unanswerable many questions surrounding women's employment in the textile industries. However, wage records reveal that manufacturers valued women's contributions to industry for reasons other than the traditional belief of women being a cheap source of labour. This makes women's influence on business decisions considerably greater than previously believed. Further studies of surviving business records by industry, region and type of goods manufactured are necessary. They should provide greater insights regarding the different roles of various groups of workers, where gender discrimination originated, and how gender relations within the workplace developed over time.

Notes

1. For discussions of gender and wages in different areas during the Industrial Revolution, see Rendall, J. (1990), *Women in Industrializing Society, 1750–1880*, Oxford: Blackwell; Hudson, P. and Lee, W. R. (1990), *Women's Employment and the Family Economy in Historical Perspective*, Manchester; Humphries, J. (1987), '"... The most free from objection ..." The Sexual Division of Labor and Women's Work in Nineteenth-century England', *Journal of Economic History*, **47** (4), 929–50; Burnette, J. (1997), 'An Investigation of the Female–Male Wage Gap during the Industrial Revolution in Britain', *Journal of Economic History*, **50** (2), 257–81; Berg, M. (1994), *The Age of Manufactures, 1700–1820. Industry, Innovation and Work in Britain*, London: Routledge, ch. 7; Rose, S. (1988), 'Gender Antagonism and Class Conflict: Exclusionary Strategies of Male Trade Unionists in Nineteenth Century Britain', *Social History*, **13** (2), 191–208. Rose states that women's wages were normally 50–60 per cent the rate of men's, for performing the same task.

2. Cotton was second only to building in value added in British industry, growing from 2.6 per cent in 1770 to 22.4 per cent in 1831. See Berg, M. (1993), 'What Difference did Women's Work Make to the Industrial Revolution', *History Workshop Journal*, **35** (Spring), 24, 27.

3. Dex, S. (1985), *The Sexual Division of Work: Conceptual Revolutions in the Social Sciences*, Brighton: Wheatsheaf Books, Ltd., pp. 116–17.

4. Berg, 'What difference', p. 31. For further support of the one-third to one-half gender-wage gap see Rose, S., 'Gender antagonism' and Rose, S. (1992), *Limited Livelihoods: Gender and Class in Nineteenth-Century England*, Berkeley: University of California Press, especially the introduction.

5. Pinchbeck, I. (1966), *Women Workers and the Industrial Revolution* (second edition), London: Virago Press Ltd., p. 144.

6. Humphries, J. (1991), '"Lurking in the wings ...": Women in the Historiography of the Industrial Revolution', *Business and Economic History*, **20**, 32–44.

7. Horrell, S. and Humphries, J. (1995), 'Women's Labour Force Participation and the Transition to the Male-breadwinner Family, 1790–1865', *Economic History Review*, **48** (1), 89–117.

8. Valenze, D. (1995), *The First Industrial Woman*, Oxford: Oxford University Press.

9. Parliamentary Papers (hereafter PP), 1834 (167), [Part I], XIX, p.39.

10. PP, 1840 (43–I), XXIII, p. 282.

11. PP, 1833 (450), XX, p. 76.

12. PP, 1841 (296), X, p. 7.

13. Evans, C. (1990), 'The Separation of Work and Home? The Case of the Lancashire Textiles, 1825–1865', unpublished PhD thesis, University of Manchester.

14. For a full age and gender distribution between these years, see Blaug, M. (1961), 'The Productivity of Capital in the Lancashire Cotton Industry During the Nineteenth Century', *Economic History Review*, **13** (3), 368.

15. Evans, 'The Separation of Work and Home?', pp. 153, 342–3.

16. Winstanley, M. (1996), 'The Factory Workforce' in Rose, M. B. (ed.), *The Lancashire Cotton Industry*, Preston: Lancashire County Books, pp. 140, 149.

17. PP, 1834 (167), [Part 1], XIX, p. 41.

18. *Cotton Factory Times*, 5 April 1885, p. 6 and PP, 1848 (957), XXVI, pp. 5–6. For the feminist historian's perspective, see Elson, D. and Pearson, R. (1981), 'Nimble Fingers Make Cheap Workers': Analysis of Women's Employment in Third World Export Manufacturing', *Feminist Review*, **7** (Spring), 87–107. Children have also been viewed as both cheaper and more dextrous labour than men. For the constraints of this chapter they have been excluded from the discussion.

19. Lazonick, W. (1979), 'Industrial Relations and Technical Change: The Case of the Self-acting Mule', *Cambridge Journal of Economics*, **3** (3), 231–62 and Chapman, S. J. (1904), *The Lancashire Cotton Industry: A Study in Economic Development*, Manchester: Manchester University Press, p. 59.

20. Freifield, M. (1986), 'Technological Change and the Self-acting Mule: A Study of Skill and Sexual Division of Labour', *Social History*, **11** (3), 319–43, argues that the breakdown of an inter-generational transmission of female skills prevented women from having and learning the necessary skills to shift from short to long and doubled mules.

21. Cohen, I. (1985), 'Workers' Control in the Cotton Industry: A Comparative Study of British and American Mule-spinning', *Labor History*, **26** (1), 53–85.

22. Turner, H. A. (1962), *Trade Union Growth, Structure and Policy: A Comparative*

Study of the Cotton Unions in England, London: George Allen and Unwin, Ltd., pp. 114, 128, claimed the exclusionary practices of male-dominated trade unions prevented the hiring of unskilled women. Berg, *Age of Manufactures*, pp. 251–2, argues that the male mule-spinners sought control of the new self-acting mule, rather than stopping progress.

23. PP, 1842 (31), XXII, Appendix 6, p. 85. See also Lazonick, W. (1990), *Competitive Advantage on the Shop Floor*, Cambridge, MA: Harvard University Press, p. 87. Female mule-spinners were common in Scotland, as shown by Gordon, E. (1991), *Women and the Labour Movement in Scotland, 1850–1914*, Oxford: Clarendon Press, pp. 39–44; and Cohen, I. (1990), *American Management and British Labor: A Comparative Study of the Cotton Spinning Industry*, New York: Greenwood Press, p. 65.

24. PP, 1842 (31), XXII, Appendix 6, p. 86.

25. PP, 1841 (31), XXII, Appendix 6, p. 85; Cohen, *American Management*, p. 65; Lazonick, *Competitive Advantage*, p. 87.

26. Lazonick, *Competitive Advantage*, p. 85; Chapman, S. J. *Lancashire Cotton Industry*, pp. 213–14.

27. Burnette, 'An Investigation of the Female–Male Wage Gap', particularly, pp. 278–9. See Coffin, J. (1996), *The Politics of Women's Work: the Paris Garment Trades 1750–1915*, Princeton: Princeton University Press, for a similar argument for France.

28. Cox, D. and Nye, J. (1989), 'Male–Female Wage Discrimination in Nineteenth Century France', *Journal of Economic History*, **49** (4), 903–20.

29. PP, 1850 (1239), XXIII, p. 4.

30. Huberman, M. (1996), *Escape from the Market: Negotiating Work in Lancashire*, Cambridge: Cambridge University Press, especially pp. 64–71 and ch. 6.

31. Although both good and bad years of the cotton industry were studied, data was too incomplete to focus on comparisons based on industrial cycles. For an overview of fluctuations in yearly business cycles, samples were taken for February, June and October.

32. In 1815, 45 per cent of cotton mills employed between one and 50 workers, with a median labour force of 54 employees. Firms with medium-sized labour forces had gained in relative industrial importance by 1841. By this time, only 18 per cent of cotton firms employed less than 50 workers, with a median labour force of 174 and 120 workers the median size for Lancashire. Gatrell, V. A. C. (1977), 'Labour, Power, and the Size of Firms in Lancashire Cotton in the Second Quarter of the Nineteenth Century', *Economic History Review*, **30** (1), 72–82. Lloyd-Jones, R. and Le Roux, A. A. (1980), 'The Size of Firms in the Cotton Industry: Manchester 1815–41', *Economic History Review*, **33** (1), 72–82.

33. Schofield, R. S. (1994), 'British Population Change, 1700–1871', in Floud, R. and McCloskey, D. N. (eds), *The Economic History of Britain since 1700*, vol. 1, Cambridge: Cambridge University Press, pp. 60–95.

34. Rose, M. B. (1986), *The Gregs of Quarry Bank Mill: the Rise and Decline of a Family Firm, 1750–1919*, Cambridge: Cambridge University Press, pp. 27–31; Manchester Central Library (hereafter MCL). C5/1/15/1. Wage Book, 1790. Initially Greg employed approximately 150 hands, which had grown to over 200 by 1790. Of these, 148 (including apprentices) were used for this analysis.

35. Rose, M. B., *Gregs of Quarry Bank*, pp. 27–28.

36. MCL C5/1/15/1 1790. Wage deductions were listed separately. For Manchester records, see Wood, G. H. (1903) 'The Course of Women's Wages During the Nineteenth Century', Appendix A, in Hutchins, B. L. and Harrison, A., *A History*

of Factory Legislation, London: P. S. King & Son, pp. 257–316. Scattered wage records remain for Samuel Oldknow and Co. during the 1790s, but not enough to make any definite conclusions. Manchester John Rylands Library (hereafter JRL), JRL.Man.816.iii, JRL RYL/820, JRL RYL/770, JRL RYL/771, JRL RYL/772, JRL RYL/815, JRL RYL/816, JRL RYL/820. See also Unwin, G. (1924), *Samuel Oldknow and the Arkwrights: the Industrial Revolution at Stockport and Marple*, Manchester: Manchester University Press, pp. 196–7, 202–3.

37. Rose, M. B. *Gregs of Quarry Bank*, p. 70. This increase was partly a result of the introduction of self-acting mules and a conversion from water-frames to throstle spinning machines.

38. MCL C5/1/15/5 Wage book, 1848; MCL C5/1/15/7 Wage Book, 1855. Collier states that both the numbers employed in weaving and their wages increased significantly with the introduction of the power-loom. Collier, F. (1964), *The Family Economy of the Working Classes in the Cotton Industry, 1784–1833*, Manchester: Manchester University Press, pp. 43–4. Mule spinning wages did not follow a consistent pattern. In February females received 90 per cent of both the rate and amount received by males; by June the situation was reversed with males receiving 82 per cent of both the rate and amount of women. Yet by October, both groups received the same rates and total amounts.

39. MCL C5/8/34 letter from Bower to W. R. Greg about the visit of short-term delegates.

40. Burnette, 'An Investigation of the Female–Male Wage Gap', pp. 268–9; PP, (1843), XII, p. 118.

41. PP, (1840), (43–I), XXIII, p. 157.

42. JRL MCK3/2/1–2 *Cotton Pickers Journal* and *Carding and Roving Journal*, 1795. Approximately two-thirds of the pickers were 'short' in June and about 40 per cent in October.

43. Hobsbawm, E. J. (1968), *Labouring Men*, London: Weidenfeld and Nicolson, pp. 347–50, as cited in Huberman, M. (1991), 'Industrial Relations and the Industrial Revolution: Evidence from M'Connel and Kennedy, 1810–1840', *Business History Review*, **65** (2), 346.

44. On short-time, see Huberman, 'Industrial Relations', p. 366. Collier, *Family Economy*, p. 15, states that in 1839 the Grant and Springside Mill, Lancashire was only running three days a week. The Fieldens of Todmorden frequently ran their mills on short-time rather than decrease output or pay of wages. Law, B. (1995), *The Fieldens of Todmorden: A Nineteenth Century Business Dynasty*, Littleborough, Lancashire: George Kelsall. See also Huberman, *Escape*, ch. 8; Huberman, M. (1995), 'Some Early Evidence of Worksharing: Lancashire Before 1850', *Business History Review*, **37** (4), 1–25.

45. In 1802, M&K had 312 operatives and by 1816 the firm had grown to 1020. Yet by 1826 M&K were running short-time hours. Lee, C. H. (1972), *A Cotton Enterprise: 1795–1840, A History of M'Connel and Kennedy Fine Cotton Spinners*, Manchester: Manchester University Press, pp. 115, 133. In 1815 M&K were the second largest cotton factory employers in Manchester, after Adam and George Murray, PP, (1816), [397], III, pp. 374–5; Lloyd-Jones and Le Roux, 'Size of Firms', p. 81.

46. MCL MISC (743) Wage book, 1876–9. Complete ledgers remain from the 1820s with few names and no details. A note with the ledger states that the entries might be the personal employees of the M'Connel family. JRL MCK DB501. Wage book, 1822–31.

47. It is doubtful that the company was running short-time hours because hours were not regular each week. MCL MISC (743) 1876–79, June and Oct. only, Feb. records missing.
48. In 1816, 48 per cent of the Strutts' workers were under eighteen. PP, (1816), [397], Vol III, p. 217.
49. MCL 01/102 Wage Book, 1801; Fitton, R. S. and Wadsworth, A. P. (1958), *The Strutts and the Arkwrights 1758–1830*, Manchester: Manchester University Press, p. 240. Female spinners, carders and reelers earned less than their male counterparts, whereas male winders earned less than the females. However, the differentials are nowhere near the margins indicated by the Factory Inspectors' Returns in the Parliamentary Papers. Reeling and winding were traditionally female and children's occupations and the significant number of male names listed might indicate boys.
50. Fitton and Wadsworth, *Strutts and Arkwrights*, pp. 241–4, includes further details regarding the Strutts' non-cash payment methods.
51. Fitton and Wadsworth, *Strutts and the Arkwrights*, pp. 230–2. This list does not include workers who left without giving the required notice. From the onset of production at Belper in 1778, the Strutts required three months' notice from all employees and imposed a system of forfeits for poor workmanship, running away or other rule infractions. The Strutts, along with other local factory masters, also refused to hire anyone without a decent testimonial from their previous employer.
52. Ibid., p. 240.
53. Boot, H. M. (1995), 'How Skilled Were Lancashire Cotton Factory Workers in 1833?', *Economic History Review*, **48** (2), 293.
54. Ibid., p. 295.
55. There is little gender variation in days worked. MCL L/1/16/3/7 Grimshaw and Bracewell Wage book, 1836–38. Lancashire County Record Office (hereafter LRO) DDCp A & A Crompton and Co. Wage books, 1837–40.
56. Records for William Gray and Sons provide no indication of hours worked and little information on rates paid. Jobs listed include many pickers, which could suggest part-time work or even outwork. Bolton Metropolitan Borough Archives, ZGR-1, Wage book,1800.
57. Data is from the same three mule rooms for each year. MCL C5/1/15/5 1848 and C5/1/15/7 1855.
58. Wood, 'Course of Women's Wages'. Wood also quotes 'Young's Northern Tour', F. M. Eden (1797), *Inquiry into the State of the Poor, The Year Book of Facts* (1879 edition) and the *Wage Census of 1886*. Wood, G. H. (1910), *The History of Wages in the Cotton Trade During the Past One Hundred Years*, London: Sherratt and Hughes; Baines, E. (1835), *The History of the Cotton Manufacture in Great Britain*, London: H. Fisher, R. Fisher and P. Jackson; Ure, A. (1836), *The Philosophy of Manufactures, or an Exposition of the Scientific, Moral, and Commercial Economy of the Factory System of Great Britain*, London: Charles Knight; and Bowley, A. L. (1900), *Wages in the United Kingdom in the Nineteenth Century*, Cambridge: Cambridge University Press.
59. Baines pp. 386–94. Jenkins, D. T. (1973), 'The Validity of the Factory Returns, 1833–50', *Textile History*, **4** (Oct.), 26, 28.
60. Jenkins, 'Validity', pp. 28–30.

CHAPTER ELEVEN

Gendering Cultures in Business and Labour History: Marriage Bars in Clerical Employment

Robert Bennett

Introduction

The rediscovery of culture continues its advance through academic disciplines, the latest to seek acceptance within this new orthodoxy is business history. Here culture is placed at the centre of an attempt to position business history at the intersection of management, sociology and economics. Fundamental to this shifting perspective has been the recognition that business organizations are socio-cultural constructs and that their performance is in greater or lesser part subject to this process.[1] In the light of this, research is being directed towards '[generating] a better appreciation of the variety of ways in which the role of culture in business performance can be understood'.[2] Despite the vigour of their support for the concept of culture, many business historians have allowed themselves to be distracted by their own histories. Often economics remains at the heart of their analyses and they fail to see the full implications of and opportunities for their initial premise. Rather than developing a full and open discussion of culture as a central motive force within institutions, their discussions continue to focus upon issues such as the development of 'a check list for assessing the economic value of different cultures'.[3]

While this chapter does not claim to present a complete and inclusive historical analysis of culture and institutions, by utilizing recent feminist perspectives on gender, discourse and culture, it does attempt to reveal the greater complexity and value of culture as a concept within institutions that is so often disregarded by the new wave of business historians.[4] It seeks to achieve this by understanding the influence of gender and class as two intersecting facets of culture which are present within the historical evolution of institutions and their regulation.[5] By rejecting the implicit simplicity of approaches that continue to prioritize economics, the historical understanding of change or continuity is given greater sensitivity to both collective and individual subjectivities. Here analysis of two organizations, Barclays Bank and the British Civil Service, has in each case revealed shared understandings of gender and class. For each organization these shared understandings were revealed within the culture of the organizations as they were translated and made concrete in institutionalized activity and rule making. In this chapter the specific example of marriage bars operating within the organizations can be seen as one such symbol of the articulation of gender and class within the culture of the organizations.

The marriage bar: past and present theorizations

During the late nineteenth and twentieth centuries, marriage bars were a frequent phenomena constraining many areas of women's paid employment. While this chapter investigates only the introduction and operation of formal or written marriage bars it is acknowledged that informal or unwritten examples played an extensive part in the restriction of women's employment opportunities. In both cases, their action was to restrict the process of recruitment to single women and, then, to force the resignation of female staff on the point of marriage. Although the power of informal bars could often be greater than that of the formal bar by appearing more natural and receiving less critical attention, formal marriage bars represent a more highly visible form of institutional constraint upon the employment opportunities of women.[6] The formal marriage bar thus offers a greater opportunity for the exposition and investigation of institutions within the labour market to which less overt processes can then be compared.

Here two case studies are utilized as examples of organizations in which formal marriage bars operated; Barclays Bank providing an example of the experience of clerical employment within joint stock banks, and the British Civil Service providing an insight into public sector clerical employment. In both cases marriage bars were implemented some time after the initial recruitment of women and upon their transfer into permanent or established posts. Each organization first recruited its female clerical staff in response to stimuli external to the daily operation of their organizations. For the Civil Service female clerks were introduced upon the amalgamation of the Telegraph Offices in 1871 while Barclays introduced this policy as a consequence of the male labour shortages during the First World War as well as the rapid expansion of the branch network following its cessation.[7] In relation to the marriage bar, the Civil Service formalized its policy in 1895 when the offer of marriage gratuities was extended to women employed in all departments. Barclays Bank formalized their bar in 1926 in conjunction with the creation of the Permanent Women Staff. Following its amendment during the interwar years, the bar in the Civil Service was removed in 1946 while in Barclays Bank it was retained until 1962.[8]

Historians that have been attracted to the marriage bar issue have done so through a prior interest in the extensive process of the feminization of the clerical labour force. It has been to this process that the marriage bar has most often been associated. Given that the interest of capitalism and patriarchy have played a considerable role in the analyses of clerical feminization it is not surprising to find that these concepts have also been linked to the emergence of marriage bars. It has been suggested that by enforcing the resignation of women upon marriage, both the interests of patriarchy and capitalism were being met. Women were restricted to low employment positions within a distinct gendered organizational hierarchy creating a body of cheap labour who were then, following marriage, constrained to unpaid and dependant domestic roles.[9] Cohn has suggested that these effects have particular salience for areas of clerical employment as there was a tendency amongst large-scale organizations dominated by clerical labour to retain traditional employment contracts specifying the payment of annual increments to both the male and female workforce. Utilizing a formal tool such as the marriage bar has been said to reduce the costs associated with such a scheme by replacing those with longer tenure and thus higher salaries with a new entrant at the basic salary level. In support of this approach, Cohn develops what he terms the 'synthetic turnover hypothesis' to describe the turnover of labour artificially generated by the imposition of a marriage bar.[10] Thus the marriage bar was seen to be an opportunistic tool adopted by employers and supported by the male employees, to maximize the cost benefits associated with the employment and segregation of a female staff.[11]

More sophisticated analyses have adopted a less overtly economic approach favouring instead an appreciation of the marriage bar as one element in the process of gender segregation and cost minimizing procedures. In these cases, the marriage bar was interpreted as a tool adopted by management in a process which justified the restriction of women to segregated employment positions. It acted to reinforce this position by restricting the length of tenure of women within clerical employment positions. By reinforcing the perception of women's position within the workforce as temporary, their segregation into poorly paid positions defined as low in skill, with few opportunities for promotion, was further justified. Here the marriage bar is a mechanism asserting a self-fulfilling prophecy restricting women to the lowest employment positions within the organization. This secured a cheap and resigned if not docile labour force for the organizations while retaining and enhancing the promotion opportunities into primary employment positions for the male staff.[12]

Contrary to these conclusions, this chapter seeks to offer a fuller understanding of the marriage bar. It suggests that such conclusions do not offer a sufficiently complete understanding of the marriage bar. By conflating the rationale evident in the feminization of clerical labour with that of the marriage bar, the economic foundations of this policy have been exaggerated. Further, the use of the problematic concept patriarchy has allowed discussions around the marriage bar to become overly descriptive. While partiarchy is accepted as an existing social system which describes a particular distribution of power, it cannot be invoked as an explanation of its own outcome: gender inequality. As Sylvia Walby suggested 'The keys to the patriarchal relations in culture are the differentiation of the discourses of femininities and masculinities, and the valuation of masculinity above those of femininity'.[13] Examining these 'keys' will lead to a far greater understanding of patriarchy, organizational culture and marriage bars.

One factor behind the initial recruitment of female clerks and the subsequent feminization of clerical work was the desire to protect the traditional male clerical hierarchy and thus men's opportunities for frequent promotion. This position has been acknowledged throughout the period of clerical feminization and a report to the Central Council of the Bank Staff Association in 1955 stated that the growth in the volume of female clerical recruits would continue to accelerate in line with increasing mechanization and that 'male recruits will correspondingly diminish in numbers, but become more important from the point of view of quality, for it will be from this source that future bank managers will have exclusively to be drawn'.[14] The Chairman of Barclays Bank in 1962 repeated more overtly that the domination of female clerks in the doubling of the bank staff since the interwar years demonstrated both the degree to which the bank relied upon its 'ladies ... to keep the machine running efficiently and sweetly,' and 'the extent of the opportunities of promotion which lie open to the young men who come into banking to-day, and indeed to all those who have joined us since the war'.[15]

It is also a truism, unchallenged by this chapter, that the introduction of an institution such as the marriage bar could enhance the turnover of female staff. It does, however, seem untenable that this institution could then by extension be seriously associated with financial or economic motives. To adopt this position would be to disregard the potential costs involved in turnover of labour and also to underestimate the tendency for female clerks to choose resignation following their marriage throughout this period.

As one senior officer within the General Post Office suggested in his report upon the amalgamation of the telegraph companies into the Civil Service, women would retire 'for the purpose of getting married as soon as they get the chance'. In this way any financial savings that could accrue from a higher turnover of female labour would be generated without needing to resort to the adoption of a formal marriage bar. Indeed, the report of the officer continued by stating that the Civil Service did not 'punish marriage by dismissal' and that women's return, following marriage, was encouraged suggesting that valuable skills would otherwise be lost. He did, however, recognize that 'as a rule those who marry will retire, and those only will return whose married life is less fortunate and prosperous than they had hoped'.[16] While it must be acknowledged that a large proportion of the female clerks recruited into commercial offices during the late nineteenth and early twentieth centuries were born into either the respectable working class or lower middle classes and may thus have experienced the financial difficulty discussed in this report, in the case of the aristocratic Civil Service and Joint Stock Banks, the female clerks tended to emerge from a more solid middle-class background.[17]

Four years after the completion of the reorganization report, with the benefit of experience gained from a longer period of employing female clerks within the Civil Service, the view that women would overwhelmingly resign automatically upon marriage received further support in a variety of evidence submitted at both departmental and state level. As the Receiver and Accountant General to the Post Office suggested in his response to questions relating to the retention of women following marriage:

> We have not had one such case where the lady has remained. Three or four ladies have married but retired. They have generally married very well ... I think that a large number of the ladies will probably marry and leave us; we have lost several by marriage ... I am sorry to say that they are going off with rapidity just now.[18]

While retention tended to be very low, in those departments where a woman had remained following marriage, the opinions of departmental controllers suggested that the traditional 'inconveniences' associated with their retention were either exaggerated or easily overcome:

> The Superintendent of the South Western District Instrument Room has married since she has been there, and has presently been confined. I am not aware that she is in any way a less valuable servant of this Department than before. The number of absences of married women through confinement is not likely to effect the convenience to the Service to any extent at all seriously ... There are two instances here of married female clerks ... their marriage makes no difference in their responsibility.[19]

During the investigation of the Whitley Council Committee established after the Second World War to consider the future of the marriage bar within the Civil Service, the tendency for women to remain in employment after marriage was again discussed. It was agreed that if the bar were abolished resignations may be delayed but turnover would remain relatively static.[20]

If the experience gained from the employment of female clerks tends to undermine the perceived need for a marriage bar as a formal tool in the promotion of synthetic turnover, further evidence suggests that, at least in the experience of the private sector, any associated financial losses associated with the retention of married women could be recouped through the manipulation of employee pay and conditions.[21] The investigation of employment policies adopted within Barclays Bank reveals a management willing and able to exploit the flexibility available in this area. Following Staff Committee concerns, expressed in 1936, over the bank's ability to continue recruiting 'suitable [female] applicants' it was agreed to amend the salary scales of the women staff.[22] The subsequent increase in salary given to new female entrants was directly financed by a reduction in salaries available to those women that had been in employment for more than six years as well as a dramatic cut in the maximum value of marriage gratuities.[23] A similar strategy was subsequently pursued in 1944 when the Staff Committee agreed to reduce the value of annual increments paid to the female staff in order to 'secure a higher salary at the marriageable age for men and to retain a longer period of scale increases for women who have not, at present, as many opportunities of commanding responsible positions above scale rates'.[24] It is apparent that a variety of policy options for the organization of staff pay and conditions were available to management and that any additional costs generated by a lower turnover of female staff could be overcome through the application of alternative strategies. Thus, prior research offering explanatory evaluations of the marriage bar have so far offered a relatively limited one-dimensional evaluation.

Central to the explanatory problems that these approaches have experienced has been their failure to look beyond the apparent functionality of institutions such as the marriage bar. That the marriage bar generates a variety of outcomes, which are more or less functional for men and capitalists, is not in doubt. However, given that a variety of employment policies were available to management, each of which held the possibility for generating similar outcomes, attempts must be made to understand what it is within this particular institution that led to its adoption in these organizations. One way to overcome this problem is to recognize that all such institutions are symbols of a particular knowledge or identity that is constructed through differentiation.[25] As shown by Kenneth Lipartito, this approach can also be seen in relation to business organization technology:

> technology, though engaged with physical reality, is socially constructed. Technology only sets limits; it does not determine outcomes ... when a society adopts a new technology, it is making a statement about itself. The technologies that a society chooses to employ say something about the values, beliefs, and self-conception of its people.[26]

Isolating the knowledge or identities that lie within institutions, or for that matter technology, and placing them within the wider context of existing discursive fields will then allow a greater level of understanding as to why they were introduced in their particular form.

The gendered identity of marriage bars

In response to the determinism evident in prior work that has observed marriage bars, developments in feminist scholarship have recently shown an increasing sensitivity to the role of gender as a constitutive factor in the construction of social relations both within and outside the labour market. While the analysis favoured by Sylvia Walby only allows culture the status of one patriarchal structure amongst six, this chapter allows it greater analytical weight.[27] In adopting such an approach, this chapter draws inspiration from the work of Joan Scott and, in particular, the recent formulations of Silvia Gherardi.[28] Following the work of Joan Scott, gender is more often being recognized as a 'way of articulating and naturalising difference' and thus as a signifier of power relations.[29] The view of discourse presented by Silvia Gherardi is equally compelling:

> discourse is an institutionalized use of language and of other similar sign systems, and it is within a particular discourse that a subject (the position of a subject) is constructed as a compound of knowledge and power into a more or less coercive structure which ties it to an identity.[30]

This stance is reflected within the context of historical research by Sonya Rose. She suggests that gender can be viewed as the primary concept in the constitution of social beings and 'through cultural processes – the elaboration of ideas, ideologies, and symbolic representations' it must be seen to be central to all social processes.[31] As

> the social meanings of masculinity and femininity are expressed in a variety of practices that constrain people's lives ... these meanings are reproduced without question, through everyday practices, and they become embedded within the structures constituted by those everyday practices.[32]

While a debate continues to develop concerning the use of these approaches in feminist and historical research, and it is acknowledged that concerns relating to issues of agency, resistance, ethics and feminist politics are still to be fully resolved, this chapter suggests that analytical benefits can be obtained if organizations are observed from a perspective that gives greater weight to the operation and evolution of discursive gendered cultures.[33] Adopting such an approach would allow the examination of the language, rituals and symbolic institutions of organizations from the context of gender distinctions.[34]

In relation to this approach and reflecting a greater sensitivity to gender in history, Leonore Davidoff and Catherine Hall have discussed the historical position and experience of clerical workers as associates of an emerging eighteenth and nineteenth-century gendered middle class.[35] Here it is suggested that gender, expressed through particular historical constructions of masculinity and femininity, was central to the emergence of a distinctive middle class: 'a conception of manhood carried with it its own laws of sexual difference – women were dependants, to be cherished and supported, protected and covered in law by their husbands and fathers. This was the foundation stone of bourgeois culture'.[36] Utilizing gender as an analytical tool and thus viewing the marriage bar in the Civil Service and banking as a symbol of gendered relationships it is possible to suggest an alternative understanding of its historical implementation and evolution.

In the minutes of the Staff Committee of Barclays Bank, one of the persisting themes raised in connection with the relationship between the organization and the female staff was the relations of the family and in particular the perceived need to secure a sufficient family wage for the male breadwinner. The emphasis given to these relationships suggested an alternative rationale for the introduction of marriage bars to those already highlighted. Amendments to the scales available to female staff in Barclays Bank were introduced to increase the salaries available to male staff of a marriageable age. Here is one example of the gendered middle-class family; the wife and child being understood as dependent upon the man and his family wage. The particular gendered meaning of femininity and masculinity existed as part of a symbolic and normative system that constructed and constrained the range of possibilities within workplace conditions and pay.[37]

Although Barclays Bank did not employ a specific formal policy which granted male members of staff a family wage upon their marriage, they did seek to provide a salary sufficient to these needs at a point in the male career when marriage could be expected. They also allowed married members of staff a higher increment ceiling.[38] In association with this policy they enforced marriage agreements which stipulated that a male member of staff could only marry at a time when a salary sufficient for the support of a dependent family had been secured.[39] For example, the marriage agreement operated by Barclays in 1931 restricted the ability of the male staff earning less than £200 per annum from marrying. This restriction meant that only those staff that had reached the age of twenty-six and had been in employment for nine years could consider marriage. This policy was upheld in all cases except those where an independent third party contracted with the Bank to supplement the staff member's salary in order to satisfy the £200 per annum minimum requirement.[40] In 1958 a female member of the staff commenting upon 'The Changing Face of Barclays' recognized the historical importance of the operation of the marriage agreement within Barclays Bank:

> When a young man joined the bank, say, twenty-five years ago, he could enjoy the happy thought that by the time he was thirty he would be able to apply to Head Office, through his Department or Branch Manager, for

198

permission to marry; by that time he would, in the Bank's view, be earning sufficient salary to keep himself and a wife. He would present his case to the Manager who, after carefully explaining the necessity of keeping up a good appearance and address, would agree to put the application to Staff Department for a decision: a week or ten days later official 'blessing' would arrive.[41]

Importantly, this rule met with resistance from the male clerks. However, critiques of the policy remained grounded within the discourse of familial middle-class respectability emphasizing not the employers' desire for the financial stability and probity of its workforce but instead the requirements of emotional and physical support. It was argued that outside of marriage '[the only resource of] the bank clerk with a prohibitory salary thinking of marrying and spending his evening rationally will be the public-house bar and music hall'.[42] Opposition to marriage agreements amongst male clerical employees also drew directly upon notions of the independent middle-class male. The marriage agreement was given the status of a marriage bar for men and vociferously criticized for its effect in challenging their independence.[43]

The Bank's 'in house' documentation revealed a central discourse, operating within and upon the organizational form. It measured the middle class associations of the organization against notions of respectability and independence available within a particular gendered family form; the independent male head of household and the dependent wife and child. The knowledge that emerged from this dominant discourse effected concerns relating to the respectability and independence of both men and women before and after marriage. While the position of the mature male clerical staff emerged in the context of the marriage agreement and the security of financial support for dependent families, these institutions did not secure the position of the female and young clerical staff.

The disciplinary effects of the gendered discourse are again seen in relation to the position of the young and dependent clerical staff where they were also sustained within the middle-class family. In this case organizations turned to the imposition of fidelity agreements. These formal contracts required the provision of a guarantor, either the individual's father or guardian, who would ensure that the clerk, until the age of 21, would be provided with sufficient board, lodging, clothing and pocket-money 'suitable to the position occupied by the clerk until he shall be in receipt of a salary of £100 per annum'.[44] After the age of 21 the clerks themselves became signatories to the contract and were thus responsible for its maintanence.

The situation of the female clerk was, however, more problematic. A particular focus of concern was the position of the female clerk following marriage. Discussions about issues of independence and respectability in the debates over the introduction of a marriage bar in the Post Office in 1875 suggest the key issues. Few problems were associated with the practical employment of married women. More commonly the concerns related to the interaction of relationships within the family and the nature of individual independence. Departmental responses to a request made by the Post Master General for opinions regarding the introduction of a marriage bar elicited the following response:

> it must be considered that the natural result of matrimony is to place the women under the influence and control of her husband and it is necessary to make the woman's admission to the service, or her retention therein dependent in some on the character and position of her husband ... [married women] are more or less under the direct influence of their husbands and much mischief might in some cases arise from that influence.[45]

Such concerns, relating to the relations between the sexes, extended beyond the family into the organization. Within Barclays Bank and the Civil Service, issues of respectability involved either the physical segregation of the staff according to sex or according to publicly visible roles. Policies adopted by Barclays Bank, except during the periods of extreme labour shortage during the Second World War, sought to restrict female clerks to positions below that of cashier. This ensured that contact between the public and female members of staff was minimized and the public image of the organization culture as masculine and independent was sustained. Similarly, within the Civil Service concern was often expressed about the public visibility of women. The maintenance of public respectability in the Civil Service received particular attention in the period before the full implementation of the marriage bar when concerns were extended to the possibility of the visible pregnant woman. As the Controller of the Returned Letter Office in the General Post Office, suggested in 1875:

> I have a strong impression that demoralisation of the Service might result from married women being employed. The female cannot be so isolated that they will not be seen and recognised, at all events as they enter and leave the office, by male employees entering and leaving about the same time, and if any become observably enceinte, they will, I fear, be subjected to rude remarks or behaviour which cannot be for their good.[46]

This position was mirrored in the views expressed by Mr Fischer, Controller of the Central Telegraph Office:

> it seems to be objectionable for married women when Enceinte to be mixed up, even with single females, as their condition gives rise to much remark and comment, which it is obviously desirable to avoid, but the objection becomes of course much stronger when it is considered that males, in some capacity or other, cannot be entirely excluded from any office where females are employed ... there is an obvious indelicacy in the position of a female among a large staff under such circumstances.[47]

The concerns over the implications of the recruitment of a female clerical staff for the specifically gendered organizational culture were also expressed amongst the male clerical staff. Male clerks, faced with the shock of a growing body of female clerks, attempted to comprehend the position of the lady clerks in relation to the discourse of middle-class respectability operating upon and within clerical work. One male clerk, employed within the clearing banks, recalled his experiences following the First World War thus:

- 1917 – return to Bank somewhat battered.
- Fascinating discovery that during one's temporary absence, ladies had arrived in the Bank.
- Appointment to sub-branch with staff of one lady clerk. The clerk-in-charge chivalrously carrying cash bag.
- Subsequent marriage to above mentioned lady clerk.[48]

That the knowledge and meaning of clerical work in the clearing banks was experiencing a period of change with the recruitment of female clerks is clear in the following passages. The first passage relates to the recruitment of women into clerical labour wherein the female clerks adopt the position of 'women travellers in a male world' in which the associations of masculine dignity within the public sphere of the Bank are challenged.[49]

THIS Moneychangers' Temple, dedicate
For many years to Ledger, Interest Rate,
Deposit Book and Loan and Overdraft
And all the other varied arts and crafts
Of Banking, stands, unmoved, upon the site
Where it has stood so many years, bedight
With dignified insignia over door
and on the window panes, just as of yore,
When solemn visaged men, in accents low,
Within its portals, said their 'Yes' and 'No'
To customers in quiet Banking Hall,
Disturbed by nothing more than here a call
For someone's passbook, there perhaps a clang
Of silver on the scales; maybe the bang
Of young clerk's ledger, as he closed the tome
And put it on the rack, ere going home.

How different now the sights and sounds we hear;
Ladies and lipstick and bright frocks appear
Where once mere man in peace had reigned supreme.
Shades of another age! Who then could dream,
In those dead days of quiet harmony,
That their still, solemn dignity would be
Shattered by rattle of a hundred keys
Tapped all day long by those same busy bees

(In make-up and bright frocks) whose former place
Was to make home a haven for their grace?[50]

In the second passage, shown below, the author analyses the implications of a reversal of the symbols of masculinity and femininity between the two sexes.

> I suggested that it is possible that, even now, woman likes to keep one foot, or at least a toe or two, on the pedestal that was once hers. Perhaps she likes to think that there is something man can do that she can't and if, in addition to admitting, man was forced into believing that she was his equal, who knows what revolutions might ensue? If the typist lit her pipe when the door was closed and offered the chief clerk a fill of her favourite mixture, what would follow? She might of course become manager in a few years, but it is probable as I suggested, that she wouldn't really like it and would prefer to get married to the Second Cashier. Perhaps the emancipators went only so far as they knew the body of their sisters would follow them, opening the door to business without closing the door to connubial bliss ...

> Pipes make for good temper and a soft heart. Pipes in the hands, or in the mouths, of the enemy are women's strongest weapon. If she takes them to herself and develops, as she must, good temper and soft heart, where will be her domination of the home? Once she feels the influence of that most perfect of mixtures, even she will not be able to ride rough-shod over the nicotine-sodden will of her men folk. And I, for one, hope that this sound reasoning will continue to hold the field.[51]

Through the narrative, the subject reasserts the relative position of his identity. This culminates in the concluding paragraph with a return to the prior division of the respective knowledge associated with masculine and feminine within the context of the family and home.

Conclusion

Recognizing the potential influence of discursive relations within and upon the organization, it can be seen that the admission of the female clerk into both the Civil Service and Barclays Bank initiated a period in which shared meanings and cultures were open to reinterpretation and re-negotiation. The introduction and operation of marriage bars must be seen as a part of that process. In the two organizations examined in this chapter, the marriage bar was part of a process whereby a knowledge surrounding the newly formed lady clerk was understood and then grounded in relation to a still ascendant discourse. When faced with the recruitment of female clerks the gendered organizational cultures, already emphasizing middle-class respectability and independence, led to the implementation of compliant disciplinary structures. As Silvia Gherardi has suggested: 'organisational cultures express values and mark out places which belong to only one gender ... Occupational segregation is a manifestation of the symbolic order of Gender which opposes the male to the female'.[52] Thus, the innovation of a formal marriage bar as well as strict occupational segregation within these organizations was both product and instrument of an organizational culture which defined the limits of the female clerk's presence. The marriage bar reinforced the central position of the gendered middle-class family, a 'manifestation of the symbolic order of gender which opposes the male to the female'.[53]

While the support of single women within the familial context of the firm was acceptable, marriage entailed dependent status within a relationship external to the firm. The marriage of female clerks was sanctified by the exclusion of the woman from her former work kin and finally the payment of a closing dowry in the form of a marriage gratuity. Within staff magazines, poetry was often the chosen means of communication and comment and the following excerpts, published in 1926, represent the attitudes of the male staff to the marriage gratuity and, ultimately, the female staff.

> A gift to each maiden who resigns
> Her post to enter wedded bliss
> Was promised; but between the lines
> The Boards advice to men was this:-
>
> Choose from the staff a damsel staid,
> Head Office will approve; nor shall you
> Be out of pocket, for each maid
> Shall have a fixed SURRENDER VALUE![54]

In making the link between the marriage gratuity and dowry explicit, the text exposes both the centrality of the family to the construction of the organization and the visible discomfort felt within the organization when 'damsels' over-extend their 'visit' and thus challenge their femininity.

From 1870 to 1920 when clerical work underwent a period of rapid change, innovation in employment policies continued to be undertaken in line with prevailing social norms and the cultural status of the organization.[55] The marriage bar emerged as one element of this process when 'shared understandings were being transformed and could no longer be taken for granted'.[56] Through the marriage bar, amongst other institutions, both the masculine middle-class clerk and the middle-class family were reconstructed under changing material circumstances. While the employment of women helped to sustain opportunities for promotion up to the position of management amongst the male staff, thus securing their middle-class social status, the operation of the marriage bar helped to sustain a specifically masculine middle-class culture based upon a dependent family.

Following the Second World War the clerk was once more under threat, this time by the declining pay differentials with the skilled manual worker. These changing circumstances were again interpreted and understood through the gendered discourse of class, family and community. As the General Staff Manager of Barclays Bank recognized in 1955:

> employers have no duty to counter the social revolution that we are going through by restoring their purchasing power fully to pre-war standards. On the other hand, to put it no higher, it is a matter of enlightened self interest that we should put sufficient into our employee's pockets to enable them to take the sort of place in the community that will bring credit to the Banking industry, i.e. to keep house and generally conduct their life and outside activities in a way that will bear comparison with those sections of the community with which we, as their employers, like them to be on terms.[57]

Possibly due to the success of a process of professionalization being undertaken within other fields of expertise including accountancy and management, the position of the bank clerk again experienced changing associations and meaning.[58] It was from within this position that, in 1962, the marriage bar in Barclays Bank was finally removed.

While this chapter has concentrated on only two organizations where marriage bars were implemented, it is felt that the approach utilized here which includes in its analysis notions of culture, discourse and identity, can be generalized to a wider variety of organizational settings and institutions. Although business historians are becoming more open to the use of culture as a tool for understanding the behaviour of organizations, the future success of these approaches relies upon their ability to allow concepts of culture priority in their analyses. Reducing culture to the position of one factor amongst many undermines its explanatory potential. In particular, the approach espoused here is not that adopted by Mark Casson where culture remains secondary to economic interest but is instead closer to that adopted by Kenneth Lipartito.[59] To maintain the prior position in which culture is subservient to economic forces, for example, continues to risk a retreat into both functionalism and essentialism.

Notes

1. Godley, A. and Westall, O. M. (1996), 'Business History and Business Culture. An Introduction', in Godley, A. and Westall, O. M. (eds) (1996), *Business History and Business Culture*, Manchester: Manchester University Press, p. 2.
2. Godley and Westall, *Business History*, p. 3.
3. Godley and Westall, *Business History*, p. 5.
4. Business historians publishing in the USA have shown a more positive response to the opportunities following from the adoption of culture in their analyses. As Lipartito has recognized: '... culture inheres in all business decisions. There

are no simple, one-dimensional, non-cultural "reactions" to market forces; all behaviour, even supposedly easy responses to unambiguous market lessons, are filtered through cultural lenses by actors all the time'. Lipartito, K. (1995), 'Culture and the Practice of Business History', *Business and Economic History*, **24** (2), Winter, 1–41, 25.

5. A useful approach to culture is one favoured by Lipartito who defines culture as '... a system of values, ideas, and beliefs which constitute a mental apparatus for grasping reality.' He further suggests that 'Business culture is that set of limiting and organizing concepts that determine what is real or rational for management, principles that are often tacit or unconscious'. Lipartito, 'Culture and the Practice of Business History', p. 2.

6. Glucksmann, M. (1990), *Women Assemble. Women Workers and the New Industries in Inter-War Britain*, London: Routledge, pp.39, 223.

7. *Barclays Bank Limited. Head Office Circulars*, 25 October 1915, (29/1603); *Staff Committee Minute Book*, 31 May 1923. Barclays Bank PLC, Group Archives, Dallimore Road, Wythenshawe, Manchester M23 9JA.

8. Public Records Office. T 162/822/3754/03/01, *Inland Revenue, Retention of Female Tax-Inspectors Following Marriage*; PRO Cab 80/46, *Civil Service: Abolition of the Marriage Bar, Consideration of Memorandum by Chancellor*; PRO T 162/822/3754/03/4; Barclays Bank Limited, *Staff Committee Minute Book*, No. 3, 13 December 1961.

9. Examples of such dual-systems theorists include Hartmann, H, (1979), 'Capitalism, Patriarchy and Job Segregation by Sex.' in Eisenstein, Z. (ed.), *Capitalist Patriarchy and the Case for Socialist Feminism*, London: Monthly Review Press, pp. 206–47; Walby, S. (1986), *Patriarchy at Work; Patriarchal and Capitalist Relations in Employment*, Cambridge: Polity Press; Walby, S. (1990), *Theorizing Patriarchy*. Oxford: Blackwell.

10. Cohn, S. (1985), *The Process of Occupational Sex-Typing: The Feminisation of Clerical Labour in Great Britain*, Pennsylvania: Temple University Press, p. 19.

11. Cohn, *The Process of Occupational Sex-Typing*, pp. 93–4.

12. Zimmeck, M. (1984) 'Strategies and Stratagems for the Employment of Women in the British Civil Service, 1873–1939', *Historical Journal*, **27** (4), 901–24; Zimmeck, M. (1987) 'We are all Professionals Now: Professionalisation, Education and Gender in the Civil Service, 1873–1939', *Women, Education and the Professions*, History of Education Society, Occasional Publications, 8; Zimmeck, M. (1988), '"Get Out and Get Under": The Impact of Demobilisation on the Civil Service, 1919–1932', in Anderson, G. (ed.), *The White Blouse Revolution, Female Office Workers Since 1870*, Manchester: Manchester University Press, pp. 88–120; Zimmeck, M. (1988), 'The "New Woman" in the Machinery of Government: A Spanner in the Works?', in MacLeod, R. (ed.), *Government and Expertise; Specialists, Administrators and Professionals, 1860–1919*, Cambridge: Cambridge University Press, pp. 185–203; Zimmeck, M. (1992), 'Marry in Haste, Repent at Leisure: Women, Bureaucracy and the Post Office, 1870–1920', in Savage, M. and Witz, A., *Gender and Bureaucracy*, Oxford: Blackwell; Zimmeck, M. (1995), '"The Mysteries of the Typewriter": Technology and Gender in the British Civil Service, 1870–1914', in Degroot, G. and Shrover, M. (eds), *Women Workers and the Technological Change in Europe in the Nineteenth and Twentieth Centuries*, London: Taylor & Francis.

13. Walby, *Theorizing Patriarchy*, p. 104.

14. *Central Council of Bank Staff Associations*, June, 1955, Barclays Bank Archives, ACC 29/1507.

15. The Chairman in his retirement speech to the company's annual general meeting acknowledged that women had represented 90 per cent of the new clerical staff recruited during the period 1945–1962. The Annual General Meeting, *Spread Eagle, Barclays Bank Staff Association Magazine* (1962), Vol. 87, p. 76. Barclays Bank Archives.

16. While this quote has received considerable attention from a number of authors, most have reproduced an abridged version which ignores the final and penultimate sections referred to here. See, for example, Walby, *Patriarchy at Work*, p. 146; Martindale, H. (1938), *Women Servants of the State, 1870–1938: A History of Women in the Civil Service*, London: Allen & Unwin, pp. 17–18; Cohn, *The Process of Occupational Sex-Typing*, p. 103. The original quote can be found in *The Report on the Reorganisation of the Telegraph System of the United Kingdom*, Parliamentary Papers (henceforth PP), 1871, XXXVII, p. 79.

17. Anderson uses the concept 'aristocratic' to differentiate a range of clerical employers, including the banking community, from commercial occupations operating in lower 'class' positions. Anderson, G. (1976), *Victorian Clerks*, Manchester, Manchester University Press. Of the female clerks recruited into the London Joint Stock Bank from 1911 to 1921, 74 per cent had fathers employed in the Registrar General's Class One or Two. Midland Bank Archives; London Joint Stock Bank, ACC274/.034; *Registrar-General's Statistical Review of England and Wales* (1921).

18. Appendix to the First Report of the Civil Service Inquiry Commissioners, *Royal Commission into the Civil Service*, 1874, PP, (1875), (cd.) XXIII. 192, pp. 175–6.

19. Post Office Archives, *First Employment of Female Clerks*, E3613/1875, Post 30/275; POA, *Married Women Employed in the Post Office*, M20612/1921, 33/329–30; *Royal Commission into the Civil Service*, 1874, PP, (1875), (cd.) XXIII. p. 192.

20. PRO T 162/822/3754/03/4 *Civil Service National Whitley Council Committee on the Marriage Bar; Minutes of the First Meeting of the Official Side and Minutes of the Second Meeting of the Committee; Civil Service National Whitley Council*, PP, (1946), Cmd. 6886.

21. Cohn, *The Process of Occupational Sex-Typing*, p. 19.

22. Barclays Bank Limited, *Staff Committee Minute Book*, ACC 80/25, 8 December 1936, p. 108.

23. The maximum gratuity payable upon marriage was cut from £100 to £32, Barclays Bank Limited, *Staff Committee Minute Book*, ACC 80/25, 8 December 1936, p. 108.

24. The suggested adaptation to the '1932 salary scales' recommended that male permanent staff aged 25 and 26, the age at which men would have previously achieved a marriageable salary, should receive salary increases of £50 and £55 respectively. This compares to an average increase for all male staff of slightly over £36. Barclays Bank Limited, *Staff Committee Minute Books*, ACC 80/25, 25 October 1944, p. 213; 'Memorandum "B", Women Permanent Staff Salary Scales'; 'Male Permanent Staff Salary Scales, Post War Considerations'.

25. Scott, J. W. (1988), *Gender and the Politics of History*, New York: Columbia University Press, p. 59.

26. Lipartito, 'Culture and the Practice of Business History', p. 25; Lipartito, K. (1994), 'When Women Were Switches: Technology, Work, and Gender in the Telephone Industry, 1890–1920', *The American Historical Review*, **99** (4), October, 1075–1111.

27. Walby, *Theorizing Patriarchy*, pp. 21, 90–108. The other five structures that Walby isolates include: patriarchal production relations in the household; patriarchal relations within paid work; male violence; the state; and, patriarchal relations in sexuality.
28. Scott, *Gender and the Politics of History*; Gherardi, S. (1996), 'Gendered Organizational Cultures: Narratives of Women Travellers in a Male World', *Gender, Work and Organization*, **3** (4), October.
29. Scott, *Gender and the Politics of History*, p. 60.
30. Gherardi, 'Gendered Organizational Cultures', p. 189.
31. Rose, S. (1992), *Limited Livelihoods. Gender and Class in Nineteenth-Century England*, Berkeley, Los Angeles: University of California Press, p. 11.
32. Ibid., p. 13; see also, Rose, S. (1993), 'Respectable Men, Disorderly Others: The Language of Gender and the Lancashire Weavers' Strike of 1878 in Britain', *Gender and History*, **5** (3), 382–97. In relation to the practice of business history, this position gains further support from Kenneth Lipartito who recognizes that structures in organizations have not only function but also meaning; Lipartito, 'Culture and the Practice of Business History', p. 2.
33. McNay, L. (1992), *Foucault and Feminism: Power, Gender and the Self*, Cambridge: Polity Press; Hoff, J. (1994), 'Gender as a Postmodern Category of Paralysis', *Women's History Review*, **3** (2), 149–68; Hoff, J. (1996), 'A Reply to My Critics', *Women's History Review*, **5** (1), 25–30; Palmer, B. D. (1990), *Descent into Discourse. The Reification of Language and the Writing of Social History*, Philadelphia: Temple University Press. For a more sympathetic response to this approach, see, for example, Kingsley Kent, S. (1996), 'Mistrials and Diatribulations: a Reply to Joan Hoff', *Women's History Review*, **5** (1); Acker, J. (1990), 'Hierarchies, Jobs, Bodies: A Theory of Gendered Organizations', *Gender and Society*, **4** (2), June, 139–58; Baron, A. (ed.) (1991), *Work Engendered, Toward a New Labour History*, Ithaca: Cornell University Press; Ramazanoglu, C. (ed.) (1993), *Up Against Foucault: Explorations of Some Tensions Between Foucault and Feminism*, London: Routledge; Ramazanoglu, C. (1996), 'Unravelling Postmodern Paralysis: a Response to Joan Hoff', *Women's History Review*, **5** (1), 19–23. Work promoting an analysis of the construction of gender within organizational cultures has recently received increased attention within the area of critical management. See, for example, Smircich, L. (1985), 'Is the Concept of Culture a Paradigm for Understanding Organizations and Ourselves?', in Frost, J. P., Moore. L. F., Reis-Louis, M., Lundberg, C. C. and Martin, J. (eds) (1985), *Organizational Culture*, London: Sage Publications; Gherardi, S. (1994), 'The Gender We Think, The Gender We Do in Our Everyday Organizational Lives', *Human Relations*, **47** (6), 591–609; Gherardi, 'Gendered Organizational Cultures'.
34. Rose, *Limited Livelihoods*, p.8; Acker, 'Hierarchies, Jobs, Bodies'.
35. Davidoff, L. and Hall, C. (1987), *Family Fortunes: Men and Women of the English Middle Class, 1780–1850*, London: Routledge; Hall, C. (1992), *White, Male and Middle Class; Explorations in Feminism and History*, Cambridge: Polity Press.
36. Hall, *White, Male and Middle Class*, p. 32.
37. Scott, *Gender and the Politics of History*, p. 43.
38. In contrast to Barclays, a number of other banks, including Lloyds and London Joint, City & Midland, did offer specific family wages to their married male staff. Barclays decided not to follow other Banks into the provision of specific family wages but would instead 'endeavour to arrive at the same results in the matter of

207

staff salaries and bonus'. Part of this process was achieved throughout the inter-war years through the implementation of Child Allowances for children in full-time education below the age of 18. Barclays Bank Limited, 'Permanent Staff Bonus', *Staff Committee Minute Books*, ACC 80/25, 8 October 1918; and ACC 80/25, 28 October 1919.

39. Barclays Bank Archives; *London & Provincial Bank Limited*, 17 October 1884, ACC 3/7; *Bank of Liverpool Limited, Book of Instructions, Staff Regulations*, 1917, ACC 3/3947; *Barclays Bank Limited, Staff Handbook*, 1931, ACC 3/2894.
40. Barclays Bank Archives; *Barclays Bank Limited, Staff Handbook*, 1931, ACC 3/2894.
41. *ESSAY*, Newsletter of the Barclays Bank Staff Association, 2 June 1958, p. 38.
42. *Spread Eagle* (1923), p. 11.
43. In relation to resistance, Foucault suggests that: 'Discourses are not once and for all subservient to power or raised up against it ... discourse can be both an instrument and an effect of power, but also a hindrance, a stumbling block, a point of resistance and a starting point for an opposing strategy. Discourse transmits and produces power; it reinforces it, but also undermines it, renders it fragile and makes it possible to thwart it.'; Foucault, M. (1981), *The History of Sexuality; Volume 1, An Introduction*, London: Penguin Books, p. 101.
44. Taken from an original fidelity agreement signed in 1922, Barclays Bank Archives.
45. POA, 'First Employment of Female Clerks', E3613/1875, *Post*, 30/275; POA, *Married Women Employed in the Post Office*, M20612/1921, 33/329–30. Similar concerns were also expressed over the potential improper influence of husbands over wives employed as Post mistresses of Post Office Sub–branches. POA, 'Employment of Married Women', *Post*, 30/3792, 1912.
46. POA, 'First Employment of Female Clerks', E3613/1875, *Post*, 30/275; POA, *Married Women Employed in the Post Office*, M20612/1921, 33/329–30; and, *Royal Commission on the Civil Service*, PP (1875), XXIII.
47. POA, 'First Employment of Female Clerks', E3613/1875, *Post*, 30/275; POA, *Married Women Employed in the Post Office*, M20612/1921, 33/329–30.
48. 'Random Recollections of a Member of the Executive Committee of the Central Council of Bank Staff Associations on Realising that He is Entering on the Last Year of His Bank Service', *Central Council of Bank Staff Associations*, December, 1955, Barclays Bank Archives, ACC 29/1507.
49. Silvia Gherardi uses the concept of women travellers in a male world to describe the experiences of women pioneers in a variety of male occupations. Gherardi, 'Gendered Organizational Cultures', p. 190.
50. Farmer, W. H. (1947), 'Mechanisation', *Spread Eagle*, July/August, p. 195.
51. P.E.S. (1936), 'Tobacco for the Ladies', *Spread Eagle*, April, pp. 210–11.
52. Gherardi, 'The Gender We Think', p. 608.
53. Ibid., p. 608.
54. *Spread Eagle* (1926), June, p. 18.
55. Braverman, H. (1974), *Labour and Monopoly Capital, The Degradation of Work in the Twentieth Century*, London: Monthly Review Press, pp. 293–358; Lockwood, D. (1958), *The Blackcoated Worker: A Study in Class Consciousness*, London: Allen & Unwin; Anderson, *Victorian Clerks*.
56. Rose, *Limited Livelihoods*, p. 8.
57. Barclays Bank Limited, *Staff Committee Minute Books*, ACC 80/26, 2 March 1955, The Remarks of Mr Boyd (General Staff Manager) to the Staff Committee.
58. See, for example, Kirkham, L. M. and Loft, A. (1993), 'Gender and the

Construction of the Professional Accountant', *Accounting, Organizations and Society*, **18** (6), 507–58; Kirkham, L. M. (1992), 'Integrating Herstory and History in Accountancy', *Accounting, Organizations and Society*, **17** (3/4), 287–97; Lehman, C. R. (1992), ' "Herstory" in Accountancy: The First Eighty Years', *Accounting, Organizations and Society*, **17** (3/4), 261–85; Thane, P. (1992), 'The History of the Gender Division of Labour in Britain: Reflections on " 'Herstory' in Accountancy: The First Eighty Years" ', *Accounting, Organizations and Society*, **17** (3/4), 299–312.

59. Casson, M. (1996), 'Culture as an Economic Asset', in Godley and Westall, *Business History and Business Culture*, pp. 48–76; Lipartito, 'Culture and the Practice of Business History'.

CHAPTER TWELVE

'Treading the Double Path': American Women's Strategies for Legal Careers in the Interwar Generation, c.1920–1941

Fiona Brown

Women lawyers were long overlooked by American historians of women and legal historians alike. In the past decade, efforts to redress this have principally taken the form of biographies of individuals or of groups on a regional or state basis.[1] Virginia Drachman's recent monograph, *Sisters in Law*,[2] gives the most comprehensive account to date of women in the legal profession in the early twentieth century.[3] Her work explores women's efforts to reconcile the 'double consciousness' of femininity and professionalism in a narrative pieced together from quantitative and manuscript sources. My own research is a much more limited case study, of women in the 'interwar generation' who qualified in law between 1920 and 1941. I have focused on lawyers active in Boston, Chicago, Washington DC and New York, where the more sizeable concentrations of women lawyers and attorneys existed.[4]

The choice of a career in law was not an obvious one for educated women of this period. The 1940 US Census recorded a total of 4185 women attorneys. This amounted to a meagre 2.4 per cent of the profession but represented a small rise in both the number and proportion of women over the two preceding decades.[5] Lawyers constituted a privileged elite of working women as a whole. They were almost without exception white, and predominantly middle class in background and outlook. Although American women's gain of the vote in 1920 clarified aspects of their status as full persons *before* the law, doubt prevailed over their supposed fitness to serve as jurors let alone attorneys. Cultural assumptions about appropriate gender roles sanctioned both subtle and more explicit forms of discrimination against women. There was resistance to the idea that a career was attainable, or even permissible, in equal measure for a woman as for a man. Gains made in women's access to legal training were offset in the course of the 1920s and 1930s by developments which sustained the hegemony of White Anglo Saxon Protestant (WASP) men within the profession. The depression of the 1930s and the rise of corporate law supported the continued marginalization of women within the profession of law and reaffirmed the pre-eminently masculine nature of its practice.

This essay aims to explore how the issues of professionalism, femininity and interwar feminism reverberated into individual lives. It draws upon a series of interviews with women who qualified between 1934 and 1941, some of whom were still active in law at the time of interview.[6] Notwithstanding the value of sophisticated postmodern approaches to textual analysis, I adopt the approach that oral histories are a valuable adjunct to, and indeed may be set in context by, more conventional forms of evidence. Directories which list women lawyers are necessary for mapping the position of women in the profession relative to men, but by themselves are rather blunt tools of investigation as they only record 'snapshots' of women's careers.[7] Manuscript collections are highly variable in the degree of personal information which they reveal and tend only to relate to the most prominent individuals.[8] Published autobiographies of this generation of women are relatively rare.[9] My interest lies with women who achieved less 'celebrity'. The lack of information available both explains the prevalence of biography in the existing literature and underlines the importance of oral histories as a way of increasing our understanding of the most basic details of their careers.

The effort to interweave personal testimonies with a variety of other sources raises substantive methodological issues. Perhaps most obviously, there are limitations to the available interview population and the processes of their selection. My interviewees do not represent a complete cross-section of city-based women lawyers of the time.[10] My purpose here is to suggest the usefulness of such testimonies in retrieving the 'human agency' which underpinned the success of women's careers 'against all odds'. I am concerned in particular to explore what motivated or inspired these women to enter a traditionally male area of work and to understand the practical ways in which they sought to resolve the major conflicts and challenges of their chosen occupation. Oral histories are the most appropriate means of exploring women's reactions and their characteristically optimistic approach to work despite the discouraging position of women as a whole.[11] I am reaching for a conceptualization of gender as a series of negotiated relationships and interactions in the workplace. Gender roles arose as a complex set of assumptions, honed in their specific historical moment. They were, however, somewhat malleable. The meaning of the post-suffrage sexual revolution was shaped by the relationships women formed with men as they entered the electorate and the workforce. Although the arguable 'certainties' of Victorian models of womanhood had ruptured, femininity – or femaleness – was not easily reconciled with a model of professionalism that had evolved in a masculine world. Women lawyers entered an environment that was shaped by 'masculine' behavioural norms such as business and financial acumen,

211

aggressive courtroom performance and competitiveness.[12] The 'double path' of their adult lives held constructs of womanhood and professionalism in tension.[13]

Gender and legal education

The established route to a career in law by the 1920s was to take a law degree before sitting the state bar examination which granted a licence to practise as an attorney. In 1920, 102 out of America's 129 law schools and all state bar examinations were open to women.[14] Thus the most blatant facet of sex-based discrimination had been removed. However, law schools varied considerably in quality. Colleges with part-time or evening law classes at reasonable rates opened out hopes of legal careers to working people, in competition with more established university law schools which tended to recruit full-time students from more privileged backgrounds. The prestige of a law school greatly influenced the likely career prospects of its graduates. Alumni networks had the potential to open – or indeed to close – avenues to vital social and political contacts. Thelma Brook Simon, for example, was conscious of the need to perform well at law school, and recognized the advantages of graduating from the prestigious University of Chicago Law School, for her future prospects:

> I'd won the moot court competition in my freshman year and then later on I
> ... was on law review ... I tried to qualify myself as best I could for a job –
> you see I had no special connections and I knew that my academic average
> and ... what could rest on the law school would be my only opportunity to
> get a job afterwards.[15]

Anne Sullivan recognized the subsequent usefulness of her law school contacts: 'I had entree to the attorney general's office, somebody I knew was in the state's attorneys' office because I had been in a class with him or something and then if he wasn't in that division he'd take me to someone who did know'.[16]

Women's pathways and prospects within legal training were influenced by a complex interplay of gender and other factors including their economic resources, family or social connections with legal circles, the region in which they sought legal education and their race or ethnicity. The quality of institution from which they gained their law degrees could thus either reinforce existing socio-economic divisions or forge new alignments amongst women lawyers. In the large metropolitan centres of Boston, New York, Washington DC and Chicago, women had a much broader choice of institution at which to study law than their counterparts in Southern or small-town America. In each of these cities women could choose from several law schools including at least one large, well established university.[17] Even so, the law schools which proved most

212

receptive to women were generally the less prestigious. This can be demonstrated with reference to the available options for women's legal education in Boston.[18]

Boston, unusually, had an all-female law school, known as Portia. The fact that Portia offered part-time study in both day and night divisions with relatively low fees bracketed it with the less esteemed 'proprietary' law schools. Although indicators of its students' performance, such as the number which passed the bar exam at first sitting suggested the soundness of its education, it was not prestigious. Women were also found in considerable numbers at Northeastern University Law School. Northeastern University had been founded by the Young Men's Christian Association (YMCA) on the principle of extending educational opportunities to working-class people, including new immigrants. Its graduates were unlikely to leave with entree to elite Boston law firms. Harvard University Law School was the top school in the Boston area. The influence of the Harvard system upon legal education at the start of the century was paramount, and its graduates constituted an elite both locally and nationally.[19] Women were not admitted to Harvard Law School until 1950. This exclusion epitomized women's lack of acceptance within the most influential legal circles. Boston University offered one of the few opportunities for women's full-time university legal education in the area, and its classes included a regular intake of women students throughout the period (see Table 12.1).[20]

Law school prepared women for the male-dominated environment in which they would build their careers. Even at the larger metropolitan law schools, the numbers of women students remained consistently low until the circumstances of the draft in the 1940s artificially boosted their proportion within classes (see Table 12.1). The small numbers of women within the student body and the scarcity of female instructors, together with the positive intellectual mentoring of male lecturers and the fellowship of male students influenced women to accept the cues of their professional training as sex-neutral.

Women approached the challenges of their legal education with self-belief and optimism. Their determination to gain the necessary academic credentials for law led them to internalize discrimination, when it surfaced, as one of the many tests of psychological rigour which they would encounter during their career. They thought they could overcome prejudice through excellence and exemplary work.[21] Eunice Howe remarked:

> I always knew I had to do a better job at anything that the men did ... You just had to. Once I got into a co-educational environment I knew I had to make better marks and then in work I always was conscientious about I've got to do it better than anyone else. So I think ... to that extent we appreciated the fact that we were handicapped ... but there was always the possibility that you could do better.[22]

213

Table 12.1 Numbers of women in graduating classes for LLB degree in selected law schools in Boston, 1920–1945

Graduating Class	Boston University Class size	Boston University No. of Women	Boston University Women (%)	Northeastern University Class size	Northeastern University No. of Women	Northeastern University Women (%)	Portia Law School No. of Women*
1920	n.a	n.a.	–	n.a.	–	–	n.a.
1921	109	9	8.3	n.a.	–	–	n.a.
1922	184	13	7.1	n.a.	–	–	n.a.
1923	184	12	6.5	n.a.	–	–	32
1924	224	17	7.6	n.a.	–	–	64
1925	159	10	6.3	n.a.	–	–	49
1926	158	6	3.8	n.a.	–	–	70
1927	264	12	4.5	188	18	9.6	66
1928	111	5	4.5	225	18	8.0	87
1929	217	4	1.8	163	22	13.5	79
1930	166	6	3.6	149	22	14.8	74
1931	161	6	3.7	213	25	11.7	78
1932	150	5	3.3	210	18	8.6	72
1933	145	5	3.5	168	13	7.7	64
1934	151	6	3.9	133	13	9.8	66
1935	124	9	7.3	114	18	15.8	48
1936	110	4	3.6	92	11	11.9	36
1937	182	10	5.5	113	9	7.9	55
1938	116	3	2.6	131	13	9.9	47
1939	85	3	3.5	112	9	8.0	55
1940	130	7	5.4	146	15	10.3	59
1941	108	7	6.5	198	22	11.1	94
1942	80	1	1.3	62	7	11.3	15
1943	38	6	15.7	21	4	19.1	6
1944	10	2	20.0	14	2	14.3	1
1945	17	3	17.6	4	1	25.0	3

* No. of Women = Class size (All-female institution during these years)
Source: Calculated from *Boston University Bulletin* (1920/1) to (1945/6); *Boston University Alumni Association Directory Centennial Edition* (1972) both in Boston University Law School Library; Northeastern University commencement programmes (1927–45) in Northeastern University Special Collections; Year Books and Newspaper Clippings, Portia Archive, New England School of Law, Boston.

At a 1933 conference convened by the National Federation of Women's Clubs, the panel of women lawyers counselled women to work harder than their male counterparts to get a foothold in the profession. One New Jersey lawyer stated:

> Only the woman who has learned the bitter lesson that she must be fully as well equipped and work twice as hard to get only half as far as men, and who has the courage to work through to success despite this knowledge can know the happy satisfaction of real accomplishment.[23]

Rita Brandeis studied law at the University of Michigan, a very large law school at which women had been admitted in the late nineteenth century.[24] She remarked of her experience:

> I went to the University of Michigan Law School between 1935 and 1938. I must say there was the first time that I did understand that I was doing something that was kind of out of the ordinary. There were two other women in my class and one of them had no idea that she was going to practice law. She just liked going to school! ... My room mate was a woman ... [in] Medical School ... so we were both kind of mavericks. But the feeling I have is that nobody laughed at us or made fun of it. There was a realisation that it would be hard to get jobs but we thought 'somehow or other we'll do it'.[25]

Women's experiences of law school provided overwhelmingly positive contact with males. As one remarked: 'The women within law school had a nice relationship with the men ... you didn't sense any particular prejudice 'cos you were women ... we were friendly.'[26] The shared educational experience of male and female students both in their pre-law college learning and as law students encouraged platonic friendships which promoted male students' widespread acceptance of their female class mates and mutual respect between students. The interwar generation of female law students were not excluded on issues of 'delicacy' in the way pioneering women law students of the late nineteenth century had been. The experience of law school and the high incidence of their later marriages to other co-educated professional men stimulated women's sense that to be female was reconcilable with work in a male-dominated field of endeavour. For the most part this reinforced ideas that had been instilled by supportive parents and families.

The themes of parental encouragement and respect for learning recur in women's accounts of what sustained them in the course of the demanding path they had chosen. Anne Sullivan's parents emigrated to America from Ireland. Her mother, one of thirteen children who all left school at a young age to help support the family, 'kind of stressed education. Never pressured us but just felt that you would not be dependent on anybody if you had a profession of some kind.' Rita Brandeis remarked:

> My mother was very, very poor and went to work at a very early age. She had practically no education ... she was really a very intelligent person; one who had a great deal of respect for education ... there was no question in their minds [her parents] that my gender had anything to do with what I would be capable of acquiring and doing. They were always very supportive ... I was encouraged ... by both my parents ... I think that they both felt that it [the choice of law] was good, but I really think that whatever I had decided they would have said go for it, that's fine.[27]

Frances Corwin stated:

> It was very unusual for parents to encourage a daughter to become a lawyer. Usually the parents, particularly Jewish parents, 'cos I am Jewish, would encourage their daughters to be a teacher or a nurse ... my parents were very unusual, I mean, they so strongly encouraged education for their daughters ... for all their children ... although their financial means were fairly modest ... and this was the time of the depression ... anything that we are we really owe to them for their encouragement.[28]

The main stumbling block for women was to how to secure employment and a viable income from law related work. No matter how receptive law schools were to female students, the exterior world of legal practice remained inhospitable. There was a large rate of wastage between the numbers of women law graduates and those who actually entered the profession. This drop-out rate reflected the difficulties of gaining employment and the high costs of establishing a private practice. It also reflected how some women chose to study law for academic interest alone, while others opted themselves out of a career by choosing a conventional marital role. It is difficult to apportion these various influences in the drop-out rate of women law graduates with any accuracy. For those determined to pursue a vocation in law but with no family connections to help ease their way, discrimination was likely to affect their efforts to find a job or establish a client base. Rita Brandeis remarked that after she graduated in 1938:

> I realised ... that there were difficulties for women that as I was just approaching the idea of becoming a lawyer I just didn't give any thought to ... I went to Washington to see if I could get a job in the federal government. And there I realised boy, the fact that I was a woman is going to be quite a hurdle.[29]

Gender identities and legal specialisms: women's footholds in law

The pattern of women's contributions to law, both in terms of the area of law in which they worked and the nature of the tasks they performed, reflected the influence of gender roles. As the work of Virginia Drachman and Patricia Hummer has demonstrated, women were almost entirely absent from large corporate law firms, rarely found as trial lawyers and tended to concentrate in the lower ranking and lower paid echelons of the profession.[30] This may be exemplified by Drachman's analysis of a 1939 directory of women lawyers, in which 66 per cent of those listed were in general practice, while the most common specialisms were probate (13 per cent) real estate (7 per cent) and patent law (3 per cent). By contrast, only 1 per cent of the sample of 336 women specialized in either trial work or criminal law.[31] Women found opportunities in the realms of legal aid, juvenile and domestic relations work, all of which were seen as congruent with their 'naturally' caring and nurturing roles. Even within law firms and public office, women tended to perform 'backroom' or support roles as law clerks, researchers or legal secretaries which reflected a gender-based hierarchy in the workplace.[32] Quantitative sources present a stark picture of women's marginalization. However, they obscure the more subtle processes of choice that also helped to shape the pattern of women's involvement in legal work. It is these processes of choice, and the dimension of 'experience', which oral histories help to bring more clearly into view.

In mixed company? lawyers' networking patterns

The central challenge for most women lawyers, especially when first qualified, was how to gain acceptance in male-dominated legal networks. If that failed they had to pursue alternative systems of professional support and guidance. For women in the large cities where there were sufficient numbers of female attorneys to establish a 'critical mass', sororities and state or city-based women lawyers' associations were crucial in helping women to secure their first footholds in legal work. An attorney's work rested on an independent work routine. The decision to tackle a legal career was in some ways an implicitly 'feminist' act, based on a belief in the possibility and capability of women to work side by side with men as rational, self-supporting professionals. The fact that lawyers were trained for professional self-reliance dovetailed with the liberal, individualistic ideologies that underpinned interwar feminism. However, the central paradox of women in the legal profession was that they were unable, for pragmatic reasons, to abandon all-female networks entirely at a time when the logic of female separatism was largely spent.

By the 1920s, local and regional bar associations proliferated. These organizations served various functions, including promoting continuing education, endorsing candidates for public office, and providing a forum for debate on substantive issues of law. Above all, membership of such associations bestowed tangible benefits in a sense of professional community and personal contacts through which individuals furthered their careers. Although by 1920 most bar associations were open to women, membership of bar associations was not compulsory for practitioners and some continued to refuse admission to women. The City Bar of New York, for example, did not admit women until 1937. Moreover, women's right to hold membership in bar associations did little to counter their scarcity on influential bar association panels or committees.

The National Association of Women Lawyers (NAWL) and prominent

217

women lawyers' associations in Chicago, Boston and Washington DC were established before 1920 in response to women's exclusion from regional bar associations.[33] During the 1920s and 1930s these women's organizations strove to fulfil similar functions to the mainstream associations, even though their members were increasingly likely to belong to the other associations as well. Indeed, although membership fees cut into women's earnings, most women combined membership in mainstream and all-female associations without apparent conflict of interest. Women's regional associations were the first obvious step for women seeking employment in an era of little formal vocational guidance, and an environment in which they were often received with scepticism.

Women of this era endeavoured to promote others within the profession by adopting strategically 'tokenist' approaches to employment. They argued that they should be replaced by other women as they moved jobs. Many interviewees described the personal recommendations for jobs or advice about likely areas for openings which they gained from women whom they met through a sorority or women lawyers' association. They also outlined their own efforts to pass on information about possible job vacancies and put pressure on their employers to hire women. Thelma Brook Simon recalled of the Women's Bar Association of Illinois (WBAI) which was based in Chicago:

> It was interesting that there was a sort of network, everyone was ... helpful to everyone else: 'There might be an opening here' ... I think among ourselves you didn't distinguish between what anybody did. There was a measure of loyalty. But it did pave the way, like [X] she started out operating a switchboard for McDermott, Will and Emory – a major law firm and from that she got to be doing some secretarial work. From that she was recognised as a lawyer – and from that she eventually became a partner ... then ultimately a hiring partner ... and she helped others along the way.[34]

Frances Corwin remembered

> When I graduated in 1940 it was extremely difficult to find a job, for men as well as women, but particularly for women. There was a lady ... [X] who was a member of the Women's Bar [WBAI]. I became active in the Women's Bar immediately and have been pretty much so all these years. She helped me to find a job so I worked for a small law firm for some months and then an opportunity came up at Legal Aid ... Until about 25 or 30 years ago I knew every single woman lawyer in Chicago ... The Women's Bar served a wonderful purpose ... of being a place of meeting and socialising and comparing notes and so forth.[35]

This effort to sustain a minimum 'quota' of women in legal jobs was practised by women who viewed such tactics as a realistic and short term expedient rather than a desirable state of affairs. Their ultimate vision remained that of a 'gender blind' future in which women lawyers would be judged on their individual academic and legal abilities rather than on grounds of sex. Women's perceptions of realistic career choices within law were influenced by the advice and actions of their female role models. This suggests that the pattern of women's clustering in certain areas of law was reinforced by the practical vocational advice shared through women's networks.

Women's bar associations also provided opportunities to rehearse and develop skills in public speaking and participation in committee work.[36] They provided an alternative 'luncheon club' to those from which women were barred either formally or informally, and a source of moral support. Eunice Howe remarked:

> A big part of being a lawyer in Boston is going to luncheon with your clients or peers, and the clubs were male ... so you were at a real disadvantage when it came time for luncheon because you just couldn't go ... The women met by themselves, shared their triumphs and their failures and reinforced each other. And also gave me something to aspire to.

The practical kind of daily support which women gained through their bar associations and sorority contacts fostered kinship and community above women's various political, ethnic, generational and socio-economic allegiances.

The activities of women's legal associations reflected the ambivalent character of interwar feminism.[37] There were prominent women lawyers amongst the membership of both the moderate League of Women Voters and the more radical National Women's Party. For the most part, women lawyers' associations eschewed conspicuously feminist ideologies. Their interest in 'feminist' issues arose from the particular circumstances of legal practice, such as their efforts to lift prohibitions on women jurors in the 1930s and 1940s. Women lawyers' networks occasionally forged cross-party alliances in support of a female judicial candidate. Lawyers no less than other women demonstrated lack of consensus over the 'big issues' of interwar feminism, such as the Equal Rights Amendment. That 'feminist' consensus was more easily achieved over matters which touched on central issues of professionalism perhaps itself reflecting the degree of focus and commitment which was necessary to succeed as a lawyer. In practice, women's bar associations were leery of 'radical' feminist schemes and of 'biting the hand' of the male professionals whose acceptance they sought.

Strategies for management of motherhood and career

Women's professional identity in the interwar generation faltered on the issue of how commitment to a career could be combined with motherhood. The expectation prevailed that women would at some point – whether temporarily or permanently – abandon the world of work in favour of raising a family. Childcare still tended to be understood as women's proper vocation. Female reproductive roles were not easily reconciled with professionalism because unbroken commitment to a lifelong vocational pursuit was one of the defining characteristics of a salaried 'professional' as opposed to a waged worker. Backlash propaganda in the 1930s against 'career women' asserted the 'a priori' obligations of motherhood.[38] Blurring the potential state of motherhood with the actual state of motherhood, it undermined women's already precarious status as professionals whether they were single or married. Press coverage of women lawyers who raised families dwelled upon their 'novelty' value. Such images ignored the sizeable numbers of women lawyers who raised families. According to census figures, in 1920 34.2 per cent of women lawyers were married, in 1930 33.1 per cent, by 1940 38.6 per cent and in 1950 44.2 per cent. Of the 948 women who appeared in Fiona Hale Cook's 1939 directory, 24.2 per cent had children. Almost 30 per cent of the women entered in a 1949 NAWL-based directory had children.[39]

The media's reportage of 'mother lawyers' conveniently glossed over the extent to which middle-class women, whether or not they were employed outside the home, relied on full time domestic help or childcare in raising their families. The question of how to combine motherhood and career without abandoning either was a central issue in the lives of many married women lawyers. In facing difficult choices about juggling commitment to children and to work, women confronted the most acute tension of 'treading the double path'. The solutions they found tested and ultimately began to alter the boundaries of gender in the world of work. Women frequently carved out career paths which incorporated interruptions or 'sidesteps' in order to accommodate the 'double burden' of home and work. Their careers were supported by their husbands' equally enlightened and courageous approach to 'companionate' marriage. Thelma Brook Simon emphasized 'the full – the real – cooperation' of her husband (who was not a lawyer) in supporting her career, and their 'mutually responsive' approach to work and marriage.[40]

Anne Chalke Sullivan graduated from De Paul University in 1937. She engineered several different ways of juggling career and family responsibilities, whilst raising eight children. While the first four of her children were young, Anne chose to break from employment for the period of their birth and infancy. Conscious of the ways in which having children might confirm employers' prejudices about women workers, Anne saw resigning as an inevitable and sensible way of managing the issue. She recalled being questioned about the issue of children in the interviews for her early posts, leaving her with a 'kind of embarrassing' dilemma about how to deal with the issue when it arose. She did not 'want to go and spoil it for people later on'. That she never directly questioned the employer's negative reaction to her pregnancy reflects the absence of radical solutions proposed at a time when few employers offered arrangements for maternity leave. However, Anne Sullivan was confident of being able to resume work at a comparable level when suitable opportunities came up. Such self-confidence was characteristic of women lawyers who engineered leverage in their working lives by resigning from jobs where necessary: a self-confidence which perhaps distinguished professional, highly educated women from those in lower white collar occupations. Confidence in their own abilities as well as the value of their professional expertise was a necessary factor in career success.

In the case of her later children, Anne Sullivan followed the pattern of many women lawyers who combined work in private practice with or on behalf of their husbands from home whilst raising young children. This inevitably reflected a degree of subordination to their husbands' work, but the sense of 'subordination' was far outweighed in these women's minds by the opportunity to remain active in legal work and to participate in a true partnership with their spouses. The particular nature of legal work lent itself to an early model of 'billable hours'. The high rate of marriage between lawyers opened out possibilities of a kind of flexibility, albeit not without compromise on women's part, which allowed the lucky few a very rare and 'modern' opportunity to creatively combine their family life and their life's work. This was an option which was just not open to other female professionals such as hospital doctors, university lecturers or research scientists of the time.

Lawyers in public service or salaried legal positions also engineered career breaks or more flexible working arrangements. Eunice Howe's career included posts in the office of the assistant attorney general of Massachusetts, the US Navy and various government positions. Faced with the demands of raising young children and full time work in a job in an assistant attorney general's office which required long hours, she decided to take a career break in order to focus on raising her children.

> After I came out of the navy I came back to the Attorney General's office ... to the Division of Employment Security where I went to court everyday on minor cases, and I didn't like that very well. No policymaking, just appearing in court with a file and representing the common law but I didn't really like it. ... I was in the process of having my two children ... and it wasn't working out very well because I was going to court and worrying ... [about] the baby ... and then I was coming home early and hadn't prepared my case for the next day ... I was at sixes and sevens. So I quit for a while ... I enjoyed being a wife and mother and I got into a lot of

volunteer work ... It kept me in contact with people and it kept my mind going.[41]

Eunice subsequently relaunched her career by becoming active in Republican politics. Other women sustained law-related work but changed jobs in order to accommodate their young children. Thelma Brook Simon, for example, took up legal research whilst her son was very young; her husband helping with childcare in the evenings so that she could do her work. Performing some element of law-related work, however mundane, was itself a priority for women who sought a way of devoting considerable time to their young children without losing sight of the intention of returning to their careers.

Highly regarded women lawyers were able to negotiate and experiment with new and 'unusual' forms of flexible working arrangements. That such concessions were won continued to fuel women lawyers' optimism that, in time, the apparent friction between professionalism and womanhood could be overcome. The Second World War, in drafting men to military service, improved the likelihood of such opportunities. This particularly benefited women who had qualified and married in the 1930s as they began to start their families during the war. While her husband was in service, Anne Sullivan was 'head-hunted' for a job which offered her a 'fabulous salary' in which she was able to 'make my own hours'. The lucky ones were able to retain the opportunities they had negotiated after the war was over. Frances Corwin worked as a house attorney for a metallurgical company while her husband was in the services. When the war ended, the company kept her on a retainer which enabled her to continue working on a part-time basis whilst raising a family. She recalled:

> I must say that while I was raising the children I had the perfect arrangement with this retainer to make my own time so that it was when my youngest was entering high school that I went back to full time ... The circumstances that were very helpful to me were that I made my own time as far as my work was concerned ... I had a wonderful lady at home and my husband was helpful.[42]

Women's accounts of the solutions which they found to combining career with family emphasize the importance of their expertise rather than merely the circumstances of war in winning concessions. Their perspectives demonstrate the degree to which women themselves idealized 'gender neutral' goals and believed themselves to be more alike than different from their male colleagues in terms of ambition. The particular exigencies of childcare rested on women's career choices rather than those of their husbands. However, these interviews suggest that some of the unstated 'benefits' which attracted women to less prestigious legal employment in salaried positions such as house attorneys or government work can be measured in the flexibility and regular hours which they offered to women seeking to 'tread the double path'.

Conclusion

Accounts of individual careers enable historians to develop a more nuanced understanding of the interplay between gender and professionalism. They serve as a necessary corrective to exploring discrimination alone as the defining note of women's working lives. Women lawyers internalized the goals of their training as sex-neutral even though the ethos and practice of the profession remained predominantly masculine. Women lawyers cultivated professional community by operating through both mainstream and all-female networks. They adopted strategies of vocational guidance and 'self help' in response to their marginalized position whilst also drawing upon the support of male colleagues, mentors and husbands.

In evolving strategies to gain acceptance within legal circles, women began to dynamically influence the boundaries of gender at work. Most significantly, they sought to reconcile the dual goals of professional and personal fulfilment by evolving strategies of career management which could accommodate their family responsibilities. The range of solutions they found to negotiate the necessary flexibility in their working arrangements varied considerably, from avoiding the issue to negotiating new modes of working with their employers.

The pattern of women's participation in the profession logically related to a hierarchy of gender. However, it was also influenced by women's promotion of 'strategic tokenism' and the positive career choices they made. Salaried employment as house attorneys or in government positions afforded women the mobility and fixed hours which enabled them to keep both professional and family goals in view.

Women lawyers in the interwar generation approached the challenge of their 'double path' pragmatically, and with optimism. Optimism itself was a conscious choice. The lives of this generation spanned the epoch between the decline of Victorian chauvinism and the rise of 'Second Wave' radical feminism. The dilemmas of femininity and professionalism were largely resolved on an individualistic basis because they espoused a world view in which the freedom to make personal choices was the most significant legacy of their mothers' fight for suffrage.

Notes

1. Recent works include: Brown, D. (1984), *Mabel Walker Willebrandt: A Story of Power, Loyalty and Law*, Knoxville: University of Tennessee; Paterson, J. (1986), *Be Somebody: A Biography of Marguerite Rawalt*, Austin, Texas: Eakin Press; Bradley Berry, D. (1996), *The Fifty Most Influential Women in American Law*, Los Angeles: Lowell House Books; Matsuda, M. J. (1992), *Called From Within: Early Women Lawyers of Hawai'i*, University of Hawai'i Press; Tuve, J. (1984), *First Lady of the Law: Florence Ellinwood Allen*, New York: University Press

of America. Of the many articles profiling American women lawyers, see, for example: Paradee, J. P. (1993), 'Delaware's First Women Lawyers: The Flow of Acceptability', *Delaware Lawyer* (Fall issue); Gorecki, M. (1990), 'Legal Pioneers: Four of Illinois' First Women Lawyers', *Illinois Bar Journal* (October); Adelman, C. (1986), 'A History of Women Lawyers in Illinois', *Illinois Bar Journal* (May).

2. Drachman, V. G. (1998), *Sisters in Law: Women Lawyers in Modern American History*, Cambridge, Mass.: Harvard University Press. Hereafter cited as Drachman, *Sisters*. See also: Drachman, V. (1993), *Women Lawyers and the Origins of Professional Identity in America: The Letters of the Equity Club, 1887 to 1890*, Ann Arbor: University of Michigan Press (hereafter cited as Drachman, *Equity Club*); Drachman, V. (1995), 'My Partner in Law and Life: Marriage in the Lives of Women Lawyers in Late Nineteenth and Early Twentieth Century America', *Law and Social Enquiry* (Journal of the American Bar Foundation) **14** (2), 221–50; Drachman, V. (1995), 'The New Woman Lawyer and the Challenge of Sexual Equality in Early Twentieth Century America', *Indiana Law Review*, **28**, 227–57; and Drachman, V. (1992), 'Entering the Male Domain: Women Lawyers in the Courtroom in Modern American History', *Massachusetts Law Review*, 44–50.

3. The few detailed monographs about American women lawyers before 1970 include: Berger Morello, K. (1986), *The Invisible Bar: The Woman Lawyer in America, 1638 to the Present*, Boston: Beacon Press; Hummer, P. A. (1979), *The Decade of Elusive Promise: Professional Women in the United States, 1920–1930*, Ann Arbor: MRI Press (hereafter cited as Hummer, *Elusive Promise*).

4. See, for example, Hummer's discussion of the geographical distribution of women lawyers in *Elusive Promise*, pp. 94–5.

5. The numbers of lawyers recorded in the US Census were, for 1920: 1738 (1.4%) 1930: 3385 (2.1%) 1940: 4447 (2.4%) 1950: 6348 (3.5%) cited in Epstein, B. (1993), *Women in Law* (second edition), Chicago: University of Illinois Press, p. 4. Census figures overestimate the numbers of women earning a living through legal work as the returns were based on the 'self-definition' of individuals. No doubt law graduates would be keen to describe themselves as 'lawyers'. The census figures probably include women working in 'paralegal' occupations such as legal secretaries and court reporters. Detailed samples which can be retrieved from directories of women lawyers are far smaller. For example, the 1939 *Martindale Hubbell Law Directory* provided Virginia Drachman with a sample of 3461 women, based on a one in five sample of registered women lawyers from all geographic areas, but only yielded income information for 482 individuals. The number of women supporting themselves through legal work in the interwar period is likely to be considerably less than the census figures suggest. See especially Drachman, *Sisters*, ch. 7 'Woman's Position in the Profession', pp. 168–90. Despite the likely inaccuracies of census figures, that the number of women lawyers increased at all contrasted favourably with their falling numbers during these years in other professions such as medicine and academia. See Cott, N. (1987), *The Grounding of Modern Feminism*, New Haven: Yale University Press, pp. 215–39.

6. Of eighteen women interviewed, thirteen qualified before December 1941, two qualified between 1941 and 1945 and three qualified between 1945 and 1948. This article draws in particular from interviews with the following: Anne Sullivan, 1934 graduate of De Paul University Law School, Chicago, admitted to bar 1934, interviewed 11 September 1996 in Chicago (hereafter cited as Sullivan,

interview with Brown); Frances Corwin, 1940 graduate of the University of Chicago, admitted to bar 1940, interviewed 11 September 1996 in Chicago (hereafter cited as Corwin, interview with Brown); Thelma Brook Simon, 1940 graduate of the University of Chicago, admitted to bar 1940 and Hon. Olga Jurco, 1938 graduate of De Paul University, Chicago, admitted to bar 1939, interviewed together 11 September 1996 in Chicago (hereafter cited as Simon and Jurco, interview with Brown); Eunice Howe, 1941 graduate of Boston University, admitted to bar 1941, interviewed 29 August 1997, in Belmont, Massachusetts (hereafter cited as Howe, interview with Brown); Eileen O'Connor, 1941 graduate of George Washington University, Washington DC, admitted to bar 1941, interviewed 4 September 1997 in Washington DC; Rita Singer Brandeis, 1938 graduate of University of Michigan Law School, admitted to bar 1938, interviewed 31 July 1997 in Sacramento, California (hereafter cited as Brandeis, interview with Brown); Mattie Belle Davis, admitted to bar 1936, interviewed on 1 August 1997, in San Francisco, California; Bereneice Gremmels, 1939 graduate of De Paul University Law School, passed bar examination in 1940, interviewed 21 September 1996 in Chicago; Laura Reynolds Helfrich, 1934 graduate of John Marshall Law School, interviewed on 14 August 1997 in Batavia, Illinois; Miriam Hamilton Keare, 1933 graduate of the University of Chicago Law School, interviewed 18 August 1997 in Highland Park, Illinois. The author thanks all interviewees in this Oral History project, and also acknowledges the kind assistance of the following in facilitating contact with interviewees: the National Association of Women Lawyers; the Women's Bar Association of Illinois; DC Women's Bar Association; George Washington University Alumni Association; Loyola University Alumni Association; Boston University Law School; De Paul University Law School; John Marshall Law School.

7. Drachman's book *Sisters in Law* is based on the following sources: Bureau of Vocational Information (BVI) survey of women in law 1920, Mss. Schlesinger Library, Radcliffe College; Cook, Fiona Hale (ed.), *Who's Who Among Women Lawyers*, Boston: Fiona Hale Cook; (1939) *Martindale Hubbell Law Directory* vol. 1, New York: Martindale Hubbell; Derry, Laura Miller (ed.) (1949), *Digest of Women Lawyers and Judges*, USA: Laura Miller Derry.

8. Major collections of women lawyers and judges' papers are held at the Arthur and Elizabeth Schlesinger Library, Radcliffe College (Cambridge, Mass.) and in the Sophia Smith Library, Smith College (Northampton, Mass.). Other collections are found at Brandeis University (Waltham, Mass.), the New Jersey Historical Society (Newark, New Jersey) and in the Library of Congress, Washington DC.

9. See Allen, F. E. (1965), *To Do Justly*, Cleveland: Western Reserve University Press; Farrow, T. (1953), *Lawyer in Petticoats*, New York: Vantage Press; Frooks, D. (1975), *Lady Lawyer*, New York: Robert Speller and Sons; McClanahan, A. M. (1958), *Her Father's Partner: The Story of a Lady Lawyer*, New York: Vantage Press; Olender, Terrys T. (1961), *For the Prosecution: Miss Deputy D.A.*, Philadelphia: Chilton Co.; and Schwartz, H. E. (1976), *Lawyering*, New York: Farrar & Giroux.

10. My sample is biased towards women who qualified after 1935. Most of my interviewees came from Chicago. I was unable to make contact with women lawyers in New York, and only one in Boston. I interviewed more women in government service or who served as house attorneys for companies than those in private practice.

11. See Chester, R. (1987), *Unequal Access: Women Lawyers in a Changing America*, Boston: Bergin & Garvey. This volume is based on extensive interviews

225

with women who qualified from law school in Chicago, Boston and Washington DC. The transcripts of these interviews are held at the Schlesinger Library.

12. See Grossberg, M. (1990), 'Institutionalising Masculinity: The law as a Masculine Profession', in Carnes, M. C. and Griffen C., *Meanings for Manhood: Constructions of Manhood in Victorian America*, Chicago: University of Chicago Press, pp. 133–55.

13. The phrase 'treading the double path' is taken from my interview with Thelma Brook Simon. She used this metaphor when discussing issues of juggling the demands of career and home. The metaphor also encapsulates what Virginia Drachman has described as the 'burden of double consciousness'; the effort to reconcile womanhood and professional identity with which women grappled in the early twentieth century. See Drachman, *Sisters*, esp. pp. 3–5 and pp. 194–5.

14. Drachman, 'The New Woman Lawyer and the Challenge of Sexual Equality in Early Twentieth Century America'. See note 2 for full citation.

15. Simon and Jurco, interview with Brown.

16. Sullivan, interview with Brown.

17. For example, in Chicago, women could attend Chicago-Kent Law School, Loyola Law School, De Paul Law School, the University of Chicago Law School and John Marshall Law School. In New York City, women could attend Fordham Law School, New York University Law School, Brooklyn Law School and Columbia University Law School from 1928. In Washington DC, women could attend the Washington College of Law, an all-female school, George Washington School of Law or Howard University Law School.

18. Drachman, *Sisters*, pp. 138–42, 157–62.

19. See, for example, Hall, K. M. (1989), *The Magic Mirror: Law in American History*, New York: Oxford University Press, pp. 219–25.

20. See Drachman's table summarizing the most popular law schools for women in *Sisters*, p. 256. According to her calculations, Boston University was the fifth most popular school from the Hale Cook sample and the ninth most popular amongst women profiled in Derry's 1949 Directory.

21. For a discussion of women's optimism in various professions and their strategies for overcoming discrimination, see Glazer, P. M. and Slater, M. (1987), *Unequal Colleagues: The Entrance of Women into the Professions, 1890–1940*, New Brunswick: Rutgers University Press; Rossiter, M. (1982), *Women Scientists in America: Struggles and Strategies to 1940*, Baltimore: Johns Hopkins University Press; Markell-Morantz Sanchez, R. (1985), *Sympathy and Science: Women Physicians in American Medicine*, New York: Oxford University Press (hereafter cited as Morantz-Sanchez, *Sympathy and Science*).

22. Howe, interview with Brown.

23. National Federation of Business and Professional Women's Clubs (1934), *The Current Outlook in the Legal Profession*, New York: National Federation of Business and Professional Women's Clubs, p. 9.

24. On women's legal education at Michigan see Drachman, *Equity Club* and Brown, E. (1959), *Legal Education at Michigan, 1859–1959*, Ann Arbor: University of Michigan.

25. Brandeis, interview with Brown.

26. Corwin, interview with Brown.

27. Brandeis, interview with Brown.

28. Corwin, interview with Brown.

29. Brandeis, interview with Brown.

30. See especially Drachman, *Sisters*, pp. 168–91.

226

31. See Drachman, *Sisters*, Table 13, p. 259.
32. See especially Hummer, *Elusive Promise*, pp. 94–9. For a more general discussion of how the allocation of office tasks reflected a hierarchy of gender see Kwolek-Folland, Angel (1994), *Engendering Business: Men and Women in the Corporate Office, 1870–1930*, Baltimore: Johns Hopkins University Press.
33. The NAWL, based at this time in New York, was established in 1899; the Chicago-based Women's Bar Association of Illinois (WBAI) in 1914, and the Women's Bar Association of DC in 1917.
34. Simon and Jurco, interview with Brown.
35. Corwin, interview with Brown.
36. Simon and Jurco, interview with Brown.
37. See Cott, *The Grounding of Modern Feminism*; Becker, S. (1981), *The Origins of the Equal Rights Amendment: American Feminism Between the Wars*, London: Greenwood Press.
38. See Scharf, L. (1980), *To Work and To Wed: Female Employment, Feminism and the Great Depression*, London: Greenwood Press; and Wandersee, W. (1981), *Women's Work and Family Values, 1920–1940*, Cambridge, Mass.: Harvard University Press.
39. Morantz-Sanchez, *Sympathy and Science*, Table 5, pp. 136–7.
40. Simon and Jurco, interview with Brown.
41. Howe, interview with Brown.
42. Corwin, interview with Brown.

Index